The Lost Field Notes of Franklin R. Johnston's Life and Work Among the American Indians

The Lost Field Notes of Franklin R. Johnston's Life and Work Among the American Indians

FIRST GLANCE BOOKS
Cobb, California

Published by O.G. Publishing, Inc.

Distributed by First Glance Books, Inc.
PO Box 960
Cobb, CA 95426
Phone: (707) 928-1994
Fax: (707) 928-1995

This edition was produced by
American Graphic Systems, Inc.
PO Box 460313
San Francisco, CA 94146

All illustrations by Franklin Robert Johnston

All photographs are from the Franklin Robert Johnston Collection
with the following exceptions:
Library of Congress: 43, 77, 103, 113
Montana State Historical Society: 69, 71, 74-75, 91, 97, 190, cover
National Anthropological Archives: 2, 11, 25, 29, 53, 54, 74, 79, 84, 85, 87, 93, 126-127, 129, 136, 151, 155, 158-159, 163
National Archives: 33, 44, 62-63, 78, 80, 94-95, 192
© The Rodney Grisso Collection: 7
Western Museum of Ethnography: 81, 88, 89, 92, 96, 140-141, 186-187

Designed by Bill Yenne, with design assistance by Azia Yenne.
Copy editing by Bill Yenne, with proofreading by Andy Roe and Joan B. Hayes.

Page one photograph: A young Seri Indian woman in face paint and beads.
Page two photograph: Zuni Governor Pahlowahtiwa.

ISBN 1-885440-05-7

Printed in Hong Kong

TABLE OF CONTENTS

INTRODUCTION

By Bill Yenne

Who was Franklin Robert Johnston and why is he important? He was an adventurer, and he was an intensely curious man with a passion for archeology and a deep interest in understanding the lives and cultures of the indigenous people of America. Most important, however, he documented, through field studies, the details of a vanishing culture before the primary source material was lost forever.

Perhaps the best way to introduce Johnston and his work is through a story of an incident that took place in the late 1930s. An archeology professor of great academic eminence had just reviewed the very field notes that are published in this book. He was obviously very intrigued, but something bothered him. Looking across his big university office desk and thoughtfully removing his half-frame reading glasses, he asked Johnston: "Where are your sources? You haven't cited your sources."

Johnston looked back at him and said quietly: "I was there. I saw it all with my own eyes."

Johnston knew Geronimo and was perhaps the last serious scholar to interview the legendary Apache chief before his death in 1909. Johnston spoke with Native Americans in their own languages, and he could read the Native American petroglyphs of the Southwest as easily as he could read *The New York Times.*

Johnston went on to spend much of the decades of the 1920s and 1930s amassing an important body of data about Native Americans by living and working with them. He also created the largest private collection of Native American artifacts in the western United States, and was probably the only man to film the mysterious Hopi Snake Dance.

He was president of the Archeology Society of Southern California and edited its bulletin, which contained many articles adapted from the field notes contained herein.

Among his most important contributions to theoretical anthropology were those that concerned the mysterious disappearance of the Anasazi culture of northern Arizona and adjacent areas, which occurred in about 1300 A.D. Johnston's theory held that this was caused by the impact of a gigantic meteorite, the massive crater from which is still a popular tourist attraction near the present city of Winslow, Arizona. His theory is detailed at length in Chapter 2.

Johnston was a member of the Adventurers' Club — along with Richard Byrd and Robert Peary — and was featured on the "I Search For Adventure" television series in the 1950s. Johnston led expeditions to the Cocos Islands off Sumatra, and located the lost treasure of the pirate Captain Henry Morgan in Costa Rica.

Right: The blanket which was given to Franklin Johnston by Geronimo during their historic 1909 meeting. It is now part of the Rodney Grisso Collection.

Recently rediscovered after more than half a century, his field notes were compiled during the early decades of the twentieth century and edited into manuscript form between 1934 and 1937, when he was editing the bulletin of the Archeology Society of Southern California. Johnston lived and worked among the Native Americans from 1905 through 1939, carefully and meticulously documenting the experience and his discoveries.

The tone and phrasing of the original field notes have been retained as much as possible. Spelling of tribal names has been corrected to modern convention in the text, but in the figure captions, which are written in Johnston's own handwriting, older spellings are retained. For example, he uses the French-Canadian term "Esquimox" for "Eskimo." While the currently accepted term for these people is "Inuit" (their own name for themselves), we have used "Eskimo" so as to stay closer to Johnston's usage. He also favored the term "pectograph" for "pictograph" in some of his earlier work, and this spelling is retained in his handwriting.

In addition to Johnston's text, based on his notes, we have used over 200 of the pen and ink drawings that he executed in the field during the decades before 1939. This work is truly one of the most important finds in ethnography to come to light in recent years.

Some of Johnston's ideas and conclusions may be controversial, but we must remember that they are based on his own firsthand observations and from his conversations and interviews with Native Americans themselves. He was there. He saw it with his own eyes and heard it with his own ears.

PREFACE

By Constance Johnston Speight

The darkness of the night was not comforting even though I could see all the shining stars through our car window. We were camped near Sand Tank Canyon, somewhere in the Mojave Desert. I was five years old, tucked with blankets on the back seat of daddy's car. I could hear the adults talking, and his voice was distinctive, but I was still very afraid.

I was always "brought along," the only child on daddy's digs and explorations. I guess I was allowed and put up with since he was president of the Archeology Society of Southern California, and a man to be reckoned with.

When the sun finally rose, I was always relieved. I happily skipped along behind daddy as he and the others explored trails that led through galleries of pictographs. I had no knowledge of the ancient artists, but I liked the faces, even the snakes and strange circles chiseled so long ago.

I often fell into disfavor on many trips because the cigar box Daddy gave me to "collect in" was always filled with more beads, arrowheads and pottery shards than the adults ever found with their screens. One irritated man asked me how I found so many things. Daddy replied "Because she's so close to the ground."

However unwanted I was by the adults, this was a unique experience for a child. Daddy also found other things of natural interest. He could locate a rabbit's warren, and he explained that wild bunnies didn't live in hutches. We would walk across a marsh, and when a bird flew up he knew exactly where her home was and parted the grass with his geology pick, revealing a perfect nest with blue speckled eggs.

I learned the cries of each bird of prey while learning to find ollas buried in the ground with only the top ring showing.

My father wasn't a physically large man, but he seemed 15 feet tall, not only to me but to those he dealt with. He gave new meaning to the word domineering. He was rarely wrong, and he had a driving curiosity and an endless need for adventure. He would have been a great pirate seeking treasure.

On the flip side, he could be a man of incredible caring and generosity with his time, as documented each Christmas when he completely rehabbed old bicycles for needy kids.

He was very respectful of all people and cultures that he encountered in his travels. Once when he was filming for Walt Disney on the Yucatan Peninsula of Mexico, he was caught in a violent storm and lost much of his gear. He found a hut, but it was occu-

Right: Franklin Robert Johnston studies a pot at one of his excavation sites.

pied. The native asked him in and offered to share his meager meal. A single pot contained water, an onion and a small fish. The man had one bowl, which was offered to my dad. The man put the fish eyes into the thin broth, which was considered a delicacy. My father told me it would have been rude not to graciously accept.

This was a valuable lesson that I learned for my future travels. I have eaten some things that I certainly didn't like, but the rewards have been new and interesting friendships. To me as a child, my father was sometimes a frightening figure, but one full of exciting knowledge about this world. I knew that he loved me deeply. I treasure the metate and pestle that he left me — which today sit on my patio — and their link to a magnificent people and to my father.

My dad walked to a whole different band. He prized his relationship with the Indians, and he treasured their artifacts.

He was a singularly unique man.

Left: Johnston and his daughter during a visit to the Navajo country of Arizona.

FOREWORD

By Michael Speight

I remember spending long summer days in a room filled with American Indian artifacts, museum cases layered with arrowheads, pottery shards, beads, old photos and items my young child's mind could not comprehend. I knew only it was all part of my grandfather's collection, gathered over some 30 years of fieldwork that he had undertaken mostly on his own.

When my brother and I were small children, my grandfather had a cabin up in the foothills of the Angeles Forest, near where we lived. My mother would take us to visit from time to time, and I remember that as we approached the cabin on our hikes, my brother and I would cry out "Yohoo Man, are you there?" It stuck. The name Yohoo Man become his moniker for a lifetime.

Yohoo Man, my grandfather, was a unique individual, one of those rugged individualists that you read about in a Hemingway novel. He traveled extensively throughout his life, to Europe, Mexico, Central America, South America and to the islands in the Pacific long before it became fashionable.

One of my greatest joys is reading his diaries from those trips: "We shipped out of Long Beach on the tramp steamer such and such, got caught in a blow off the coast of Costa Rica. Everyone at the rail."

They make movies out of lives like his.

For me, he was the most interesting figure a young man could possibly have to look up to. He was always there for me whenever needed, and he taught me much about life. He had a green thumb, a warm heart and an inquiring mind.

He had done things and seen things that we can't even imagine today. During World War I, he was a field artillery observer, working behind enemy lines, calling in the cannon shells from the great guns of the day. In this role, he met Colonel Remey of the French Underground. They became lifelong friends, and during World War II they worked together documenting the Nazi atrocities.

My grandfather took some of the first photographic evidence showing the horror of the death camps. I still have vivid images from my childhood of those photos, bound in their leather book, but I cannot imagine what it was like to have seen such things firsthand.

It is a great pleasure for me personally to share this heretofore unpublished work: My grandfather's notes, an early glimpse of one man's attempt at documenting the lives of our original citizens.

Compared to what we know today, there may be wrong assumptions or false understanding within these pages, but there is truth of observation, and an honest rendering at a moment in time.

Above: Lone Wolf of the Kiowa with a presidential medal. The Kiowa were among the tribes that Johnston studied.

CHAPTER 1:

WORSHIP THE GREAT SPIRIT

Although there was a variation in the religions of different tribes, the Great Spirit was the one to whom they all looked for succor, whether it be in battle, the hunt or for rain to make the crops grow. Some believed the Creator came from the inner regions of the Earth, others from the sky, and still others from the ocean, thus giving a variation to the interpretation of the religious ceremonies.

Each tribe had its own sacred animal—bird, fish or reptile. All known animals, in some form or another, were gods. So complicated were their orders that it is hard to decipher the paternal clan or gene relations of one to the other. Most tribes have left pictographs or petroglyphs and rock writings that have aided in reconstructing their tribal life, but very often the petroglyphs in one district had quite a different meaning from those found in another section of the country. Great care had to be taken in their interpretation, especially if associated characters were added.

The frog was associated with the rain god. It was found on pottery designs, in basketry, and even on stone and pottery fetishes of worship. The gods of lightning and thunder were also important figures. No form of thunder fetish is known except where the thunderbird is referred to as flapping his wings and causing great rumblings. Lightning was represented by a zigzag pattern.

Fire was held in reverence by the American Indian, though not worshiped as it was by the Toltec further south, in Mexico and Peru.

The various clans could be compared favorably with our secret organizations, except none ever admitted a woman. The clans consisted of the hunting clans, the priests and the shaman. The hunting clans were divided into groups according to the animals worshiped or the region or territory in which they lived—bear, eagle, deer, otter, hawk, coyote, etc.

The priests or shaman were the real rulers of the tribe, supreme in power. Nothing of importance was ever carried into action without their sanction. They held ceremonies for the hunt and blessed the clan hunting fetishes and the hunters prior to the hunt. In times of abundant game, this was not such a serious matter, as almost anyone could procure a supply; but in times of scarcity only the most skilled hunted. Only after a big ceremony could the hunters then go forth to hunt.

If there was to be a war, whether for an attack or to secure plunder, it was the priest who worked the warriors into a frenzy by his chanting and exhortations before the battle, the chief having first been worked into the proper mood. The priests set the time for holding festive prayers and offerings to the gods prior to planting crops, for imploring the rain gods for rain, for the harvest, and last-

Right: The Sun Goddess, identified as such by Johnston because of the position she held among the thousands of petroglyphs at Sand Tank Canyon in the Mojave Desert.

ly for the grand ceremony of blessings for the bounty of that which had been given them.

The eagle was reverenced in some form of ceremony by all tribes, due no doubt to its strength and sagacity. It was shown in winter counts, pictographs, petroglyphs, pottery and basketry in some form by all American Indians. In 1602, the expedition of Spanish explorer Sebastian Vizcaino, visiting Santa Catalina Island, said the Indians there were worshiping two great black crows (which were probably condors).

The bear was worshiped for its prowess, strength and fearlessness. The claws were worn as a badge of valor, as were the talons of the eagle. Bear skins were greatly sought, although in many tribes the meat of the bear was never eaten. The coyote was venerated for its fleetness and cunning by all tribes except the Chinook, who said the animal was a medium for the Evil Spirit. The snake, because of its close association with the Earth and its supposed wisdom, was sacred to many American Indians. The Pecos associated the serpent with Montezuma, the rain god, and the Pueblo Indians prayed to the serpent for rain.

The Eskimo did not recognize any superior deity but a number of supernatural beings, the evil ones seeming to predominate. At all times they carried on their person some small carved talisman as their protector and aid in the chase and in fishing.

With the Aleuts, the sun, stars and moon were worshiped. Their great religious dance was held in December, at night. Wooden idols were carved for the occasion and carried to some island where they were set up. The participants, both men and women, first donned masks, then stripped and danced naked under the moonlight around the idol. They could see only their feet, and woe to the one whose mask should come off. To look at the idol or one of the opposite sex was as fatal as the glance of a demon and one was marked as dead. When the

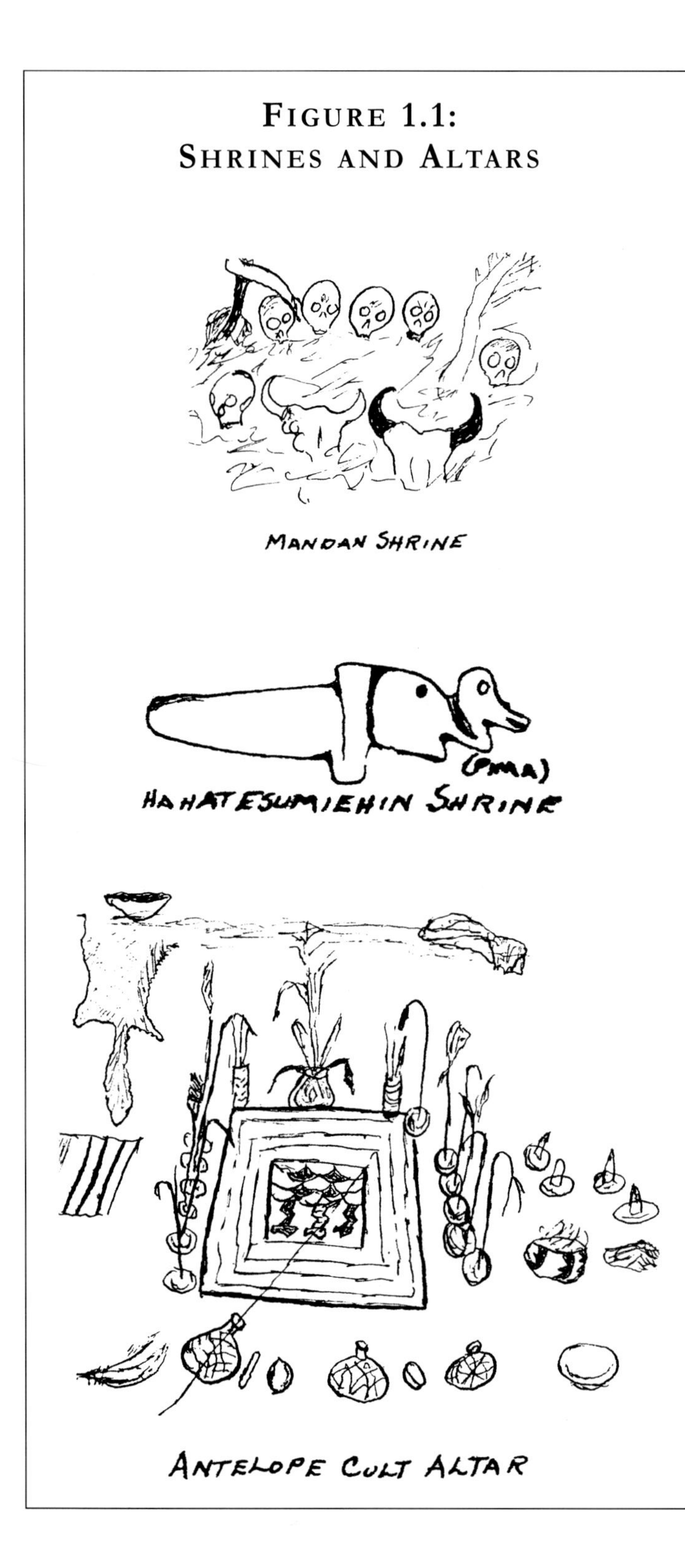

FIGURE 1.1: SHRINES AND ALTARS

dance was over the idol and mask were broken and cast away.

A ceremony of the northern coastal Indians was celebrated in January and was called the "immersion of the bladders." More than a hundred bladders taken from animals shot only with arrows were blown up and fantastically decorated and painted. They were hung horizontally along the wall of the kashim. Four birds carved of wood, an owl with the head of a man, a sea gull and two partridges were set up so they could be moved as puppets; the old owl fluttered his wings and moved his head; the gull struck the boards with his beak; and the partridges pecked each other. Lastly, a stake covered with straw was placed in the center of the fireplace. The men and women danced before these effigies in honor of Jugjak, the spirit of the sea.

Each time someone stopped dancing, some of the straw was lighted until all was consumed. The bladders were then taken down and dipped into the sea, which was the greatest part of the ceremony and its conclusion. When these northern coastal Indians were asked why they performed such a ceremony, they usually replied that they did so because their fathers had always done so.

One of the gods of the Californians was Chinigchinich, which means "almighty." One day, when there was a great gathering, he appeared before them dancing, dressed in a petticoat of feathers and a high crown, also of feathers; his body was painted red and black. He told them he had come from the stars. He talked with them and confirmed the powers of the chief and the medicine man, as well as taught them worship and how to construct their places of worship. He then prepared to die and the people asked if they should bury him. He warned them against such a thing, saying, "If ye bury me ye would tread upon my grave. Look to it then that ye do not bury me, for I go to where the high stars are and my eyes will see all the ways of men." Thus he was cremated.

Some of the Columbia tribes pictured the future as two large rivers flowing out of a dark lake. The good entered the stream on the right, which sparkles with constant sunshine and supplies them with an abundance of salmon and berries, while the wicked pass into the left stream and suffer cold and starvation.

The Salish described the happy state of the hereafter as the bright land where all things abound. The wicked, on the other hand, abide with the Black Chief and are constantly tantalized by the sight of game, water and fire that they cannot reach. At the cremations, others believed the smoke curling and floating upward carried the soul from the funeral pyre to the regions of the rising sun.

Every group had a punishment for those who had, during their life, transgressed the sacred laws of the tribe. The Navajo believed that at death they returned to the place whence they originated; below the earth, where all kinds of fruits and cereals grew from the seeds lost above.

The paradise of many of the American Indians lay to the south, where it was perpetual summer and there was always plenty of game. There they had all the comforts and the pleasure of seeing their friends and relatives again. In this paradise there were no wars or disturbances of any sort, no bodily pain and all lived in harmony.

Departed spirits may return to their native habitat and manifest themselves in dreams. If the relatives had not mourned sufficiently or kept food in the grave vessels or attended the dead respectfully, they would be annoyed by whistling sounds and startling apparitions.

Many tribes believed that man was not the lord of the universe, being equal with only the rabbit, the deer and the young corn plant, and they should be approached circumspectly if they were to give and lay down their lives for him. All must have sacred songs sung to them and certain rituals performed.

One of the things that was taught by many of the more advanced tribes was that rectitude of conduct produced length of life, and that evil inevitably reached the offender.

The Midewin societies of the Great Lake regions were teachers of the best that was in the American Indian according to these standards.

A certain sketch shows the Midge path of life from youth to old age, the tangent at each angle representing a temptation. There are seven of these temptations in life. The first comes to the young man, who, if he yields at this time, will not live long. The same is true of the second. The third temptation regards the young man's reli-

FIGURE 1.2:
SYMBOLS PAINTED ON HIDES

FIGURE 1.3:
EXAMPLES OF PICTOGRAPHS

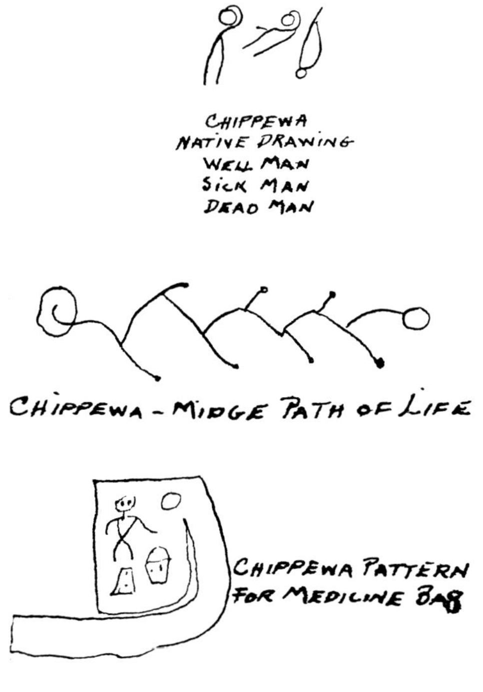

CHIPPEWA
NATIVE DRAWING
WELL MAN
SICK MAN
DEAD MAN

CHIPPEWA - MIDGE PATH OF LIFE

CHIPPEWA PATTERN
FOR MEDICINE BAG

Above: Teha, at the age of 125.

FIGURE 1.4: SAND PAINTING

gious life. The fourth comes in middle life, and the fifth arises as he begins wondering if he has always been respectful to old age. The sixth and last concerns the fulfillment of all his religious obligations; the seventh, whether or not he has been respectful through all ceremonies. If not, he is doomed; if, however, he has been respectful through all, he will be allotted the old age due to man.

The Choctaw regarded the sun as a deity because it was ascribed with the power of life and death. They thought that if it continued to look down upon them they were safe; but if the sun turned away, some of their tribe would die. This explains their dread of an eclipse. The sun was their succor in war through the influence of Hushtahli, the Supreme One. They also referred to Ishtahullo, who no doubt was one and the same, although they did not have any spiritual conception in connection with him.

If they needed rain they applied to the rain maker or rain god and not to Hushtahli. Likewise, for fair weather they appealed to some other source and not the man above.

The rainbow was supposed to be the beautiful dress of the thunder god. He loosened it when he wished to climb down to the Earth.

FROM INDIAN LEGENDS

In the beginning, A'wonawil'ona lived with the sun father and the moon mother, and with them lived Shi'wanni and his wife Shi'wano'kia. They were super-beings who labored not with their hands but only with their minds and hearts. A'wonawil'ona's breath was the clouds from which the rain formed. Therefore, when an American Indian breathed upon a fetish he was bathing it with the life or breath of the Creator and the action was divine.

Shi'wanni and Shi'wano'kia were the parents of A'shiwi, who was created in the underworld. By sprinkling a pathway of sacred meal, he was able to lead the people out of the darkness of the underworld. Then they came to inhabit the present Earth, which they reached as the Evening Star (the second warrior of the sun father) rose above the horizon.

Then came the birds who sang songs of praise to A'wonawil'ona. At the end of the ninth day, after many prayers, A'shiwanni was directed by the Divine One to build a house, as prior to this time they had none.

Some of the Indian legends say that in the beginning they had webbed feet and stub tails, which they amputated after a time. Other tribes say that they came in human form as they are now, and those who had to change their form came afterward.

The Divine One, wishing the world to be guarded by keen sight and smell, visited Shi'papolima, who conversed with his medicine man and the beast god Po'shaiyanki. They converted the cougar and gave him the north over which to reign; the bear received the west, the badger the south, and the white wolf guarded the east. The eagle was given the zenith to guard, and the rattlesnake and ants were to preside with wisdom over the Earth.

Above: Ga'be'nah'gwey'wence (John Smith) at the age of 128.

SAND PAINTINGS

Indian mythology records said the gods were the first to make pictures in the sand, while another account said that they first made the paintings on the clouds; but as man could not do likewise, they were taught to use sand. Still another account said that the eagle taught them to paint. All legends agree that paintings were made in sand instead of on cloth, like the first painting originally made by the gods. By making them on sand, no one could steal them and cause strife or fights in the tribe.

In making the paintings, white sand represented the east, blue the south, yellow the west and black the north, while red was the symbol of sunshine. Black was male and blue was female. Different tribes made paintings for various purposes—boys' and girls' puberty ceremonials, as well as season dances, such as the snake dance, antelope dance, etc. Desert Indians were the greatest makers of paintings, but many other tribes did similar work, sometimes in meal, pollen or earth. At times the shaman used a sand painting as a last effort to cure a sick man, but if the affected one did not recover he was sure of a happy ending if thus honored. All paintings were destroyed the day they were made.

FIGURE 1.5
SAND PAINTING

CHAPTER 2

CULTURES

Cultures may be traced more definitely in one district than in another. Changes in climactic conditions and the abundance or lack of game were responsible for many shifts and migrations, while in other sections a tribe may have stayed in a certain district regardless of the variations that have taken place, as for instance in Southwest Arizona, New Mexico and nearby bordering regions.

We find the Basket Makers Number I were the earliest group in the Southwest. They were more or less nomadic people who depended principally upon caves for their shelter and on small game and wild vegetation for their livelihood. Basket Makers Number II were a semi-hunting, semi-agricultural people. They stored their corn and supplies in pits lined with stone, but still clung to caves as their main shelters. They made better baskets, twine and sandals, and had progressed to some extent. Next came Basket Makers Number III, who made pottery. They had advanced in many ways. With stone and sand they faced up their cave fronts, thus making a better habitation. They raised more grain and vegetables in their cultivated patches than did their predecessors.

The next group in this section was Pueblo I. These people added to the walled-up caves a number of rooms of masonry. They made cotton fabrics and domesticated the wild turkey. They practiced cranial deformation. Pueblo II continued to advance, dwelling in small, individual houses which have been called the unit or one clan house. All masonry construction was entirely above the ground, with a kiva located under the central court. Corrugated pottery and painted ware were made by these Indians.

Pueblo III developed large, urban centers and the finest examples of Pueblo architecture. They created pictorial decorative pottery, with each center having its own individual designs. Pueblo III existed around 1100 to 1300 A.D. Pueblo IV, from the last of the Pueblo III until the arrival of the Spanish, was a rather declining period, in which many of the great early centers were completely lost or absorbed by other groups. During this time a general dying out of cultures occurred.

Some six and a half centuries ago, an Indian civilization flourished in Arizona. Then—as if in one breath—this civilization disappeared. Out of the sky came a meteor weighing from 10,000,000 to 12,000,000 tons. The crater which it made is about 40 acres in size, even today.

The wake of destruction left by the meteor spreads out 225 miles in all directions from the great hole. It forms a circle 450 miles across. It wiped out the civilization which, as all scientific evidence shows, disappeared from Arizona about that time.

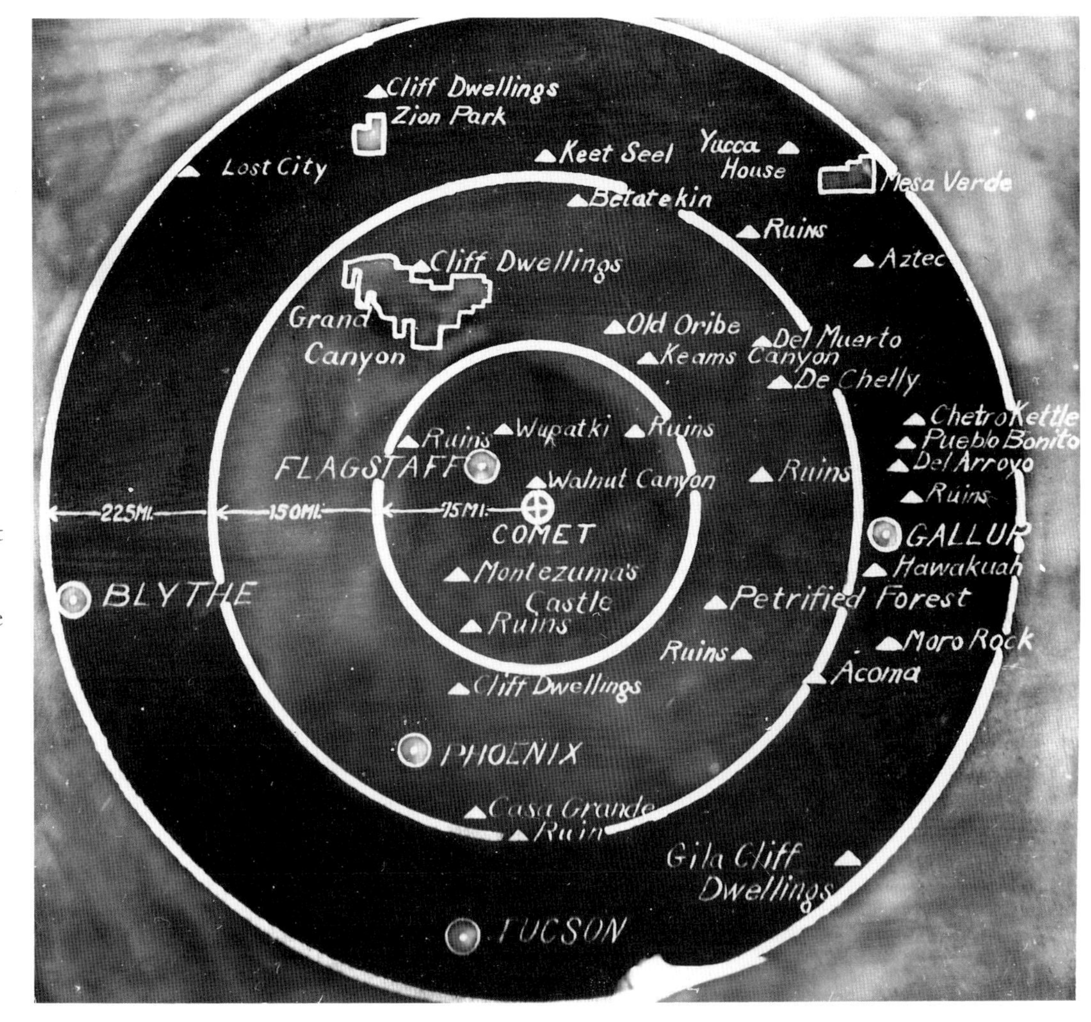

Right: Locations of important pre-Columbian cultural sites within a 225-mile radius of the meteor crater in northeastern Arizona.

The huge chunk of ore is known scientifically as "the Arizona Meteorite." The large area around the 225-mile radius was left desolated. The Great Spirit had no reason to be angry with the cliff-dwellers, a peaceful people, who lived under a democratic form of self-government, and apparently were at the peak of their "golden age" when the crash came.

Mummified human beings have been found sitting upright in family circles inside of ruined buildings, exactly as if something had suddenly sucked the life out of them. In a tumble-down cliff house near the great bee-hive dwelling known as Yucca House, there were three aged adults and a child, the adults sitting with their backs to the wall, while the child lay on the floor. You could hardly call them skeletons, because the skin had dried to the bones. They were sitting amid plenty. A pot with charred sticks under it shows that a meal was being cooked, and beneath a thick coat of plastering a cache of corn was found. Many persons have viewed such scenes, in widely separated villages, before the ruins were ransacked by souvenir hunters.

"Those sitting mummies were very old or very young persons," stated Russell, Dugan and Stewart in "The Solar System." "Hence the cataclysm occurred during the daytime, when the hunters were on the ranges and all the younger women were in the fields. The evidence appears very strong that this crater has been produced within modern times." (The fall of the Arizona meteor is a moot question; some competent authorities hold that it fell before the dawn of man in America; others place its fall around 1278.)

Due largely to the work done by Dr. A.E. Douglass, director of Steward Observatory, University of Arizona, the definite dates when about 40 old towns were started and finished have been ascertained from tree rings in beams buried amid the debris. And the timbers which told the most were charred—some of them burned into charcoal. So far as various searching parties were able to discover, the last tree used in the building of White House Pueblo was cut in 1275. Likewise, the last tree used in Wind Ruin was cut in 1275. Betatakin's last log was cut two years later, in 1277, which is the last date for many moons. The tree-chopping and house-building sud-

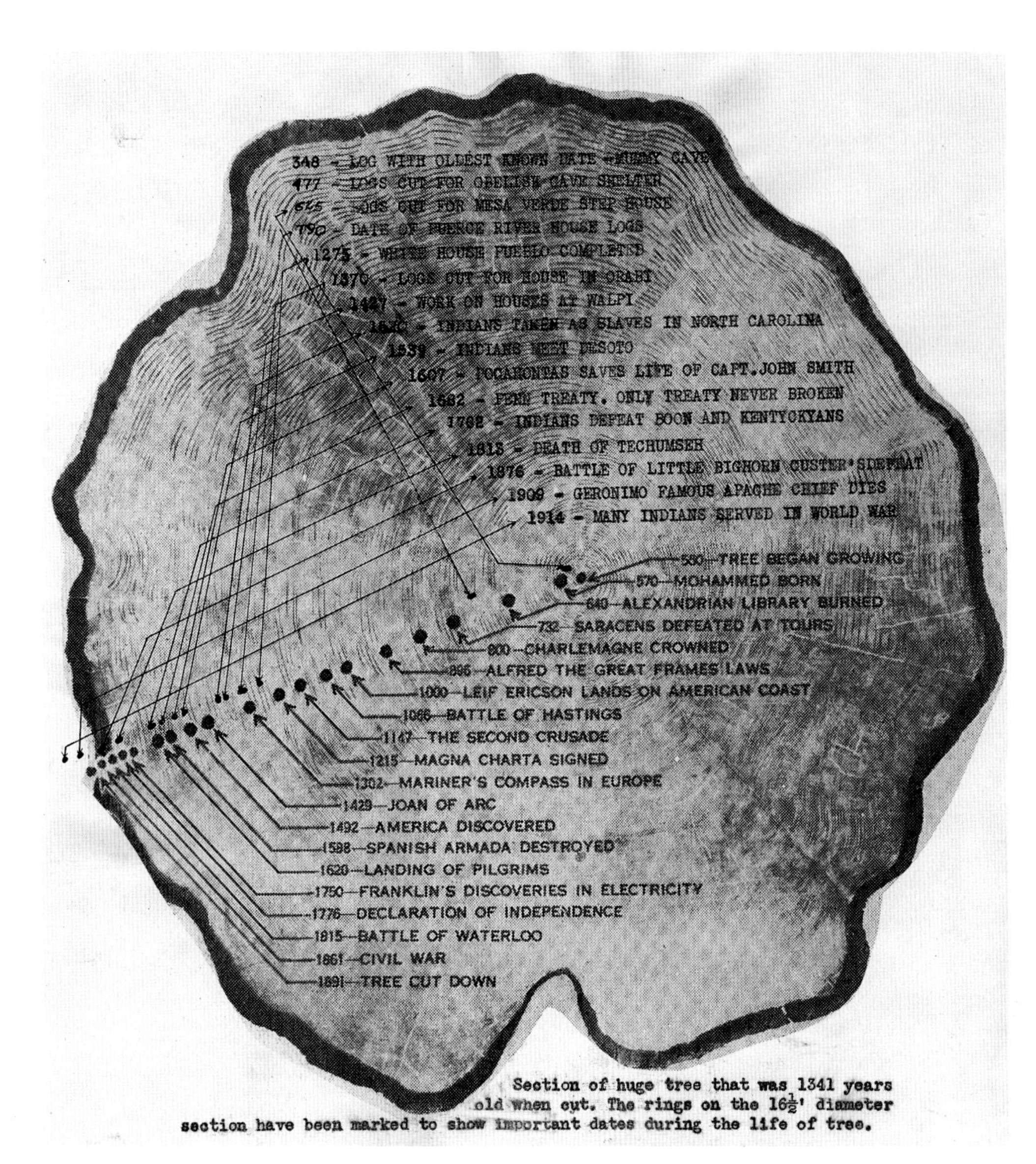

Above: The tree cross section that Johnston used to demonstrate the history of North America's indigenous cultures.

denly ceased. This may have been the time when the comet crashed.

To be sure, building operations were resumed later on (at Oraibi in 1370, at Walpi in 1427), but most of this later tree-cutting was town-building done by another newly-arrived group of people—a people that decorated pottery with Hopi yellow instead of the more primitive polychrome-on-red. "It was easy to note the difference between prehistoric wood and modern fragments," says Dr. Douglass. "The old timbers had disappeared entirely except in the form of charcoal or near charcoal."

Pueblo V is the period of the modern village and extends from the subjection of the Pueblos by the Spaniards to the present day. In making excavations, it is found that many of the periods overlap. Nowhere in the Americas is it as easy to trace through times of occupation as in the Southwest. The arid conditions have preserved specimens of all sorts to a far greater degree than elsewhere.

A much debated question among students and archaeologists is how many ages of occupation there have been. Their discoveries and explanations are like those of the three blind men and their description of the elephant.

One might dig to a certain depth in a given former Indian village and find refuse objects that tell a clear enough story of the people.

Associated items, bone, etc., give a fair idea as to the age of the site. Another archeologist comes to this site, goes on down a few feet more or many feet more, and finds, after having gone through a seemingly undisturbed layer, another similar to the one above. This has been done for as many as five different layers in some of the deposits on Santa Catalina Island.

Along the California coast, it is not unusual to find three distinct ages of occupation, one over the other. An example of how easily this could happen was forcefully shown recently when at the site of an excavation an extremely heavy rainstorm came up. After a day and night, the original contour of the camp was not only obliterated, but a service station that had stood on the highway that bordered this camp was completely buried. The only thing visible was the gas tank vent pipes. This flood condition clearly showed what had happened to the Indian villages in the past. Later, another group of people came along and thought this a favorable place, not knowing the fate of those before, and so on through the cycle of time. An excavation in the south recently uncovered items of extremely early Indian origin. Then in another layer were items brought in by De Soto, while another layer contained items from a later date, and so on.

In collections from caves where there has been the least amount of moisture, the remains have been found better preserved. The coniferous trees furnished timber for building and firewood. Deciduous trees helped out also. The shrubs and brushwood yielded material for bows, clubs, digging sticks, prayer sticks and basketry. Bark was put to many uses—cordage, nets, bedding and costumes. The smaller vegetation was used for arrow-shafts and ceremonial offerings; flutes were made of the

THE SOUL

What we term the soul, many of the Indians term heart. When a person dies it may be said that the "heart goes away." Sickness is an attempted departure of the heart.

THE AGED

The Gillinomeros and a few others killed the aged. They were led away from the camp, thrown on the ground and a pole was placed across the neck, upon which others sat until strangulation was complete. More often, however, the aged were treated with respect.

FIGURE 2.1: ARTIFACTS FROM AHUITZOTLA, MEXICO

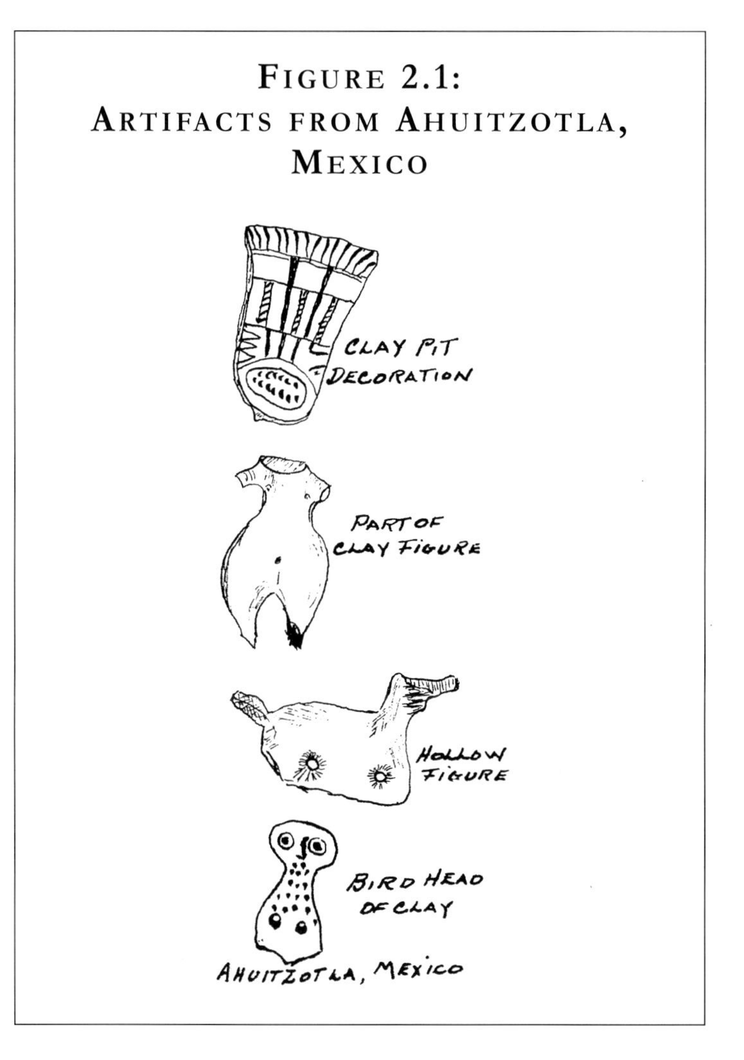

FIGURE 2.2: FETISHES

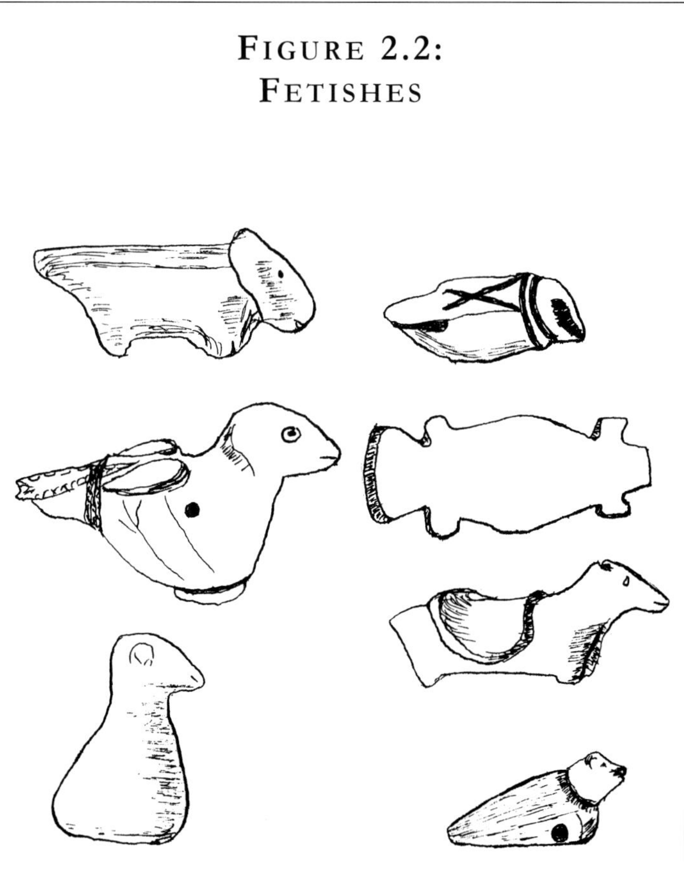

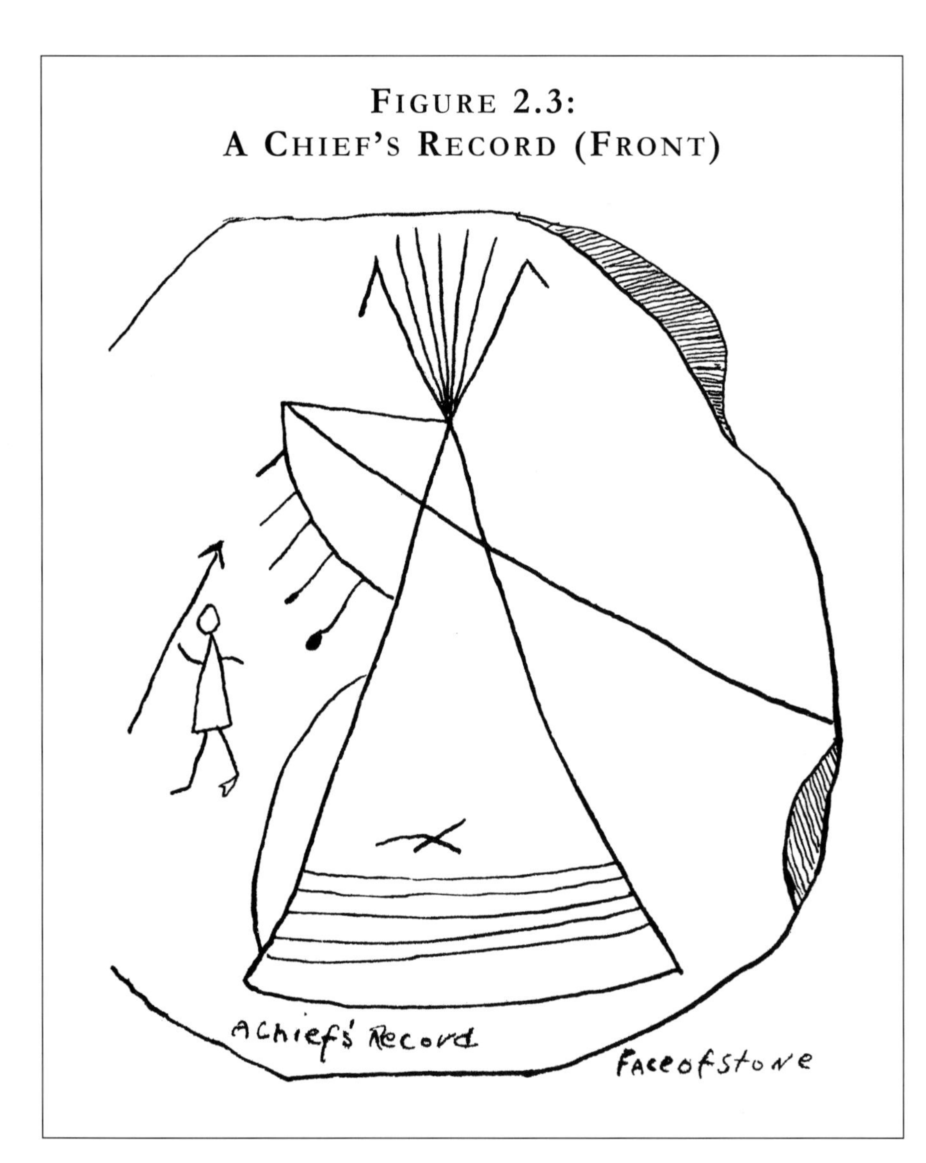

FIGURE 2.3: A CHIEF'S RECORD (FRONT)

reed; mats of tule; baskets, sandals and storage hampers of willow, yucca, dasyliron, etc. Fibers, food, medicines and dyes were made from the wild plants and roots, pinon nuts and acorns. Besides the cultivation of corn, squash, beans and gourds, cotton was grown in many of the warmer districts.

These evidences, along with the remains of certain bone, flint and stone things from the usual camp refuse, give a fair knowledge not only of the life of the people, but also of the things they had about them, both vegetable and animal.

In other places, shell mounds and kitchen middens serve to establish a culture by the items found there, especially along coastal districts where shell food formed a goodly part of the tribes' food. In the desert regions where the dwellings were stone or adobe, and in most cases partly excavated, much is written of these house ruins.

In determining the antiquity of man in America, Columbus will have to look to his laurels, for 1492 no longer is the "earliest date" in American history. Future schoolboys can start with 643 A.D.

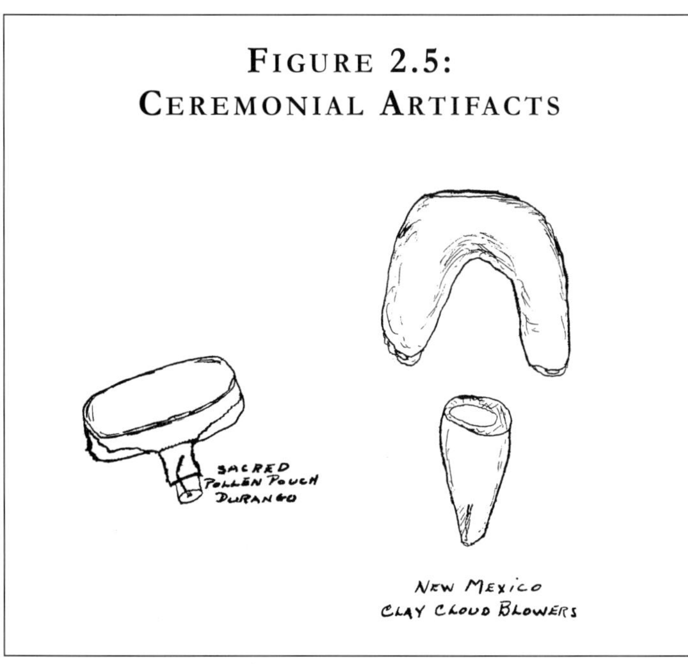

FIGURE 2.5: CEREMONIAL ARTIFACTS

The "dated" history of the United States was pushed back to the year 790 with the Smithsonian Institution's announcement that a house, identified as having been built that year, had been found by an archeological expedition near the Puerco River in Eastern Arizona.

This "dated" house will take a lot of guesswork out of America's ancient history. As definitely as a history book it reveals when its builders, the early Pueblo Indians, were flourishing in the Southwest.

The tree growth rings in the roof timbers made it possible to "date" the house as accurately as if "790 A.D." had been carved on the cornerstone. The timbers, with their rings, had been preserved through 11 centuries because they were charred by a fire that partially destroyed the house.

The roof collapsed, preserving a complete set of house furnishings of the style of 790 A.D. The house itself was little more than a shallow pit roofed over with poles, brush and plaster.

Knowing the date of the old house is important, said Smithsonian archaeologists, because it was built almost at the beginning of the rise of the Pueblo civilization, one of the most remarkable in the New World before the coming of the whites. The tree ring method already has been used in dating some of the later Pueblo dwellings built in the so called "apartment-house" style.

If considered only from the point of the number of languages and dialects that were used—more than 65 languages and four times as many dialects—it would seem almost impossible to accurately determine how long it would take to develop so many different tongues among an aboriginal people.

They were a people who could and did adapt themselves to the different existing local conditions and environment. Whether east, west, north or south, they made use of the materials they found at hand and progressed, according to artifacts found. A crude implement usually means a poor material to work with, and when better material was obtained we find a better artifact.

FIGURE 2.4: A CHIEF'S RECORD (BACK)

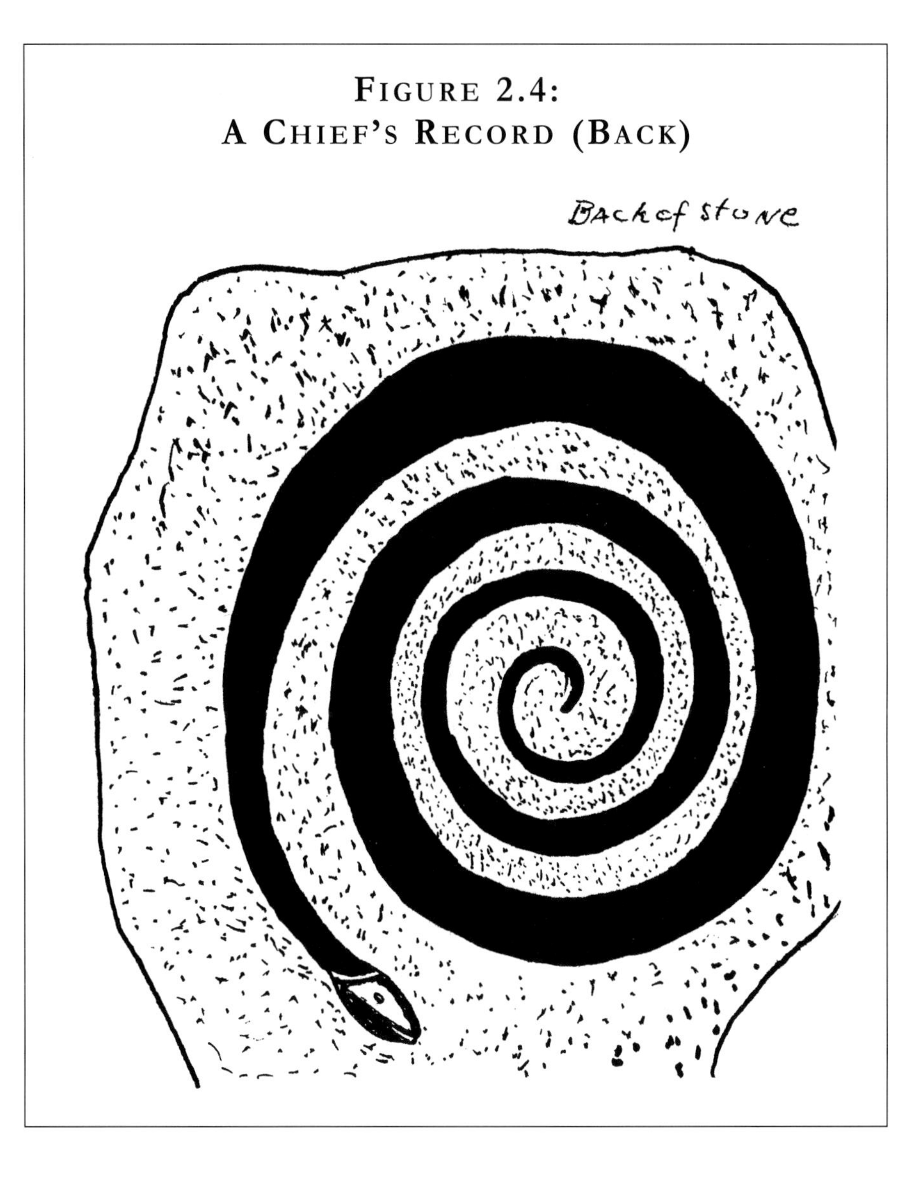

MEXICO

The finds in the northern Mexican districts and excavations were not so different from those of the California Mexican border, except where there were a few of the Aztec type specimens or the predominance of an Aztec influence. Clay figures, objects and many facial designs of relief work were found in fragments. Pottery forms similar to those farther north are commonplace. Slip glaze, incised textile and stamped designs are all found here. The clay spindle whorl is also found to be in use. In general, unless you go into the heart of Mexico and the vicinity of Mexico City you will find the country not so different from those districts bordering thereon.

CHAPTER 3

CHIEFTAINSHIP, WAR, TRIBUTE

Trespassing on lands, encroaching on hunting and fishing rights, abduction of women and supposed witchcraft were the greatest causes of war among the Indians; slaying a man might be righted by paying a certain sum or delivering slaves, but the former acts usually called for a greater revenge. The Juaneno never waged war for conquest, and this was true of many of the tribes.

In the West, conflicts as a whole were not so fiercely waged as was commonly supposed—being more noise and sham than actual battle. With the desert and Pacific Coast tribes the fall of the first enemy usually signalled a halt to the tumult. With the Eastern Indians, however, it was often a fight to the finish. Not until those that were not desired as slaves had been killed or had escaped, and until the village had been pillaged and burned, did they call a halt. Throughout the East, all the tribes were more active and naturally carried things to a more complete end.

In some of the tribes, when a chief intended to start a war party he selected some prominent part of the camp, usually a tree, and there he deposited his war club, a bow and arrows. They were placed on the side facing the enemy. All who wished to join the war party presented themselves to the chief and declared they wished to learn the art of war under his guidance. The chief then caused a drink to be brewed, of which they partook. After counseling, final preparation (which usually lasted days) and a final dance, they were ready to start on their journey.

Council and speech-making and painting of bodies with much ado always preceded any conflict, no matter how great or how trivial. The council lodge is taboo to women and children during councils. The leader of the council sits opposite the doorway, and the tribesman next in importance sits to his right, until the assembly is completed. Pipe and tobacco are laid directly in front of the chief personage, usually the chief, with the sacred fire in the center.

To be admitted as a warrior a young man had to pass certain ordeals, having first, by some feat, established himself as worthy. A day was appointed when one of the braves, acting as sponsor, introduced him to the chief who had placed himself in a circle of warriors; after addressing the candidate, he took from his pouch an eagle claw and proceeded to score the body all over until the blood ran freely. The candidate was expected to show no signs of pain. If the ordeal went off to the liking of all assembled, the chief then presented the young man with a bow and arrows and gave him a new name. Then each of the warriors gave him arrows to show their approval. In the campaigns following his initiation, he

Above: Yellow Bear, the chief of the Cheyenne.

would be assigned to the hardest and the most dangerous duty. He must continue in this manner until a new candidate appeared to take his place. (A translation of one of the Hidatsa songs is "I am simply of the Earth—need I be afraid?" With that thought in mind, is it any wonder they were courageous?)

Attacks were usually made early in the morning before the enemy was up. To those just awakening and somewhat bewildered the attacking party would seem more terrible than it actually was. In firing an enemy's place, firebrands were attached to arrows and shot into the roofs or where it was most likely to ignite.

As a rule few male prisoners were taken unless it was for some special reason, such as torture. In battle they struck quickly and were on the move to the next fight, stopping only long enough to scalp. Many of the women and children were treated to the same fate, and if prisoners were taken it was likely to be them. The Pawnee wore their hair in a scalp lock. In the taking of the scalp, the hair was grasped and a knife run around the base of the hair. The foot was then placed on the victim's neck and the scalp jerked off.

Warriors always painted themselves prior to going to war, partially to frighten the enemy and also to ward off evil spirits. Also with many tribes, there is a firmly fixed belief that the hour and conditions of every Indian's off-shuffling of the mortal will be perpetuated in the existence to come.

With the Maidu Indians, the bow was used in warfare, but a stabbing spear was their main weapon. They used no shield, but some of the Northwest tribes had rod armor coats that protected the chest and had the form of a high collar behind which the warrior could shield his head.

Shields or breast coverings were made of elk skin and other tough hide, shrunken to the greatest possible degree in order to thicken and toughen it. Protectors were also made of small sticks, bone or shells placed together on jackets or leggings.

The Comanche were one of the few tribes that made arm shields; a light basketwork frame is covered with two or more thicknesses of shrunken buffalo hide. Between the layers of hide is a stuffing of hair, making such a shield impervious to all weapons except a good rifle. They usually exposed their side, as it was thinner

FIGURE 3.1: WAR FETISHES

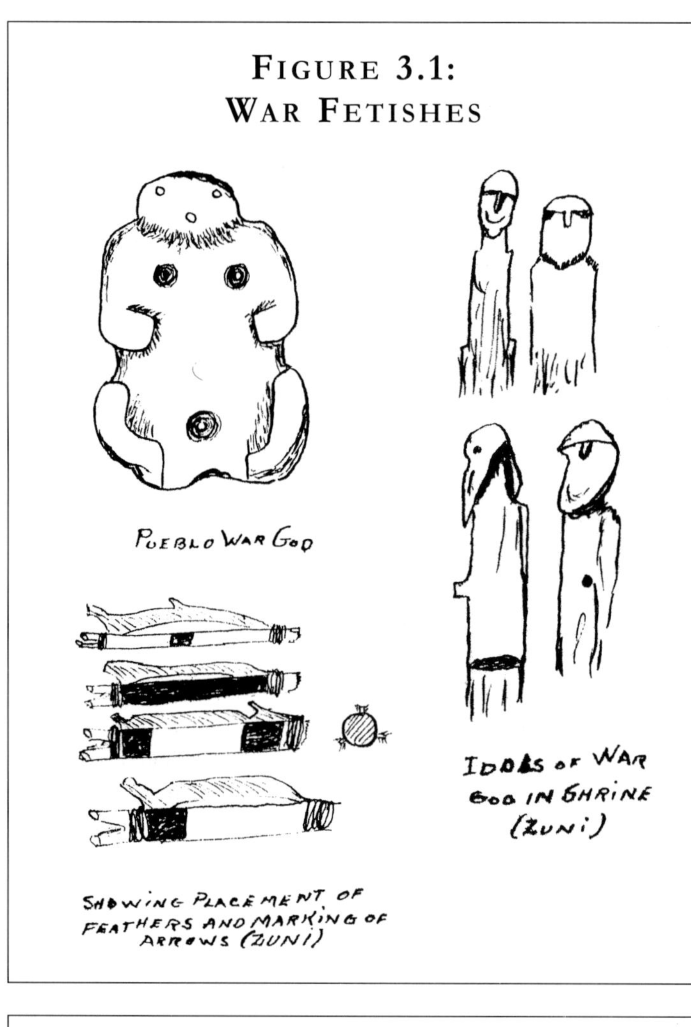

FIGURE 3.2: STONE AX HEADS

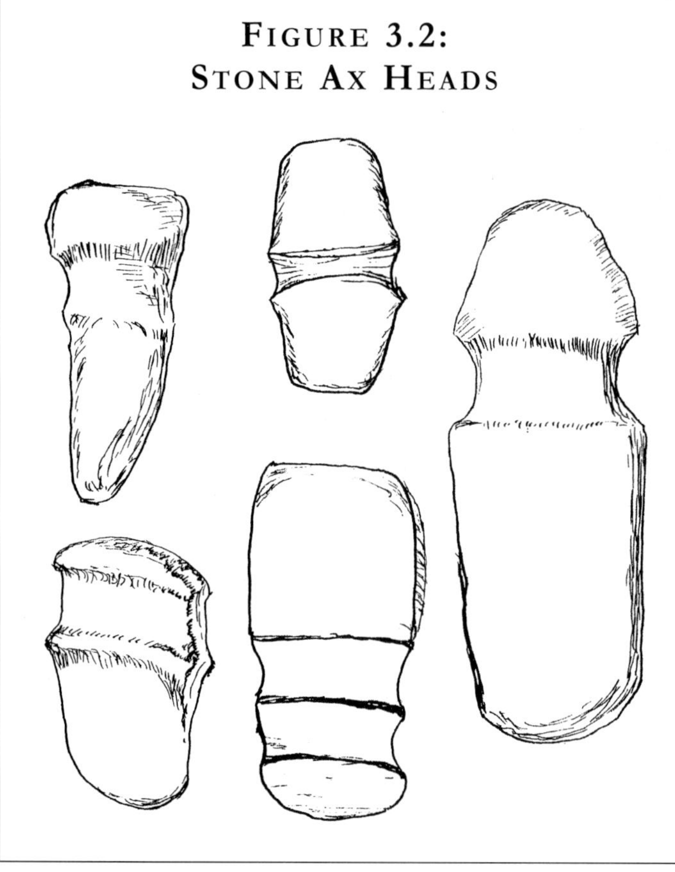

Above: Artifacts from Johnston's collection representing Native American ax technology from the Stone Age to the nineteenth century.

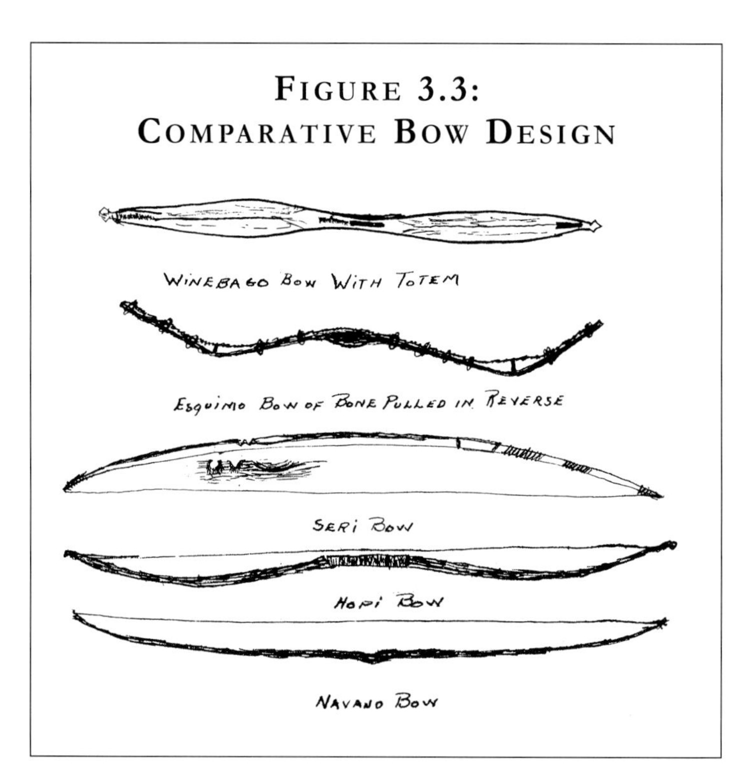

FIGURE 3.3: COMPARATIVE BOW DESIGN

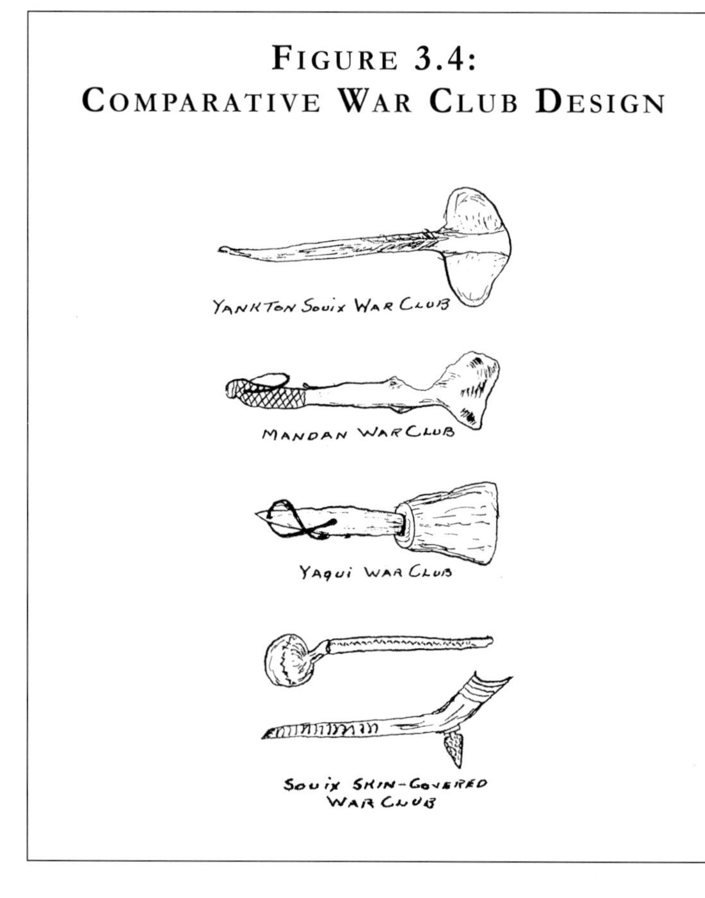

FIGURE 3.4: COMPARATIVE WAR CLUB DESIGN

than the front view. They placed great reliance on dodging arrows, being always on the jump or in a dancing movement.

The bowstring of the war bow was of fiber or sinew, as thongs would be liable to stretch if they became wet. The only exception to the use of thongs was the use of the neck of the snapping turtle. This was cut spirally, and it is said that no amount of moisture would affect it. No doubt at times thongs were used.

The arrows of the Indians were tipped with flint, stone, slate, bone, ivory and fire-hardened wood. Swords of a sort were made, some with flints inserted along the edges, others with just hardwood.

TRIBAL RIGHTS

Chieftainship was not always hereditary among the Indians. The chief was sometimes elected, and often chosen because of wealth or property or bravery. At no time was it an invariable rule that a father was succeeded by his son, unless the son was a fit person to fill the trust. In the East, the tribal chief was usually the war chief also; however, among the Western Indians this was not always true. It is often found that when the chieftainship was hereditary the chief did not exercise as much authority as the war leader.

Some tribes would attach themselves to a chief of their own choice, paying him certain tributes from the produce of their hunt and labor. Other Indians lived without such government, and some elected a chief only when going to war.

There were certain tribal or community rights observed among the Indians. Each gens had a right to the labors of all its women in the work of the camp and field. Each gens had a right to the male members in avenging wrongs, and the tribe had the right of the service of all males in time of war. To reveal the secrets of the medicine preparation or to give information to an enemy or one outside the tribe was regarded as treason, and in all cases was punishable by death.

If an Indian was adjudged guilty of witchcraft by the grand council, he had only one appeal, and that was to supernatural judgment. He must pass the test of fire. A fire having been built on the ground in a large circle,

Above: Bird Rattler, chief of the Blackfeet. The number of feathers in a headdress designated the number of good deeds done.

FIGURE 3.5: COMPARATIVE ARROW POINTS

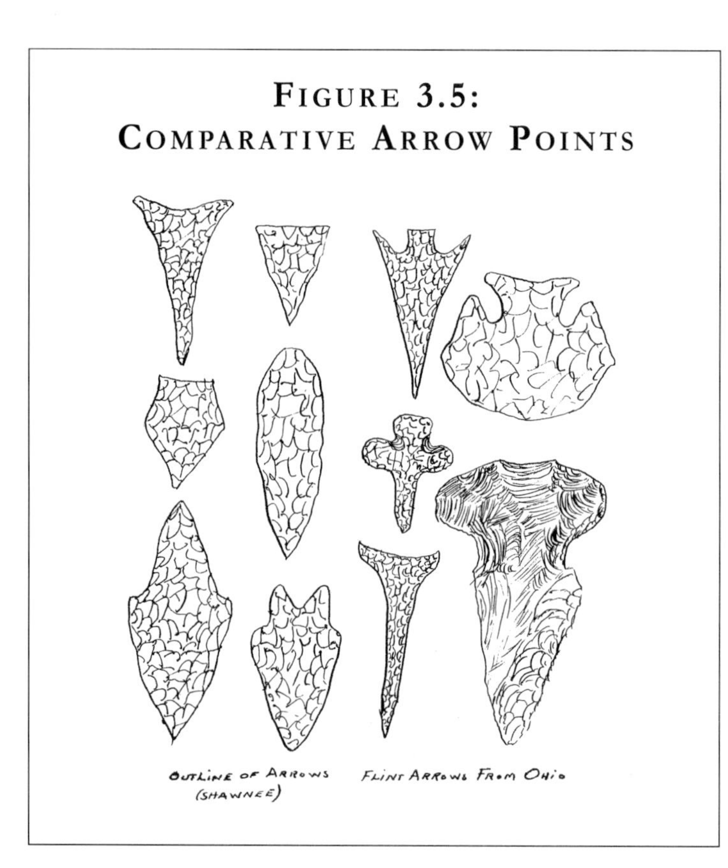

the accused must run through the fire from east to west and north to south. If uninjured, he is adjudged innocent; if injured, or if he stumbles in the procedure, he is condemned.

In the sacred war tepee of the Omaha there was a bladder in which the heads and fangs of four rattlesnakes were kept. For a serious offense the malefactor was given a choice of either losing all his horses and other belongings, or of forfeiting his life. Some trustworthy man of the tribe was designated to strike the culprit. This was done by dipping a staff in the bladder and prodding the offender on some part of his naked body.

Some of the stronger and more hostile warring tribes demanded and received yearly tribute from weaker tribes. The tribute consisted of slaves and supplies of their choice. The Pomo had a famed salt deposit near one of their villages. They demanded payment from other tribes who gathered salt there, and this led to many wars and feuds.

Above: Flint and obsidian arrow and spear points from Johnston's collection.

Above: A Plains Indian spear point and elaborately-beaded sheath from Johnston's collection.

Chapter 4

HUNTING AND FISHING

The specter of hunger hung continually over the Indian home, as it did with all indigenous peoples. Although some tribes had developed a rudimentary agriculture, animals and fish were the main foods of many. Lacking modern methods of storage, this search for food, hunting and fishing, was a steady and ceaseless occupation of the male members of the tribe. The implements used in these pursuits were the bow and arrow—frequently thought of in connection with warfare, but far more often used in the humbler work of filling the family larder.

The slow and tedious labor of manufacturing needful weapons and accessories consumed the greater part of the American Indian's time when not actually engaged in hunting, fishing or warfare. The type of implements were developed largely in accordance with the kind of game found in the area wherein they lived. Barter and exchange with tribes of other districts helped to spread tools which might not have been developed in certain localities from necessity alone. These factors also tended to modify some of the designs.

The Plains and desert tribes would be less likely to create fishhooks without the benefit of experience from those living where water was abundant. The variety of implements and the materials from which they were made were astounding.

Hunting bows were generally longer than the war bow. In size they varied from about 32 to 72 inches in length with a thickness of 3/8 to 1 1/2 inches, and a width of 1 to 3 1/2 inches. The most suitable wood found in the locality was utilized, generally ash, hickory, yew and willow. The wood was worked so that the outer part of the tree was on the inside of the bow. To curve the ends of the bow, it was sprung into shape and held over a slow fire until set. Frequently the bow was strung with sinew, often with sinew backing and bound at four or more places to prevent splitting. The war bow, however, was more often strung with fiber, as sinew stretched when wet, which would have been a deadly handicap. A rare variation of this was a thong bowstring, which was cut spirally from the neck of a snapping turtle. This material did not stretch. Bone, ivory and antler were used infrequently as materials for the manufacture of bows; however, generally, this was done in the North.

Arrows were universally similar in style, varying accordingly as to the wood or cane used for the shaft and as to general length. A fair average was approximately 25 inches. Some localities abounded in large reeds of "arrow weed." Into the hollow ends of this shaft, as with cane, a wood foreshaft was fitted to furnish ballast in flight. The arrow point was secured to one end by inserting it in a split and then binding it with sinew and tarring

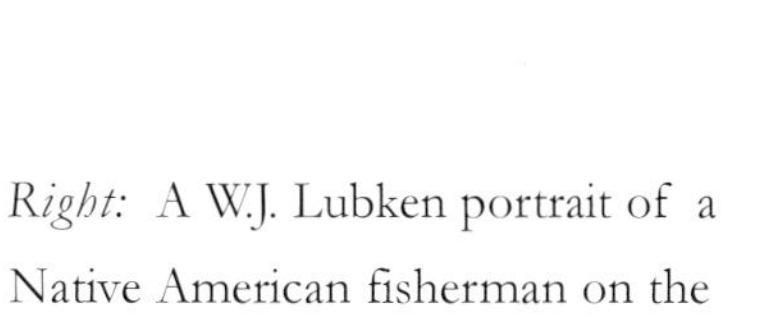

Right: A W.J. Lubken portrait of a Native American fisherman on the Colorado River, August 16, 1907.

or pitching. The other end was notched and winged with feathers to make it travel in a true course. The feathers were split lengthwise for ease in fastening. These were pitched or bound on with fiber or sinew. Some tribes used two or three, and sometimes four, feathers.

The arrowheads offer a wide variety of design and material. Flint was the most popular, as it was the most serviceable; however, other materials were utilized. Often, fire hardened wood, shell and bone were worked into suitable form and shape. In hunting, the arrow was often retrieved intact and used repeatedly if not damaged, but in war it seemed to be a practice never to use the arrow point a second time.

One of the reasons for having a foreshaft in the reed arrow was that if an attempt was made to withdraw the arrow, the point would remain in the wound. This was especially true in warfare. In this case, however, an unnotched arrow point was used to make doubly certain the point could not be withdrawn.

Quivers were usually made from the skin of some animal, most often from one of the hunting animals, such as the wildcat or wolf. A few made of reeds woven together or braided yucca fiber have been found in the desert country. Skin covers were devised for protecting the bow when not in use.

Small game was often killed with a blowgun and darts. This weapon, most popularly associated with the

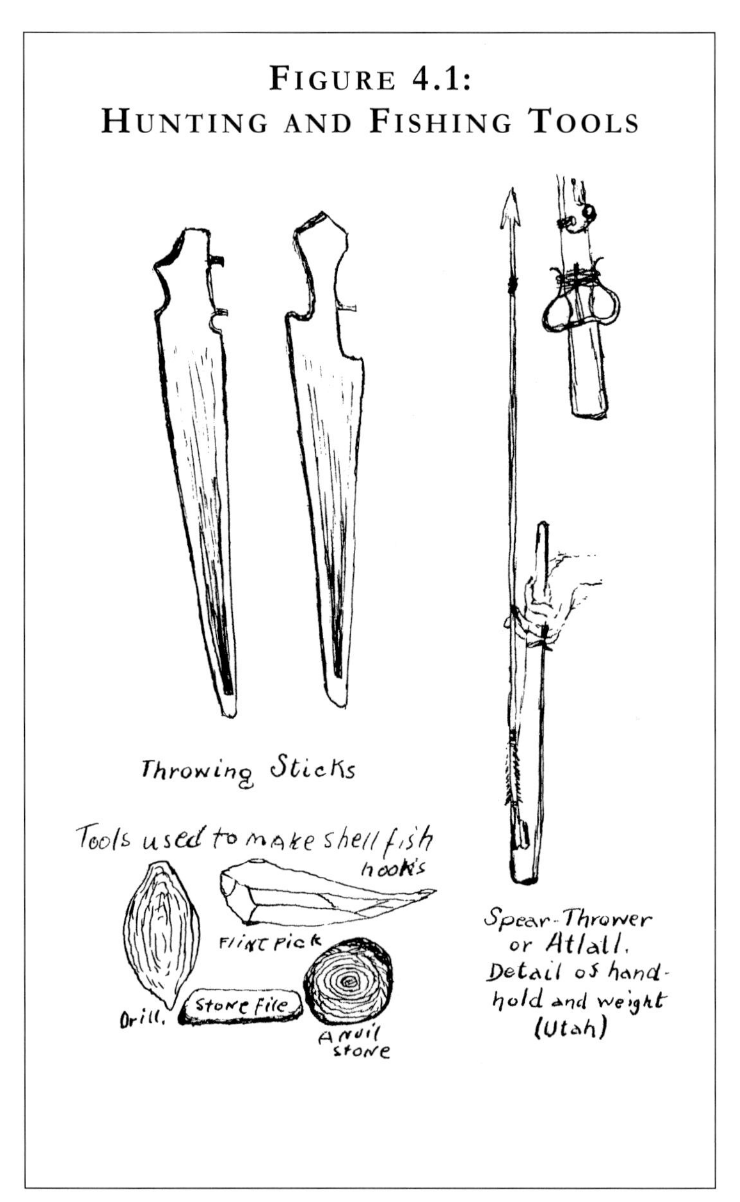

South Sea islands, has been found to have been more widely used by the American Indians than was previously supposed. The arrows, which were blown through the tube, were slender pieces of cane, often feathered with thistledown.

The earliest knives were made of bone, flint, stone and slate. After the first contact with the white people, the American Indians secured trade goods and made knives with steel blades, which had a variety of handles. The purpose for which the knives were designed created patterns such as: one for woodworking, one for eating, and one for a different type for hunting. These patterns seem to have been universal. Saws were especially sought for making knife blades.

The extent to which the knife was used in hunting is varied. Likely, with larger animals, it was used to deliver final blows. It was also the implement for skinning and severing the flesh for food from the carcass. Hence, it was an indispensable part of the equipment of the hunter.

As with quivers and bow covers, skin was the most used material for making knife scabbards. Almost all sheaths were made from leather of some sort. It is natural that many handsome examples are still to be found, due to the fact that it was the most readily worked material available and a plentiful supply was always at hand because of steady hunting.

The use of the throwing stick dated from an early age, and is one of the lesser known means of hunting employed by the American Indians. How widespread this may have been is a matter of conjecture. It is certain that the Southwestern tribes practiced this art up until recent times. The dry desert air of this region is more conducive to the preservation of wooden artifacts than elsewhere, though this evidence does not prove these tribes were the sole users of this method. The rabbit stick, thrown with deadly accuracy by the desert tribes at the rabbits that abounded on their plain, are an excellent example of a people who use the throwing stick, even in present times.

The atlatl, or spear throwing tool, was used extensively by the early people. The projectile was similar to the arrow, except much longer. The atlatl was held in the user's hand, above the shoulder, the butt of the arrow at the tip of the atlatl. With a forward whip-like movement the arrow was thrown with great force and accuracy. The desert ruins have yielded numerous parts and a few complete atlatls. Although these implements have been located throughout the entirety of this region, the throwing sticks may probably be explained by the dry atmosphere, which naturally preserved the wood much longer than would be possible elsewhere. This implement antedates the bow and arrow.

The use of copper for spearheads and other implements was limited to those tribes where the metal could easily be procured, and when it was procured it was often in a crude fashion. While more copper has been found in the Rocky Mountain region than elsewhere, it also appears nearer the surface in the Great Lakes area. As mining was practiced only minimally among the American Indians, it is no surprise to find that its use started in the latter region. The spear was used from the very earliest times to the modern period, with only slight changes. It was a long heavy shaft with a point attached. The method of making the harpoon varied from the straight fire hardened stick to the Seri turtle harpoon method, which entailed inserting the head or spike in the split end of a shaft and lashing on well made harpoon heads with fiber or sinew. Bone, antler and similar materials were best suited for making harpoon heads, as they were lightweight, tough and easy to create the serrated edges necessary to perform their functions.

The Eskimo developed the harpoon art to its highest degree. Their harpoons have a main shaft and a point that is detachable when it strikes the game, the head being secured to a line which is reeled out when the harpoon is thrust. The shaft is secured by a halter that causes it to drag, thus retarding the animal's progress. Sometimes, no line is used and two or three harpoons are thrust into the animal, and, with the shafts dragging, its progress is retarded so that the hunter can overtake it in their boats and dispatch it readily. Even to this day, the white race imitate these methods in their whaling practice. Having the harpoon head affixed to a line, but detachable from the shaft, is the principle of the whale gun of today.

The use of axes, clubs and mauls for warfare, for killing already wounded prey and for household work was very widespread. Stone was the principal material used. Water worn boulders (conveniently shaped to

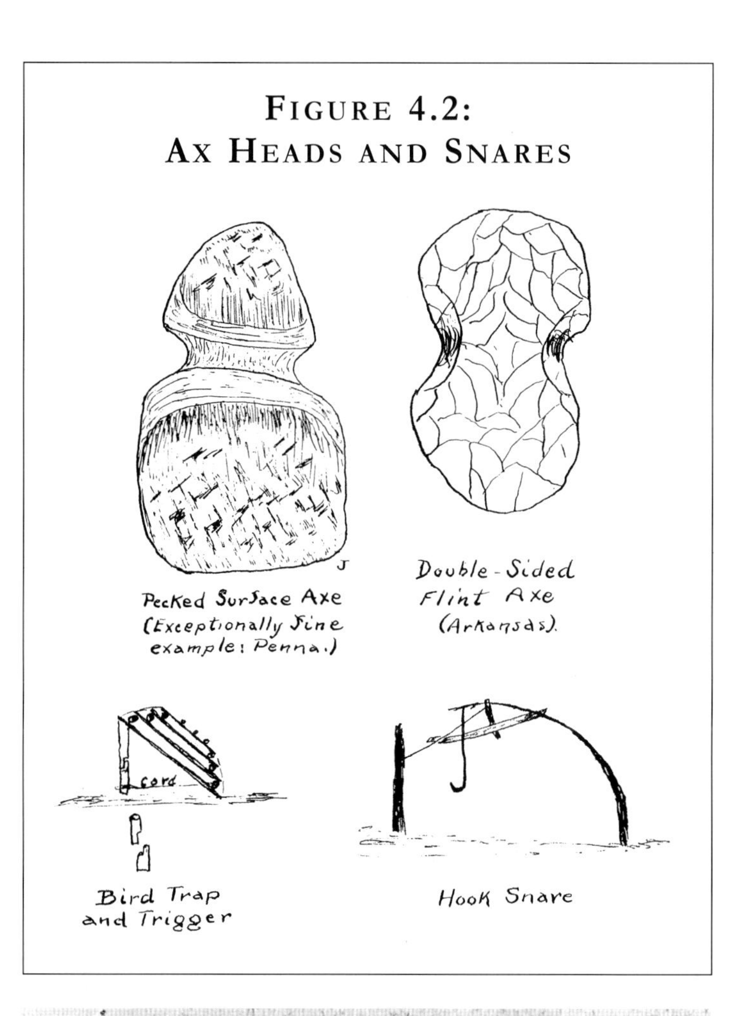

Above: Arrow points of weathered stone (21) and obsidian (22).

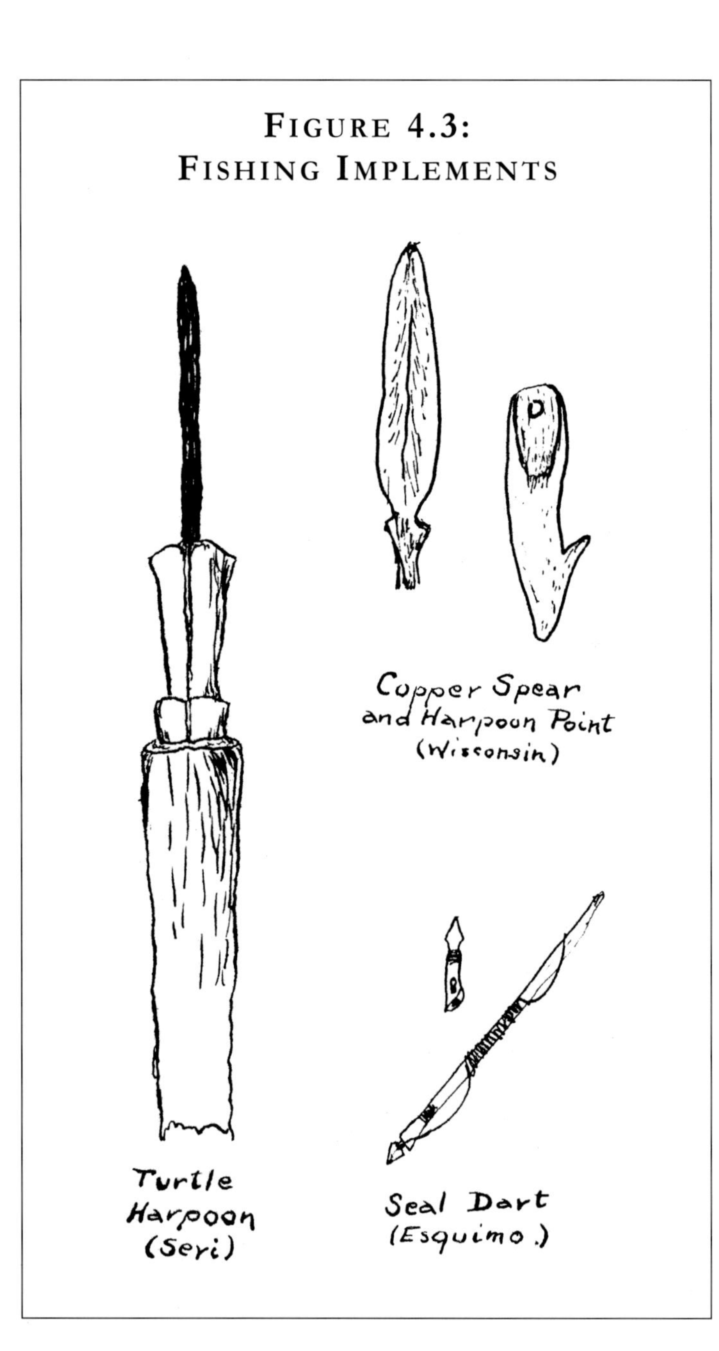

FIGURE 4.3:
FISHING IMPLEMENTS

begin with) were pecked away at with harder stone until the hafting groove and cutting edge had been achieved. Some of the harder stones kept this form, having been found in a fine state of preservation. Those of softer stone did not last so long, and their misshapen forms are frequently found. Near the old buffalo wallows, many stone mauls were found. It is understood that these were used for breaking the bones of larger animals to secure the marrow and for driving the pegs of tepees.

The hafting of the ax varied little with the different tribes. A crotched stick frequently was convenient. The head was lashed in with wet sinew or fiber cord, which shrunk as it dried, and was often reinforced with pitch. Occasionally, a more pliable wood was utilized.

In following the hunting expedition, scrapers were needed to remove the final scraps of flesh from the skins in preparation for drying and tanning. Bone, flint and stone implements of this type have often been found in great quantities. They also served other purposes: in the limited woodworking done in the home and in the preparation of the implements.

FISHING

Some writers have denied the use of fishhooks among the Indians, asserting that such items were solely utilized for ceremonials. However, many made of flint, shell and bone have been found, and thus we may conclude that their use for actual fishing must have been very widespread.

The few tools used in making fishhooks served admirably and were well-adapted to their special needs. In making the shell hook, the abalone, petkin, olivella and clamshells were generally used. A blank was roughed out and the center punched so the reamer-shaped drill could produce a smooth hole the size of the inside of the hook. A stone file was then employed to work down the outside, cut the line notch and work the point, thus finishing the product. One found rare clamshell hook had been chipped, much in the same way as flintwork is done. However, this is an exception to the rule. Some hooks were attached to the line directly, while others were secured to a short shaft and then to the line. In making the bone fishhooks, the leg bone of the deer was used. An elongated hole was worked in the bone by making a series of holes with a flint drill, and then smoothed with a stone file. The length of the hole corresponded to the length of the hook. The outside was then cut away to the desired thickness of the hook shank. By cutting just above the loop on opposite sides, two hook blanks were produced. The notch and barb, if one was made, were then cut to finish the hook.

Although a few hooks have been found with barbs, the general principle was the snag method of fishing. Many tribes had fish as part of their diet, and for many, especially those on the sea coast, rivers and lakes, it was their principal food. They developed means of drying, freezing and curing to preserve the fish in order to maintain their food supply and to supply their dogs with much needed food.

Due to the salmon's habit of ascending streams at certain seasons for spawning, they offered easy opportunities for spearing. In fact, spearing or trapping would be the only means of securing them at that time, as they did not feed during the spawning period, and hence could not have been caught with hook and line. It is quite possible that this obvious chance taught the American Indians how to use these spears, which were later adapted for other purposes. The Pacific Northwest was the scene of the most extensive fish trapping. The habits of the

FIGURE 4.4: COMPARATIVE FISH HOOKS

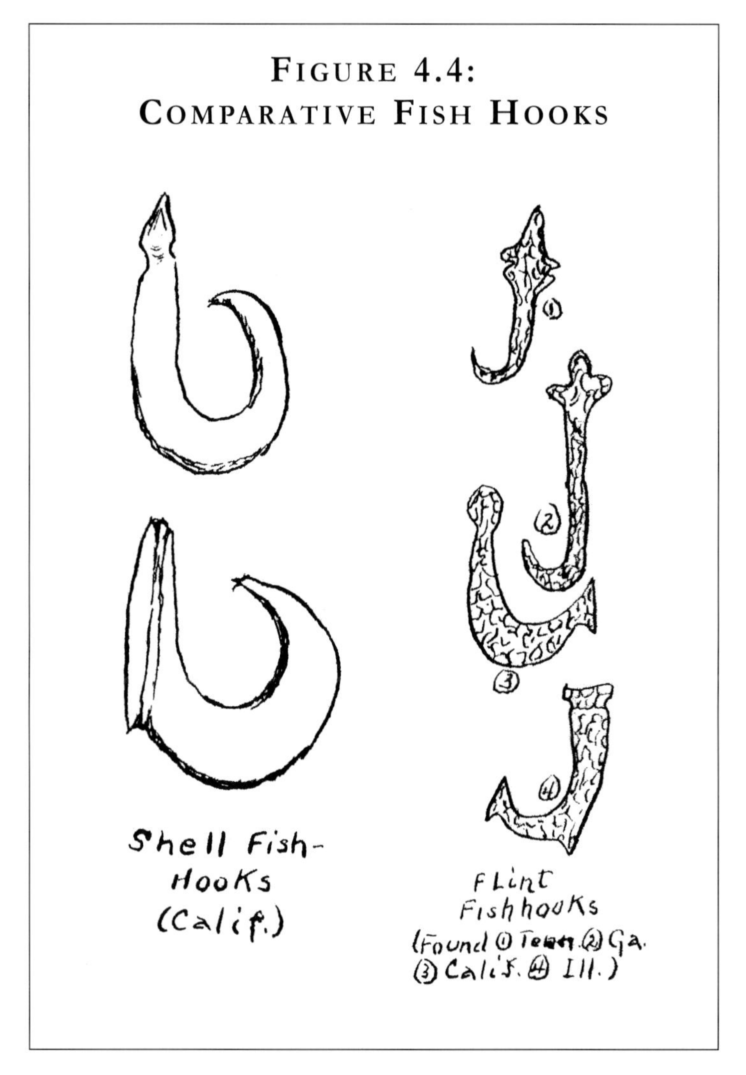

Above: A Native American salmon trap constructed on an Alaska river.

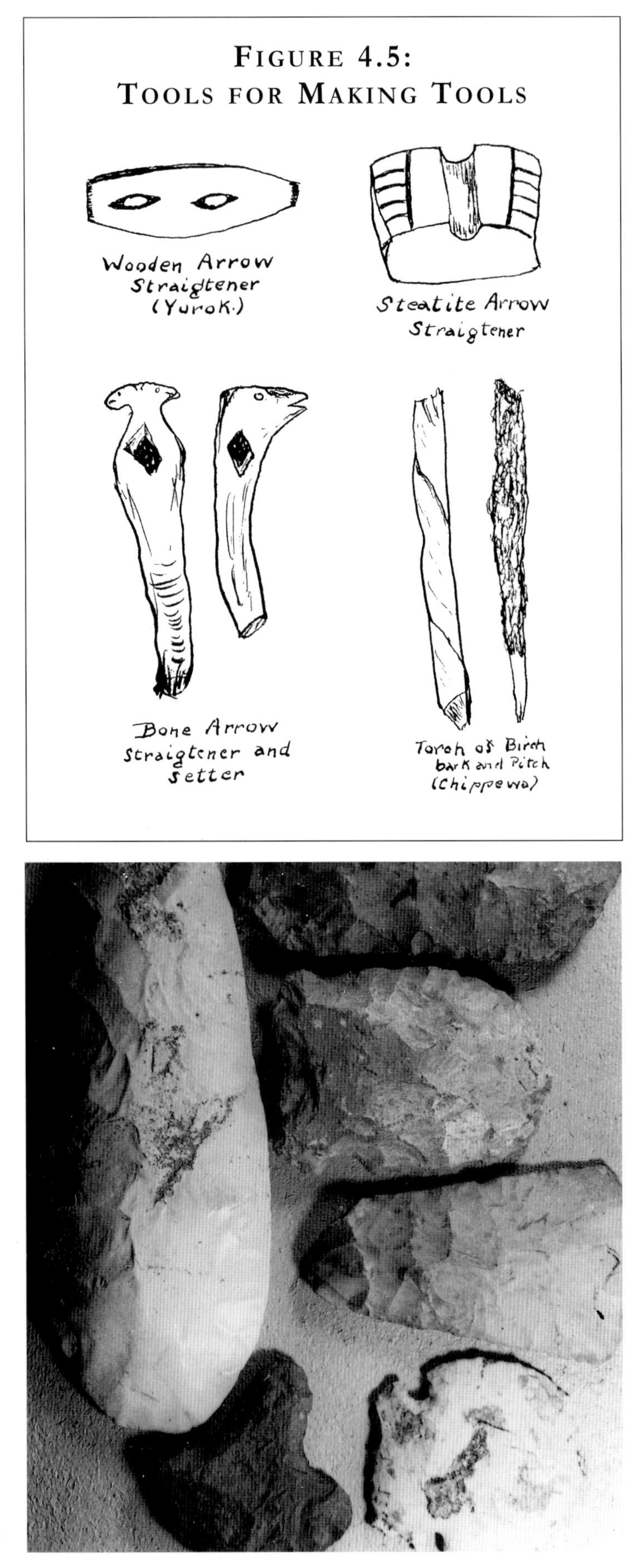

Above: Stone age tools from the Mississippi Valley.

fish abounding in these waters were conducive to seining. Both seines and traps were made of net. Many of the tribes became experts in the making of fishnets.

The nets were set near the shore and hauled in each day, or as they needed more food. In handling the nets, as well as making them, these fish-eating tribes became remarkably proficient. Thus, they were able to provide a more continual supply of food. The stones attached to the nets for sinkers, as well as the implements for weaving and such aids as a net spacer, show the high development of this industry. These items are particularly interesting artifacts in comparison with those used by the South Sea peoples.

Another means of catching fish used by some of the inland tribes was to have a number of spring traps set on the riverbank, probably with a baited hook. However, it would appear that this type required constant watching if it were to produce results.

MAKING IMPLEMENTS

The manufacture of implements for both hunting and fishing and for warfare was the principal occupation of the males when not actively engaged in one or the other. The final products of these crude tools are little short of marvelous. What was lacking in precision of equipment was made up for in persistence and patience.

They made adzes with bone and wood handles and fitted cutting heads of stone, ivory, slate and jade, as the materials were available to them. Others used plain stone adzes, with both straight and curved blades.

The use of the arrow shafters and straighteners seem to have been universally employed in preparing the projectile. The shaft of wood was drawn back and forth for a long time through the straight groove until the desired size and smoothness was secured. The adze was widely used for woodworking, and served both to prepare the wood for the arrow, as well as to shape the bow. Sand and constant rubbing with stones served the purpose of modern sandpaper. Later, grease was applied to preserve the wood.

The material used to make arrow straighteners varied considerably, depending upon the tribe. Generally

Above: Native American implements, including a traditional bone harpoon point (*top left*), fish hooks and ladles.

FIGURE 4.6: SPECIALIZED TOOLS

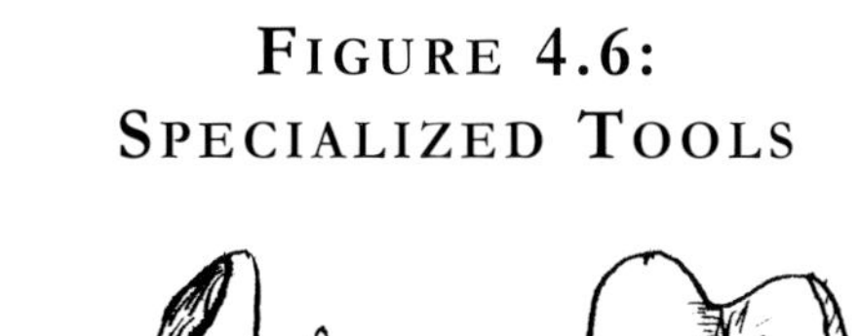
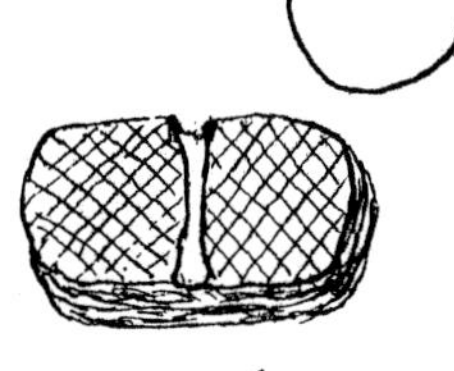
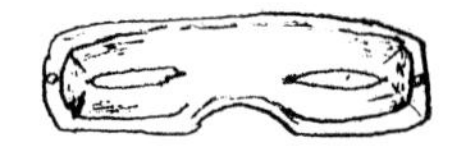

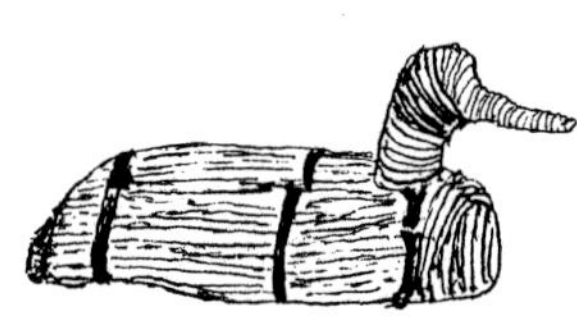
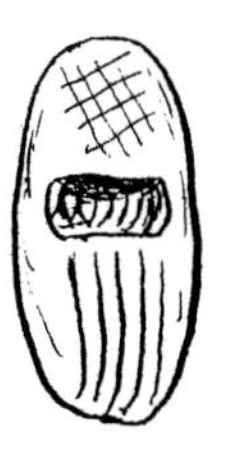

speaking, the most convenient material to be found in a tribe's area was used. It is possible that different individuals in each tribe preferred different kinds of tools, just as craftsmen the world over have always displayed their idiosyncrasies.

The use of the horn wedge and the stone maul for riving timber may have been as varied as similar implements that are used today. The manufacture of flint tools was done by means of flaking. For this, special tools were used. The methods varied both in percussion and by the slower, but more accurate, means of flaking.

SPECIAL AIDS

In night hunting and on other occasions, satisfactory illumination was a problem. The American Indian wanted to be able to see themselves but not be seen or have their presence known to enemies. The Chippewa, as well as other tribes, made a torch of birchbark and pitch which served the purpose well, although as a rule they relied on their own eyes and stealth instead of the aid of a torch.

One of the most surprising hunting aids developed by any tribe were the snow goggles of the Eskimo. True, they lacked lenses, being merely narrow slits in a curved piece of whalebone or wood; but they served to reduce the amount of glaring reflection from the snow, which the eye must absorb in the far north. They also prevented snow blindness, which can lead to death.

TRAPPING

Though extensively practiced in some regions and despite the constant need of food supply, trapping was not a general occupation of the American Indian. The wooded regions invited the development of the art of snaring and deadfalls. Large animals, such as bear and deer, were taken in pitfalls. The pit was dug on a well-used trail and carefully concealed. A branch placed in front of the pit and slightly above the ground would cause the animal to jump, light upon the obscured screen and fall into the pit.

Above: Native American knives and awls.

CHAPTER 5

FOOD

The American Indian faced what is perhaps the fundamental problem of all living beings, that is, the problem of acquiring food. The ease with which the various tribes procured their food had definite bearing on their advances and culture. While the coastal tribes retrogressed because their food supply (shellfish mainly) was so plentiful and easily obtained, the hunting tribes advanced steadily.

Berries and wild fruits of all kinds were used, in many cases the fruits being dried for future use. Roots of many plants and bulbs were eaten, as were insects, beetles, grasshoppers and other foods which the people of today would consider inedible.

The acorn played an important part in the food of all tribes wherever oak grew. The mesquite bean and other nuts were used like the acorn.

The wild potato is indigenous to America and was first used by the American Indian. Many of the native tubers—the *Cynara scolymus* or wild artichoke, the *Phaseolus* or big potato and the nuna—were used by the Indians, even among those who did not practice agriculture. The nuna is a form of the *Phaseolus*; it is now used to designate the cultivated potato.

In the early days, the potatoes were gathered and eaten both raw and cooked. At times they were treated the same as the corn and wild rice, and later some of the tribes practiced agriculture and the nuna (white potato) became one of the staple foods.

One of the foods of the American Indian which has not been mentioned by historians but has played an important part in their diet is wild rice. This was a native crop of 16 different states. It was introduced into 13 other states, as well as into parts of Canada, New Brunswick and Newfoundland. Wherever there were ponds, lakes, river bottoms and delta lands flooded, the wild rice established itself, if the conditions were at all favorable. Where the soil was alluvium, the grain was distributed by the current of the stream, by the waterfowl in its flight and by the Indian who carried it to his favorite lake or pond.

The French explorer Jacques Marquette wrote of wild rice in 1673. He mentioned that in some places it had grown so thick that it was hard to push boats through when it was green. One early writer speaks of a field five miles long and two miles wide. Another tells of fields extending as far as the eye can reach.

With the exception of four states, all of the East Coast was a rice area. This area extended well into the Plains country, but did not extend all the way to the West Coast.

The diet of many of the Eastern and Central Indians was maple sugar and fish in the spring; fish and

Right: A Hopi farmer at work with a hoe in a communal corn field, circa 1900.

game in the summer; and wild rice, nuts and seeds of other sources for the fall. More industrious Indians and those with a bit of foresight gathered and stored wild rice for use throughout the year. After their contacts with the whites, when game decreased and was harder to procure, the American Indians did more storing and planning ahead.

The wild rice is a plant that springs almost spontaneously and does not have to be cared for. It matures in August and September. Before harvest time, the women went to the rice fields in their canoes and tied the stalks in small bunches to keep them from falling into the water as they ripened. Tying was usually done with strips of bark. They tied bunches and left them forming rows, which later could be easily reached from a canoe and gathered. When the time for harvest came, they returned, each to the patch she had tied in bunches. With a hooked stick she drew a bunch over the side of the canoe; with her free hand she used another stick to beat the heads, thus loosening the grain so it fell into the canoe. In this way, by reaching first on one side and then the other, she covered quite a path. When the canoe was filled, she returned to shore, where the rice was placed in baskets and carried to the camp. At the camp it was then dried or cured before threshing to remove the husk.

The Dakota (Sioux) dried their rice on a scaffold from 20 to 50 feet long, eight feet wide and for feet high.

Above: A Navajo family, with corn drying, photographed at Canyon de Chelly, Arizona in 1873 by Timothy O'Sullivan.

The scaffold was covered with grass and reeds upon which the rice was spread. A slow fire was kept under it for 36 hours. This slightly parched the hull and changed the color of the rice, but did not damage it. Many methods of threshing were applied to remove the husk from the rice. One of the most common was to put the rice in a large basket or woven bag with open top. This was then placed in a hole in the ground, which was dug to fit the basket. By tramping or using a long stick with a knob on the end as a pestle, the hulls were loosened. At intervals the basket was taken out and the rice poured into a shallow winnowing tray and winnowed. This process was repeated until all was threshed. Another method was to put a deerskin in the bottom of the hole and tread the rice on this. Other tribes used a tub with wooden staves, in which the grain was placed in order to be threshed.

The rice was prepared in many ways. Some tribes parched it and ate the whole grain. Others cooked it whole in boiling water, while some ground it into a flour and used it in baking, in thickening soup and in gruel, which was often cooked with pieces of venison. When rice was stored it was buried in the ground in fiber or bark bags to prevent its being stolen.

The mythology and ceremony of the rice is as follows: The bear was the first totem, the eagle the second. The first was the head of the thunder phratry and the second brought rain. The Good Mystery came in the question of who gave the Indians maize (corn)? The Indians visited the Bear Phratry and offered maize and fire in exchange for wild rice, which was the property of the Bear and the Sturgeon. The bargain was made and since that time the Bear and the Sturgeon Phratry have lived together.

The American Indians have many ceremonies before and during the rice gathering season. They were usually preceded by periods of fasting and prayers to the Master of Life for the crop. The first kernels gathered were set aside for the spiritual, or holy, feast. If rice was offered to a guest he could feel that he had indeed been honored.

The following is a list of plants that were cultivated before the coming of the Europeans: arrowroot, barnyard grass, kidney bean, lima bean, chili pepper, corn and maize, cotton, gourds, Jerusalem artichoke, papaw, prickly pear, pumpkin, squash, sweet potato, apple, wild rice, yam, wheat, cacao, tomato, etc. It is estimated that four-sevenths of the agricultural products were domesticated by the American Indian.

Sunflowers were cultivated by nearly all tribes who did any agricultural work. The flower was used for ornamentation and worship, and the oil was extracted by boiling and used for anointing the hair.

Wild onions were used raw and cooked by the Plains tribes. The apple was gathered, and some early writers think they cultivated it for food. Practically every type of melon we now have was raised in some form by the American Indian. Watermelon, squash, cucumbers and types similar to our musk melon and pomegranate were raised. They also had the wild cherry, grape and a type of fig.

The Eastern and Southern Indians are credited with placing fish in the hills to act as fertilizer when planting their grain.

The cactus was one of the universal foods of the desert Indians. During the fruit season, July and August, the tribes would leave their permanent abode and travel en masse to the cacti, eating the luscious pulp and becoming very fat. Some of the plants were dried or prepared according to their own methods for future use.

Another important desert food was the mesquite bean. They were gathered in large baskets and taken to the mortars, where they were ground and pulverized for

Figure 5.1: Food Processing Vessels

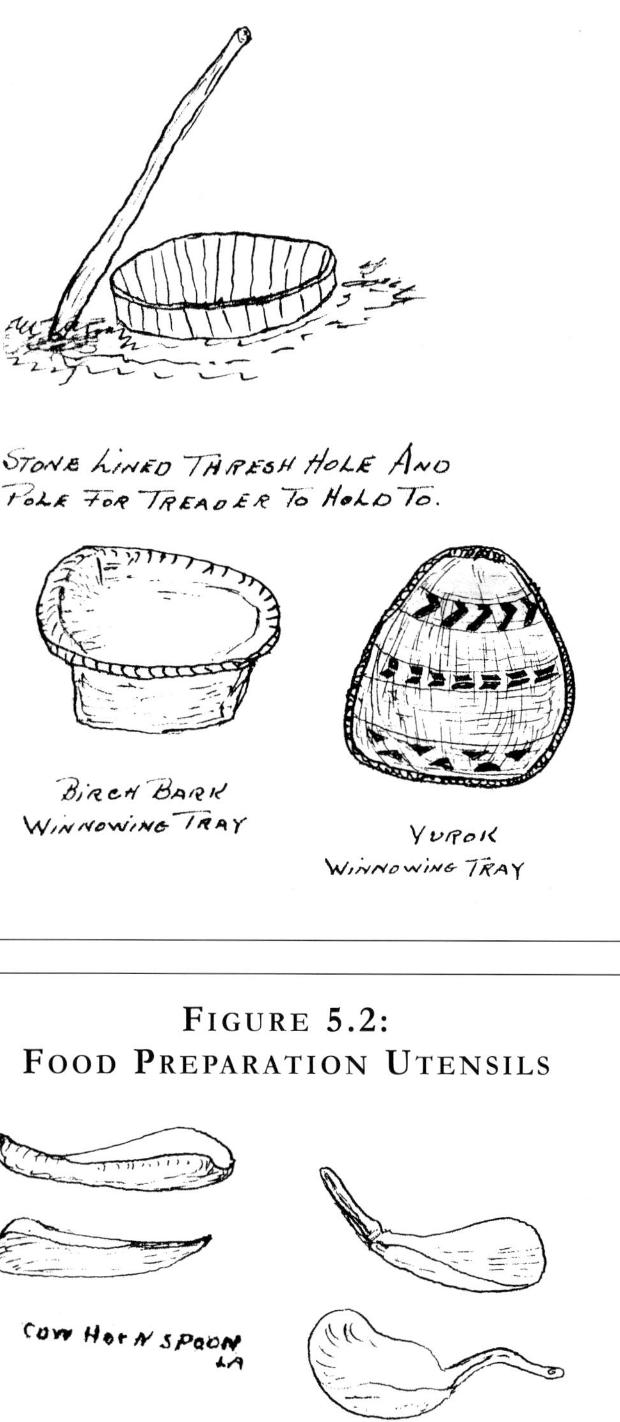

Figure 5.2: Food Preparation Utensils

FIGURE 5.3: STONE TOOLS FOUND IN CALIFORNIA

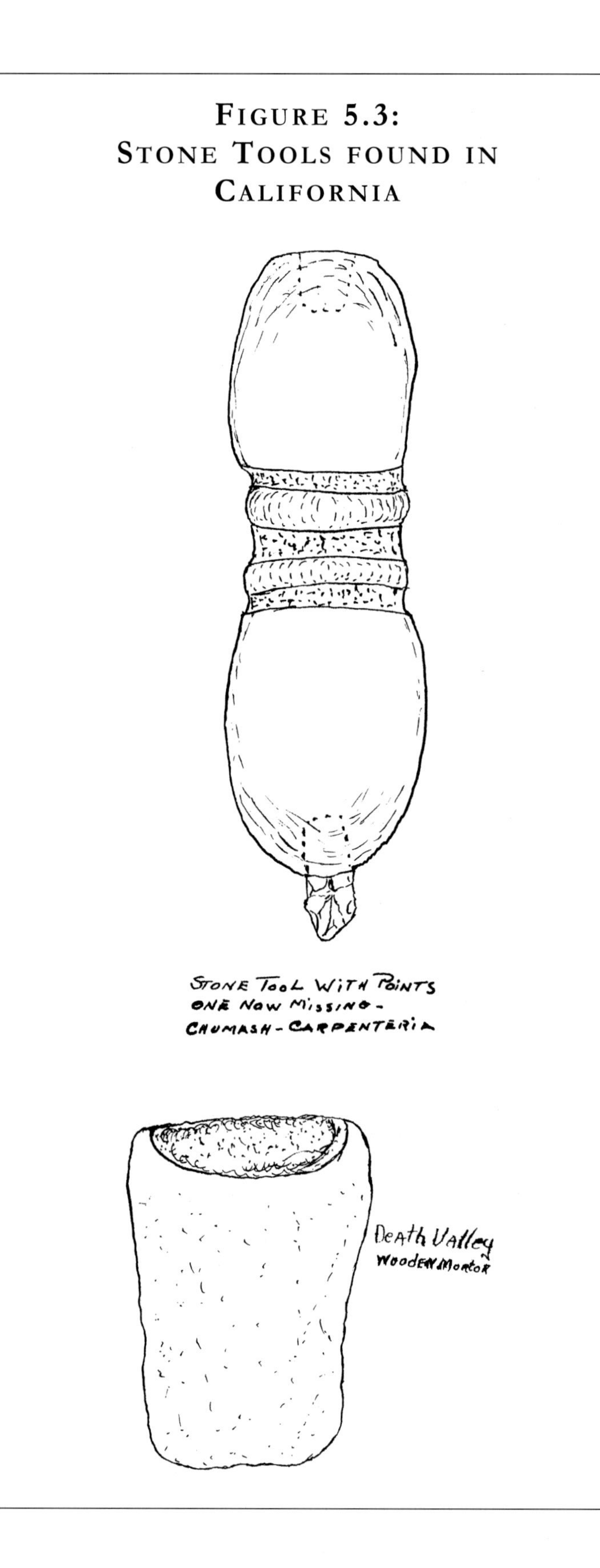

food. Some of the meal was eaten raw, but it was usually mixed with water and cooked. The meal was often stored for future use. Many other seeds and grasses and bulbs were gathered in season and eaten by the tribes who inhabited the area in which they grew.

The Menomini, who lived in the vicinity of the maple groves, made use of the sap for making maple sugar. They tapped the trees in a manner similar to the way the settlers later did, and gathered the sap in pails make of birch bark. This was cooked down until of the proper consistency, and was put in makaks for storage until needed. Sometimes they would dump the thick, hot syrup on the snow, where it would form a sort of sugary wax, which they were very fond of.

Many of the tribes gathered berries in great quantities in the berry season and stored them by drying or mixing them with maple sugar or other sweetenings. A number of the tribes caught grasshoppers in shallow baskets. They were regarded as a great delicacy. Mushrooms were used as food by the American Indians, as well as wild celery.

The Iroquois legend of the origin of corn is as follows. The corn plant sprung from the bosom of the mother of Sic, the Great Spirit, after her burial. The spirit of the corn, bean and squash are represented as the three sisters (trinity). They were supposed to have been beautiful maidens who delighted to dwell together. Thus, the three will grow together from the same hill.

With most tribes, the main supply of food was from the hunt. From the buffalo down to the ground squirrel, each filled a place in the menu. Each tribe had some animal which they worshiped and which they would not kill for food. At times, such animals could be killed for their skins, but their flesh was never eaten.

When a kill was made, the American Indians would gorge themselves, leaving not a bit of any portion, even the entrails. In the buffalo hunts, where the main idea was to get the meat supply, the hunters would follow the herd as long as possible, the women following behind, cutting and skinning the carcasses and making jerkin for the winter.

The river tribes dried fish in the same manner. The Oak Grove people stored their acorn meal, and the Navajo stored corn and pumpkins. The more hardy and aggressive groups usually had a store of provisions.

The buffalo were usually hunted on horseback. The riders rushed into the herd, shooting with bow and arrow as long as they could keep up with the herd. Others used the spear in a similar fashion.

In deer hunting, the American Indian used various methods of stalking, pitfalls and driving into a defile where hunters were stationed, or over a cliff. The antelope were driven up steep canyon sides by one group, while another group stationed themselves at the top in order to take up the chase of the fatigued animals, thus making the slaughter easy.

Small game was quite often taken in snares, by throwing sticks or by shooting with blunt arrows. As the skins of the smaller animals and birds were used as adornment, the blunt arrows were used to stun the game, which could then be captured without damaging the pelt or making it bloody.

When a hunt of any kind was decided upon, there must first be prayers to the God of the Hunt. Preparations must also be made. The rabbit hunt, for instance, was quite unique. At the time of the decision of the hunt, a cottontail and a jack rabbit were killed, and hung up on the roof beams, where they remained until after the hunt. While the men bathed and washed their hair in yucca suds, the necessary home preparations were made by the women. At the appointed time, the participants all left the village and went where the Ko'yemshi (great father) and his deputies were seated near some tree, each facing a different direction. The hunters set themselves in a circle and the great father gave a prayer, which was then repeated by the deputies, each clasping the hand of the other. The prayers were for the crops, the hunt and the health of the people; they were also made so that they may not die, but in time sleep and awake as little children. The ceremony closed with a smoke, joined in by all. They then went to a fire that the great father had prepared. He gave them bits of bread, which they threw into the flames. After passing their rabbit sticks through the flame and exhorting the gods to be good to them, the hunt started. The great father remained with them until the first rabbit was killed. He dipped his fetish in the blood and then returned.

On returning home, the rabbits were laid out side by side in rows, with their heads to the east and with an ear of corn between the paws. They were all sprinkled

Figure 5.4: Food Processing Tools

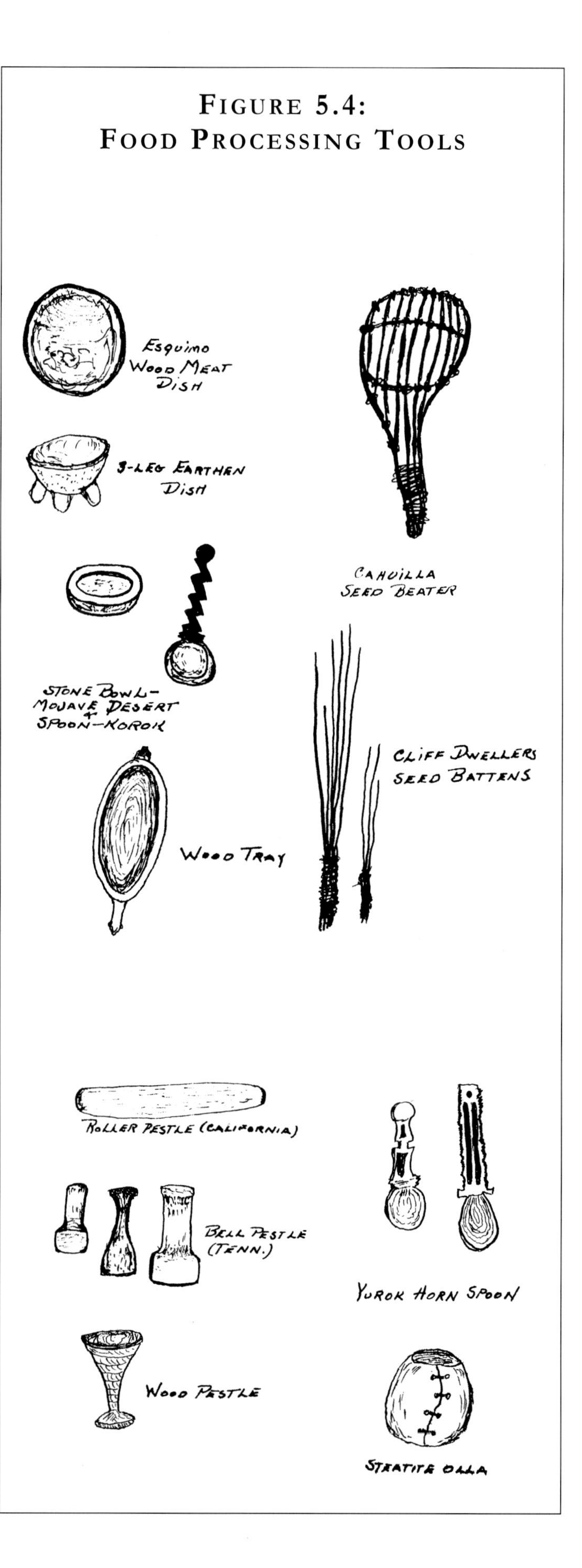

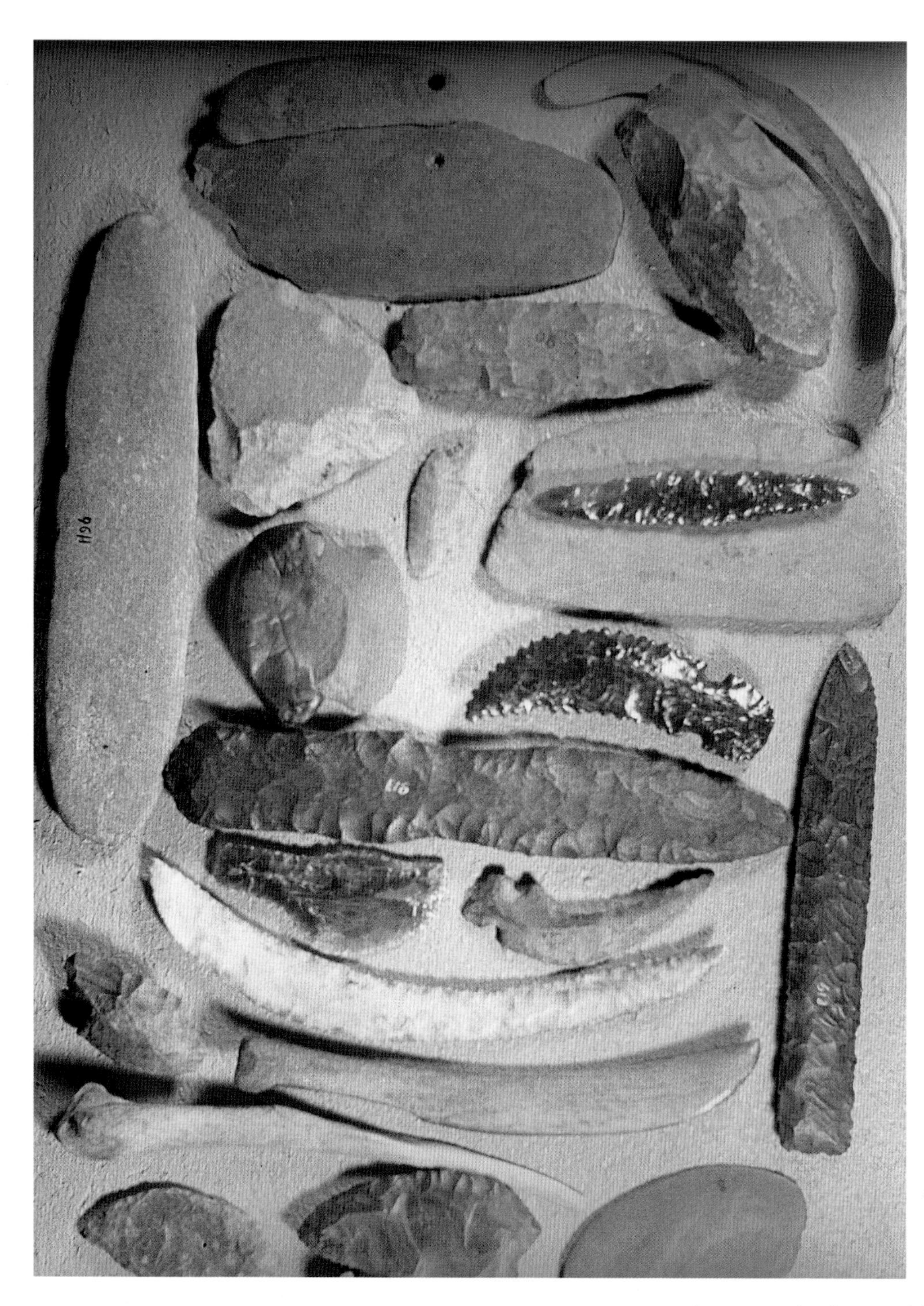

Above: Native American knives and food processing implements.

with sacred meal so that many more rabbits might come. After this, the rabbits were flayed. Spearing the fish with a long spear was a favorite method of the American Indians for obtaining their fish supply. Nets were used extensively, as were fish traps. Hooks were additionally used, some of which were very ingeniously made—chipped of flint, cut from bone or shell, and by assembling various materials together. Lines were made of different kinds of fiber, and sometimes of skins. They would often fish at night from boats with a torch. Many of the tribes who relied upon fish as their main food split open their catch and hung it to dry for winter use. The Indians of Nova Scotia dried their fish and dipped them in brine or sprinkled them with salt during the process to help preserve them.

Along the Pacific Coast, the seal and shellfish were great sources of food supply. Other fish, deer and small game furnished the meat needed in their diet. They used acorns wherever and whenever they were found, as well as the mesquite bean, chia seed, and various small roots and berries, all of which supplied the balance of their food requirements.

For the most part, the food supply of the Navajo was taken care of by the stock they raised, which also furnished wool for cloth and skins. They had droves of sheep and some cattle, although in later years their herds were smaller.

The older Navajo tell of the time prior to the period when the animals were introduced by the Spaniards. At that time, the people lived by the chase and the cultivation of maize, and on wild fruits, pinon nuts and seeds or grasses. As time went on, they devoted more time to the fields and to the cultivation of pumpkins, beans and similar foods.

We usually think of dried venison as jerkin, but the American Indians cut into strips all game they had in abundance and dried them in the sun or over slow, smoldering fires until they were dry and hard. The fire of green wood burned slowly and was easily tended. The smoke kept the flies away and gave the meat a more pleasing taste. Buffalo, deer, elk and bear, and later cattle and horse meat, were all treated the same.

The wild pithaya was much sought during its ripened season and some tribes lived on it almost exclusively at that time. The Cochimi had a habit of picking up the undigested seeds from their own bowels and, after parching and grinding them, made a meal of them.

Going to the salt grounds or licks was one of the great ceremonies of all tribes. From time immemorial, the salt deposits were neutral ground among all Western Indians; in the East some of the wickedest attacks were at salt places. The tribes would gather at the salt grounds at different seasons of the year; or, if they gathered at the same time, they would form different camps and pay strict attention to their work. Many would build altars, where they worshiped the gods who were responsible for the supply of the salt.

Any baking or semblance of such was accomplished by heating slabs of stone, on which the batter or other ingredients were poured and allowed to bake. Peki bread was baked in very thin sheets.

FIGURE 5.5: AGRICULTURAL IMPLEMENTS

STONE SPADE WITH HANDLE

DIGGING STICK AND CROOKS

PIMA AGRICULTURAL IMPLEMENTS WOODEN SHOVEL, DIGGING STICK AND HOE

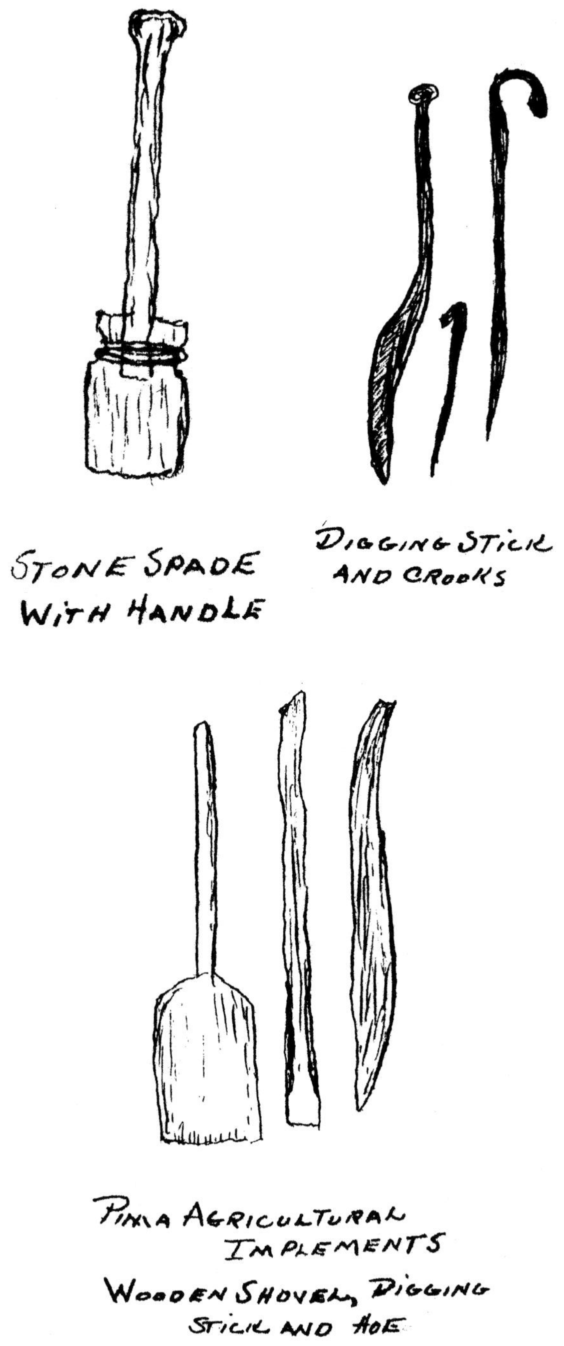

IMPLEMENTS

Spades of flint, slate and stone of many forms are found throughout the places occupied by the American Indian. In drier, arid regions, wooden items such as digging sticks and shovels have been found. Many of the flint and stone implements were used as they were found, while others were hafted to make their use easier. Some of the desert Indians completed and used irrigation systems, which cause one to wonder how they were made with the simple tools available. Hoes of flint were the finest type found. Some were notched for hafting, and others were merely long,

Above: Drying peaches at Isleta Pueblo, New Mexico (circa 1900).

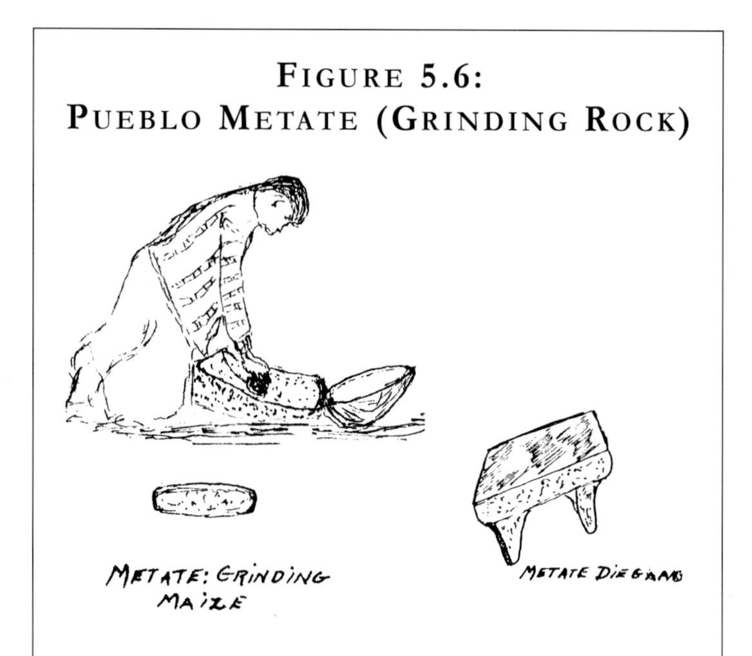

FIGURE 5.6: PUEBLO METATE (GRINDING ROCK)

thin flint blades, sometimes as large as 4 x 15 inches. Many very fine ones have been found in Johnson County, Illinois, on the old George Rogers Clark Trail, running from Fort Massac to Fort Kaskaskia. The notched type are also of stone in many forms, some rather thick and heavy. Hoes in some form of stone, flint, shell or bone were found in all localities where crops were cultivated, and in scattered distribution over a much larger area, where they were used for digging graves and food caches, although pointed sticks were often also used for these purposes.

Drills were made of every material known to the Indians: stone, bone, antler, flint and reed, which were used with sand or coarse earth as an abrasive. These did remarkable work, as attested to by the drilling of their slate pieces and some of the hard stones that at times are found with the core still standing. Pump drills and bow drills were likewise used by twirling the shaft between the palms of the hand and holding the point in the fingers.

Celts are ungrooved axes in general, and were oftentimes hafted for greater ease in using. They also served as aids in skinning and splitting wood, and as a cutting and scraping tool where needed.

Mortars were made of several materials, and were of many shapes and patterns. The stone mortar with the stone pestle was the most common, since they wear the longest and the grinding is more rapid. The wooden mortars and pestles were used a great deal among the Eastern and Southern Indians, while the Western Indians had the basket mortar, which used a small boulder for the grinding base, with a bottomless basket tarred on to act as a hopper. This construction provided a much lighter mortar to transport, especially to the acorn-eating people, who moved about a great deal. Metates were used more than mortars in the West and Southwest, and into Mexico. Quite often near the oak groves or districts where the mesquite beans were gathered, large boulders were found with as many as 30 holes ground out. This was where the women of the tribe worked together to prepare the season's meal.

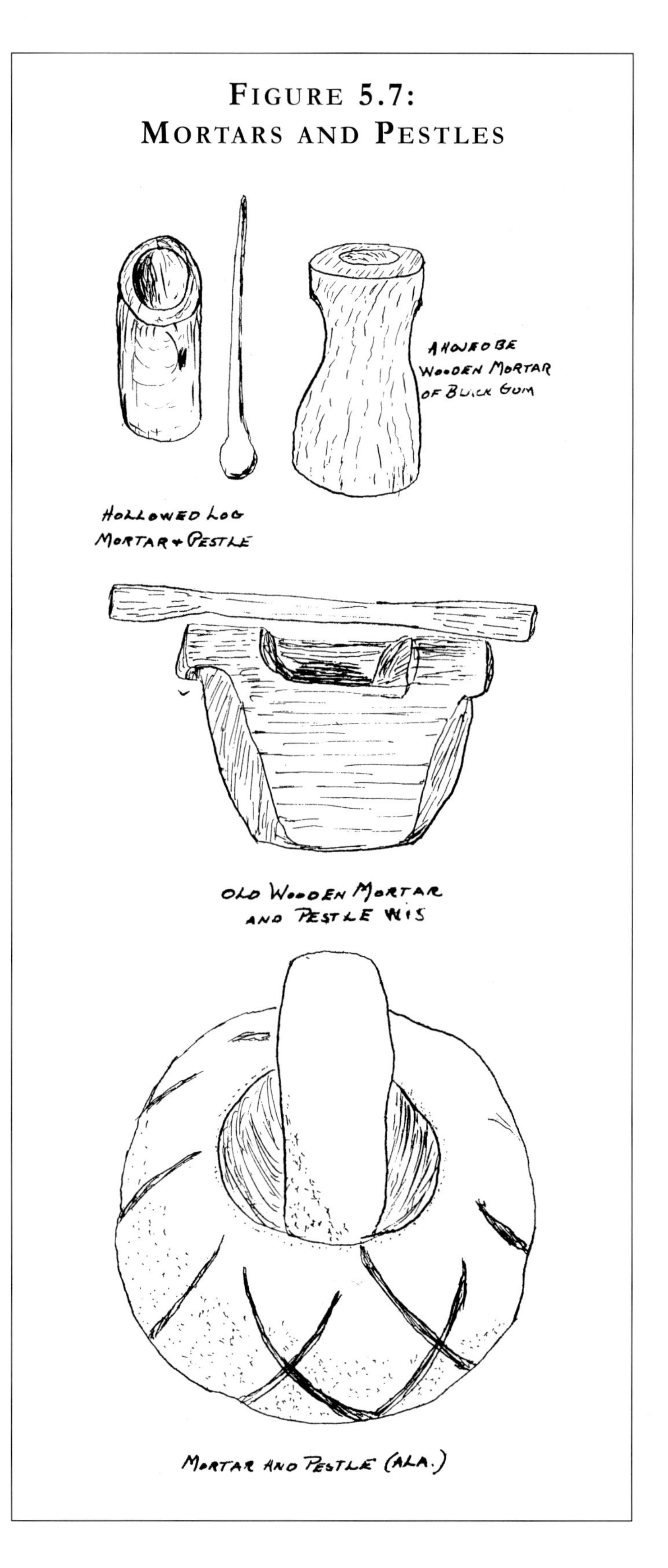

FIGURE 5.7: MORTARS AND PESTLES

Bone awls were used for opening the acorns, which had to be treated in order to remove the bitterness. Different methods of treatment were used, one being to put them in cord or fiber bags, and then place the bags in a stream so the water could run over them. Another way was to place wood ashes over them, while another method was to bury them for a time.

Many baskets and containers for gathering and storing food were made of birch bark, especially the containers for maple sugar, wild rice and dried meat; wherever the bark was obtainable, it was used to store most items.

Spoons were universal in distribution in some form. The Eskimo had them of ivory and wood; the elk horn served as a material for the Yurok and neighboring tribes; those in the mountain districts further south used the mountain sheep and goat horn; the Plains Indians made them of buffalo; and in the South the shell was made use of, and no doubt each tribe had them made from the material most easily obtained and worked.

STANDARDS OF VALUE

It would be an endless task to begin to tell of the value of Indian items or the equivalent of them, but a few examples might demonstrate their conception of value in regards to trade, gambling, and exchange. A gourd was equivalent to a basket; a mortar or metate equal to a small shell necklace; a basket, a blanket and a string of blue beads were equal to a pony; 12 feet of blue glass beads equaled a bag of paint; and a large basket of corn and beans equaled a cooking pot.

In measuring, the distance from the center of the breast to the tips of the fingers was the humaka, or standard of measure used by some; another was the arm, the distance from under the arm pit to the beginning of the fingers; and the shortest measure was the length of the index finger. No doubt a big Indian would rather buy than sell by his own measure.

Chapter 6

PRE-COLUMBIAN TRANSPORTATION

Before contact with Europeans, boats and dog sleds were the usual methods of conveyance among the Indians, although, of course, these differ in form from place to place. Each tribe developed its own transportation out of its own particular needs and limitations. The Eastern Indians made bark canoes by covering wooden frames with birch bark.

The Northern Indians had canoes similar to these, but the people of the Northwest, in some instances, hollowed out logs or made their boats from planks lashed together. They used stone sleds and elk horn wedges to rive the planks out and sealed the seams with gum. Further down the coast, the Californians had tule boats for their sloughs and inshore use, but for offshore boating and for inter-communication with the islands they fashioned boats of sterner stuff. These were boats of planking, made by grooving the planks together, securing them with thongs and fiber, and thoroughly caulking them with asphalt to make them watertight. These boats are the largest type made by Indians. Some held as many as 20 men, and were hardy enough to withstand the rough waves of the ocean during their trips to and from the islands, some of which were 80 miles offshore. In contrast to this highest development, some tribes used a log with an outrigger to keep it righted and just poled along. So each type of boat grew out of the necessities of the immediate environment. One type of canoe was hollowed out of a single log, a section having been dug out where the boatman sat and paddled. Most of this section was removed by the use of fire, charring and scraping it until the desired shape and depth were attained.

The Menomini made canoes by hollowing out the log of the butternut tree (also by using fire), and then the charred parts were scraped away and the process repeated until the desired depth and dimensions were attained. A single piece of wood was inserted near each end to give the vessel support and to strengthen it. After this had been done it was usually filled with urine and allowed to stand for many days. This was supposed to toughen the wood and to keep it from cracking so readily. The oarsman used a single paddle, and placed tufts of grass under his knees to relieve him and to act as a cushion on the bottom of the canoe.

The Chinook made a dugout from the log of the common white cedar; according to the reports of Lewis and Clark, they ranged from 10 to 50 feet, depending upon the waters they were to navigate or the load they were to carry. Although this differed a little in shape, the principles and methods used in its construction were similar to other canoes. The people also made birch bark canoes, the frames of which were made of white cedar, the ribs being very thin and all lashed together with the

Right: A Blackfeet family with a horse travois, circa 1900. The horse travois evolved from the pre-Columbian dog travois.

thin roots of spruce. After the frames were completed, the bark was sewn together and the edges rolled over the upper sides of the frame; then all small holes and the ends were smeared with pine resin. In the bottom, fine withe rod with a bark mat over it were placed as protection, both from the load carried and the oarsman. The oar was about four feet long and made of cedar. The Californians developed this particular craft by gathering tule and binding it into large bunches, and then tying them together to form a boat.

Bull boats were used by some of the Plains Indians to cross rivers. They were made by stretching buffalo skins over frames of slender poles lashed together. Bull boats could be dismantled for easier transportation. These boats were identical to those used at the time when the pyramids were built in Egypt.

Kayaks were built to carry only one man. They were developed principally by the Eskimos, made of skins and built upon a frame of driftwood or whalebone. The entire boat was covered except for a small opening for the torso of the boatman, thus no water was allowed to enter. This makes a very seaworthy craft; being light and buoyant, they are easily propelled through the water at great speed.

Land Transportation

Dog travois were used by the Cree, who had a roving disposition and followed the buffalo and other game. They lived in transportable skin tents. Only a small load could be carried by a dog; however, because they had many dogs it was an easy task to get considerable goods transported. These dog travois were of very ancient origin. When horses were later acquired, they were used as a method of transporting goods. In using the horse travois the women generally walked, leading the horse, while the children rode either the horse or the travois.

The Mandan used dog sleds for winter travel. Some of these sleds were 10 feet long, and were bound securely together with thongs. They were capable of carrying quite a load. As most of their foods were kept in caches, they used this method to bring the food in as it was needed. The dog harness was a rawhide collar wound with pieces of blanket or cedar bark. A main strap was

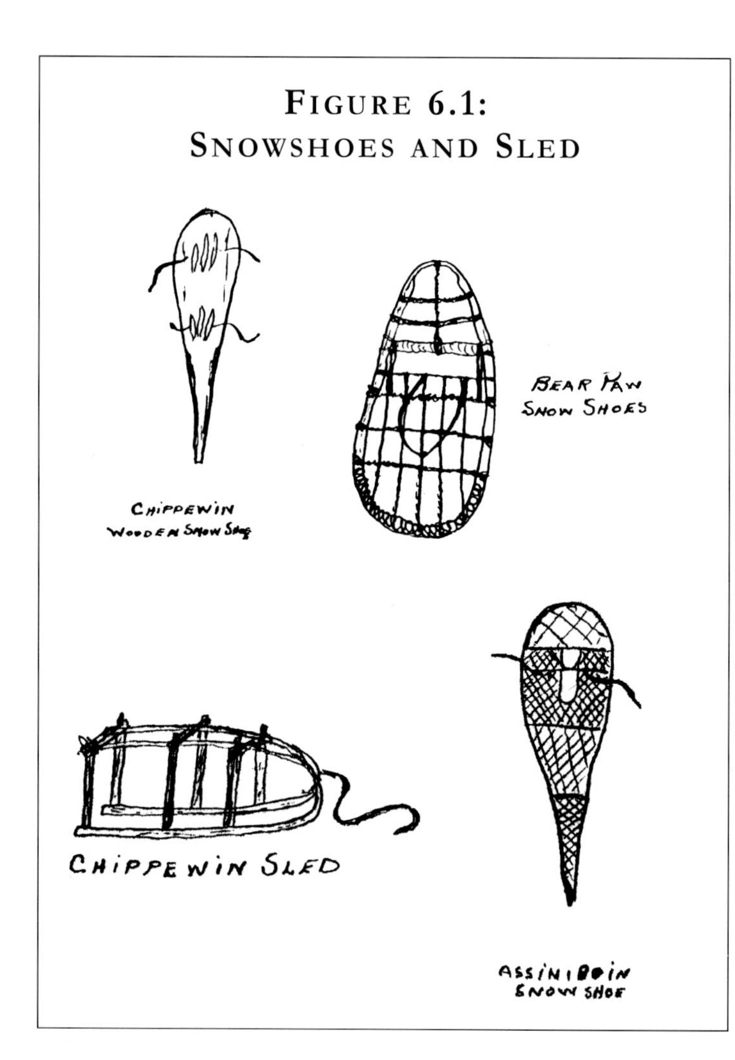

FIGURE 6.1: SNOWSHOES AND SLED

attached to the sled, and the various dogs were fastened to this main lead by short straps. They were placed in single file or one on either side of the main lead, one in back of the other, never in pairs.

Since snowshoes were a necessary part of their very existence, the Eskimos developed the art of using snowshoes to a level of high efficiency. Their different adaptations show some ingenuity.

BOAT BUILDING

Gouges of stone and flint have been found scattered over a wide area. Their appearance indicates they would have best served in building boats of the dugout type, but as a rule most of the wood was removed by fire, first charring and then scraping it. The gouges may have been used for this purpose, although they have been found in areas where no boats of this type were built. Of course, trade among tribes and acquisition by seizure may account for this.

Pitch was used in making the boats waterproof and in making torches. In the spring, the Indians would visit

Above: When this Cheyenne dog travois was photographed near Lame Deer, Montana in 1922, Johnston was already doing fieldwork.

the pitch bearing trees and scrape the bark off in places. Later they would return and gather the pitch in containers of bark, and repeat this process until the desired amount was secured.

In making torches, sometimes a stick was just coated with pitch, while at other times small bunches of bark were rolled together and coated. These were used in the house as needed, and also for fishing at night or stalking deer, never for traveling at night, however, as their eyes were trained so that this was unnecessary. The use of a torch might attract enemies.

Twines and cords were made from whatever the district produced: yucca fiber and wild iris made the best cord (where obtainable), but outside leaf produced two fibers only. This shows the tedious task required to make it in large quantities. Interior bark of the bass wood, elm bark, some of the cedars, cotton and sinew were also used. Certain nettles made twine, which was used in the making of fishnets.

Many people think that the tar which the West Coast Indians used in tarring their boats and fastening their implements was obtained from the La Brea asphalt pits and the pits at Carpenteria. However, tests have shown the tar used was practically 100 percent pure. Tar from these pits needs considerable refining. It was later discovered that the tar found in small lumps along the seashore was of the same density and purity as that used by the Indians.

This came from the deposits in the ocean and the centrifugal force of the waves, which had whipped all the impurities out of it. For example, the oil wells and tar deposits at Somerland, California, which are a quarter to half a mile out in the ocean (the wells are set on pilings), give an idea of where some of these deposits in the ocean came from.

FIGURE 6.2: NATIVE AMERICAN BOATS

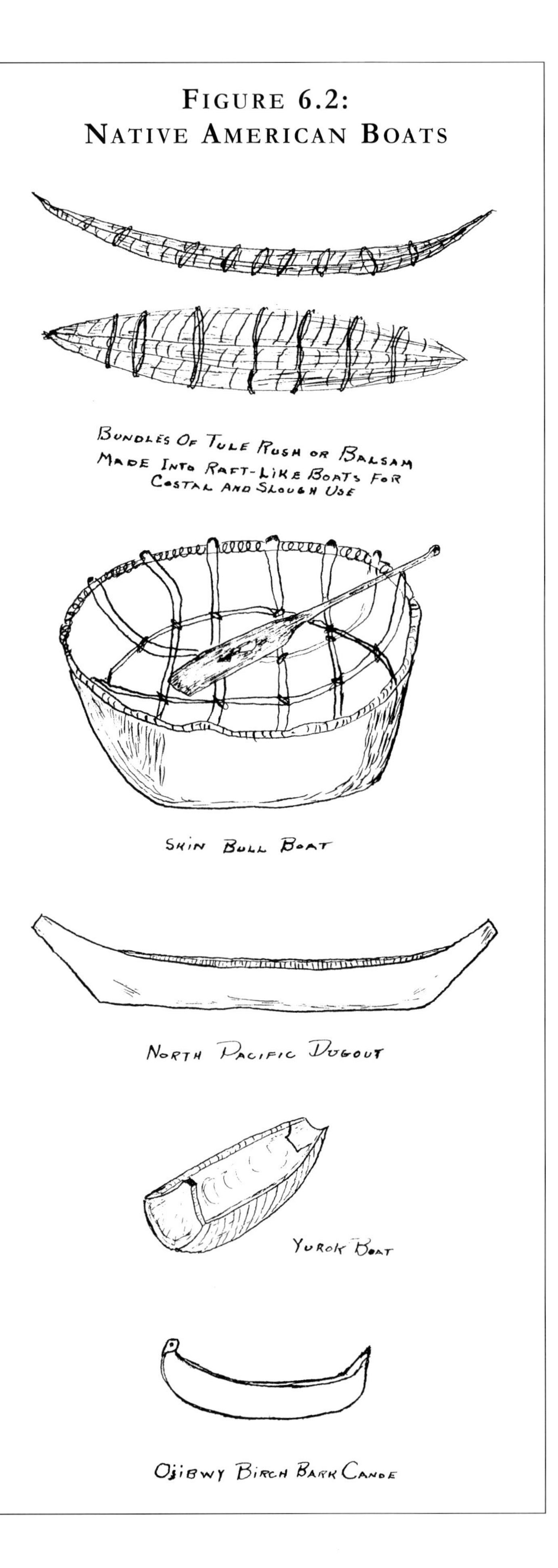

METHODS OF MEASURING

Short measurements were made by the finger, hand or arm, while distances were reckoned by a man's ability to traverse a certain space in a day or days. Measures of quantity were made by the handful or swallow.

Chapter 7

DWELLINGS

The architecture of the American Indian was influenced largely by the character of the country in which they lived, the materials available and the climate. In one legend concerning the original dwelling of the American Indian, the poles were made of precious things—white shell, turquoise, abalone, obsidian and red stone. The inside was lined with four shelves of white shell, four shelves of turquoise, four shelves of abalone and four shelves of obsidian. Each corresponding pole was of precious stone, and thus combined the cardinal colors of white, yellow, blue and black in one glorious edifice.

The floor of this structure was laid with a fourfold rug of obsidian, turquoise, abalone and white shell, each spread over the other in the order named, while the door consisted of a quadruple curtain of screed of dawn, sky blue, evening twilight and darkness.

Among the most revealing elements pertaining to the American Indians are the dwellings which they occupied. There was a wide variation of types of abode; however, conditions such as geography, climate and the building materials available were not the sole governing factors in the development of the various types of dwellings.

The constant necessity for a steady supply of food hovered over the Indian community. With nothing but the most primitive storage methods, this never-ceasing need determined the location of their homes. It decided whether residence could be had throughout the year in one place, or whether seasonal migrations were imperative. This naturally influenced the building of permanent, semipermanent or transient types of dwellings.

Furthermore, the development of various tribes had not in the past followed parallel lines. Some had reached a close community life centering on the tribe, similar to the "clan state" of civilization as evidenced in Europe and Asia. Others had reached the state where the large family, rather than the tribe, was the central unit; while for others, individual or small groups was the rule. These conditions for human relationships and the resulting customs played a certain part in the type and locality of dwellings.

The habits and temperament of various tribes differed enormously. The peaceful agricultural tribes tended to have more permanent abodes. The war-like and raiding types leaned to seclusion and mobility; for example, the Apache built their hogans not only quickly for convenience, but also because they were less likely to be readily observed by outraged victims of plundering expeditions.

The dedication of the Indian home took place after the house was completed. First, a fire was built. Then some staple food was rubbed on the walls on the cardi-

Right: A Shoshone brushwood hogan, which Johnston photographed in the field.

nal points. After, with a sweeping gesture to indicate the sun, the man distributed meal around the outer edge of the hut, observing strict silence all the while. He then chanted, sprinkling meal on the fire so that it would always serve them, before finally throwing meal toward the smoke hole and out the doorway. The woman then repeated the same ceremony, and the dedication was over. Thus a thorough consideration of the dwelling occupied by the American Indian furnished many ideas of the character, habits, customs and conditions of a particular tribe.

In the Northeastern section of the United States, the Iroquois (six tribes) reached a high state of tribal organization. Their dwellings were usually referred to as "long houses." These were permanent shelters for a varying number of families. In size, they varied from 50 to 150 feet in length, and from 15 to 25 feet in width, but were nearly always 20 feet high at the ridgepole.

The construction was by means of a frame of forked poles set in the ground. On these poles the first roof supporter was placed. The roof was formed by bending slender poles to make the ridge. No heavy ridgepoles were used. Then, horizontal poles were lashed to the sides and roof. These, in turn, were covered with bark shingles or slabs. The bark slabs were obtained by girdling trees with an incision when the sap was rising. Later, the bark was peeled off in six foot lengths, and as wide as the circumference of the tree, which was frequently several feet. After being rolled lengthwise to complete drying and offset the natural curl, they were fastened in layers on the roof and sides, overlapping in a fashion similar to that employed in shingling. These bark slabs were fastened to the framework by splints or bark rope. On the outside, poles were lashed, corresponding to the inner pole of the framework, giving added strength. This helped tile roofing to carry the snow load in the winter. Smoke holes were cut in the roof, one for each family. Some effort was made to close these in bad

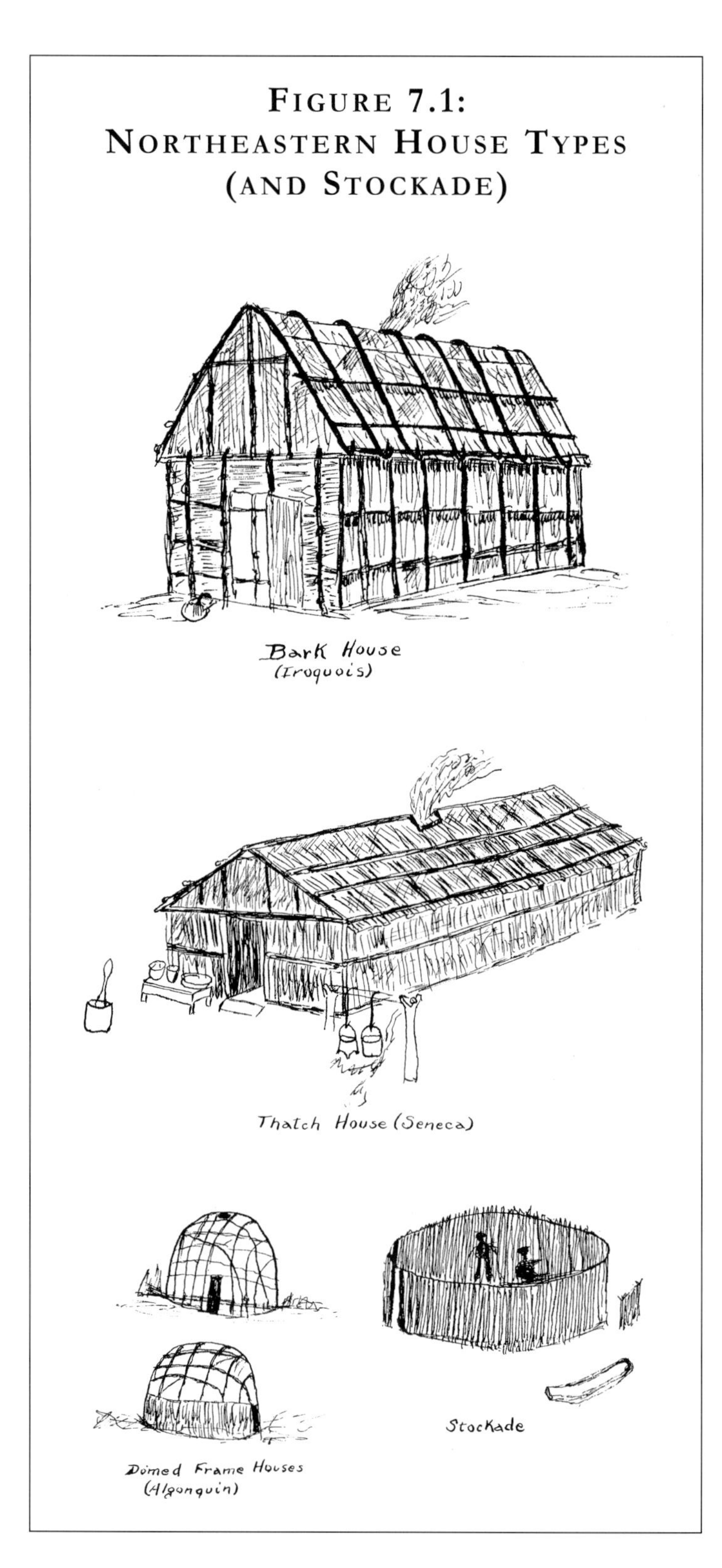

FIGURE 7.1: NORTHEASTERN HOUSE TYPES (AND STOCKADE)

weather by means of an oversized bark sheet, which could be shoved in place by using a long pole. Doorways were placed at each end of the building. The doors were bark covered frames, which hung on crude wooden hinges or leather thongs.

The Seneca "thatch house" was very similar in construction to the Iroquois long house. Dried grass and reeds took the place of bark. Although as wide, they were never as large as the long house. There was only one smoke hole cut in the roof, due perhaps to greater danger of inflammability, or because the occupants were members of one large, central family group.

Though not resembling in shape, but closely approximating in method of construction, the Algonquin tribes built single family dwellings which used more flexible poles and were completely domed. The Algonquin also built log palisades reinforced with earthworks to form a defense.

These strongholds frequently covered several acres and enclosed a village. Large logs were set deep into the ground, and stood from 10 to 12 feet above, set as close together as possible, with a single opening shaped by overlapping ends of the circle. The shape of the stockade varied, but the circular type prevailed.

The tepee was the portable dwelling of the Plains tribes, and of other groups for summer homes. Eight to 20 or more poles, about 20 feet in length, were set in a circle with the top ends tied together. The diameter was generally around 15 feet, though many were more than twice as large.

A covering placed over this basic framework was stretched by sewing together skins of the larger animals, usually the buffalo and elk. It was held in place by pins driven in the ground; wherever it happened to overlap, it was tied with thongs. When the weather was warm, the cover was rolled up from the bottom. When used as a permanent residence, or in cold weather, the interior was dug out to a depth of two or three feet. The earth removed was banked around the outside to add warmth and protection from the winds.

The entry was formed by an overlapping section of the hide covering which was left unfastened. At the top, a hole was left for the smoke to escape. The smoke was kept from the tepee by two flaps of the covering rising a little higher, thus deflecting the downdrafts. These were controlled by a long pole which was fastened to the upper corners of the flaps.

The interior was sparsely furnished. Skins and woven mats were the only sleeping accommodations. Weapons and other equipment, as well as food supplies, were suspended from the framework.

The earth lodge of some of the Prairie tribes was an adaptation of the tepee principle, although it closely resembled the construction of the "bark house" of the Northeastern tribes. Four large posts were set into the ground. A few feet outside of these four more posts of half the height were placed.

Crossbeams were lashed to the tops of the uprights. Against the framework thus constructed, heavy poles were placed, reaching an apex above the center of the four higher inner posts. When the poles were lashed in position, layers of small poles and brushwood were added. On this, bundles of grass and sod were arranged in overlapping layers. After some time, there was a sufficient admixture of dirt, and rooted plants grew and blossomed when in season.

From a distance the structure appeared to be a mound, except when smoke issued from the single vent at the top. The doorway was generally a passage of several feet, built of logs and covered with earthwork. A skin was hung over the entry. The earth lodge of the Navajo was usually referred to as a "hogan." It was a much simpler structure than the other great earth covered dwellings of the Prairie Indians. Three forked poles were set in the ground as the main framework. Then brushwood, poles and bark were placed in layers to receive the sod and earth covering. The doorway was built out like a dormer window on the east side, and over this a blanket was hung.

The Navajo summer dwelling was only a shelter from the sun. On a slope they set two upright posts in the ground, with notched ends up. A crossbeam was laid on this; then they leveled the earth from the upper slope to make the floor. Cottonwood boughs with the leaves were placed against the bank and allowed to rest on the cross beams to complete the shelter. As the leaves withered, they added fresh boughs.

The permanent abode of the Pima was often built on the same plan, though smaller, as the earth lodge of the Prairie Indians. Their dwellings, however, were not

FIGURE 7.2: PLAINS EARTH LODGE

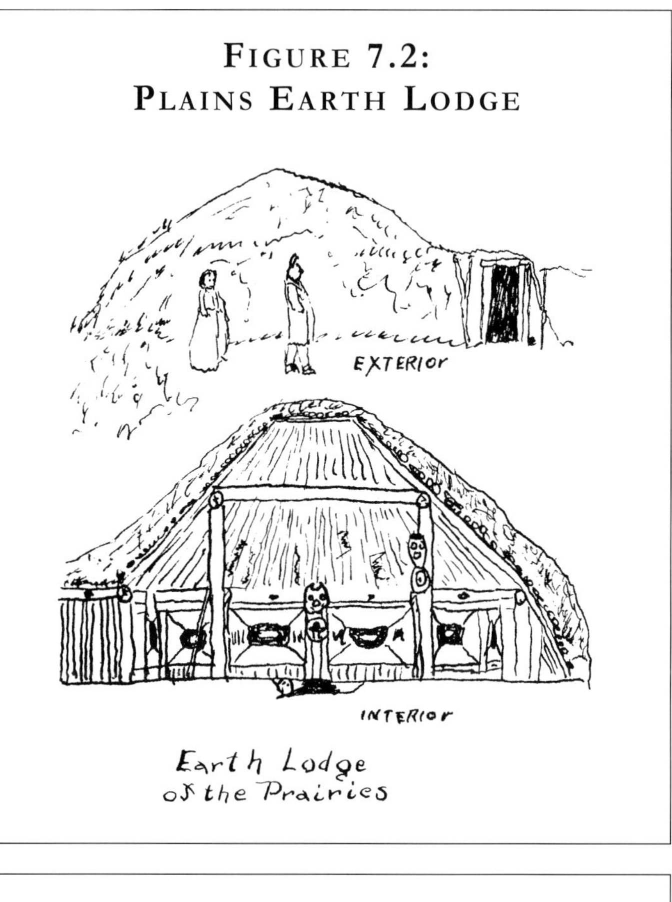

FIGURE 7.3: PLAINS AND SOUTHWEST HOUSES

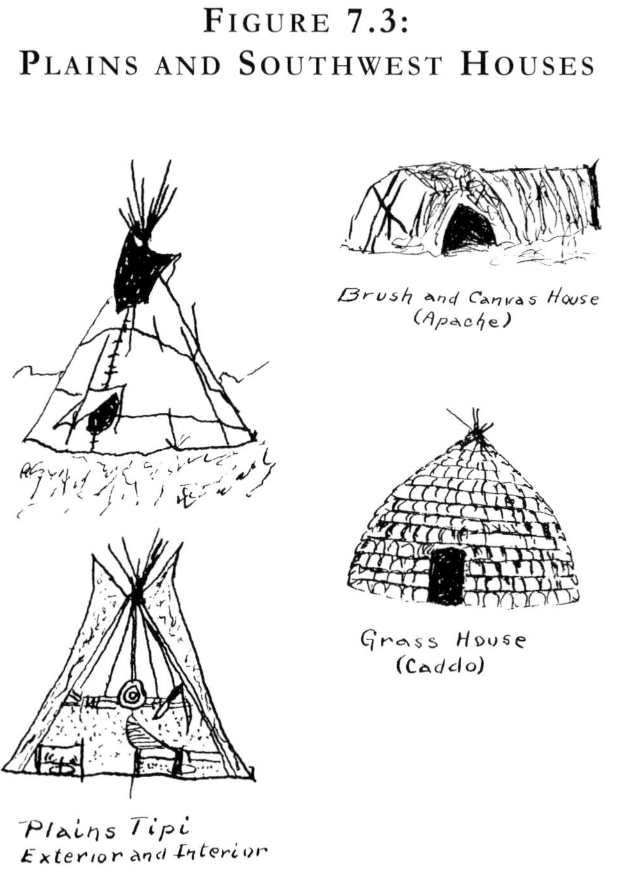

FIGURE 7.4:
THE NAVAJO HOGAN

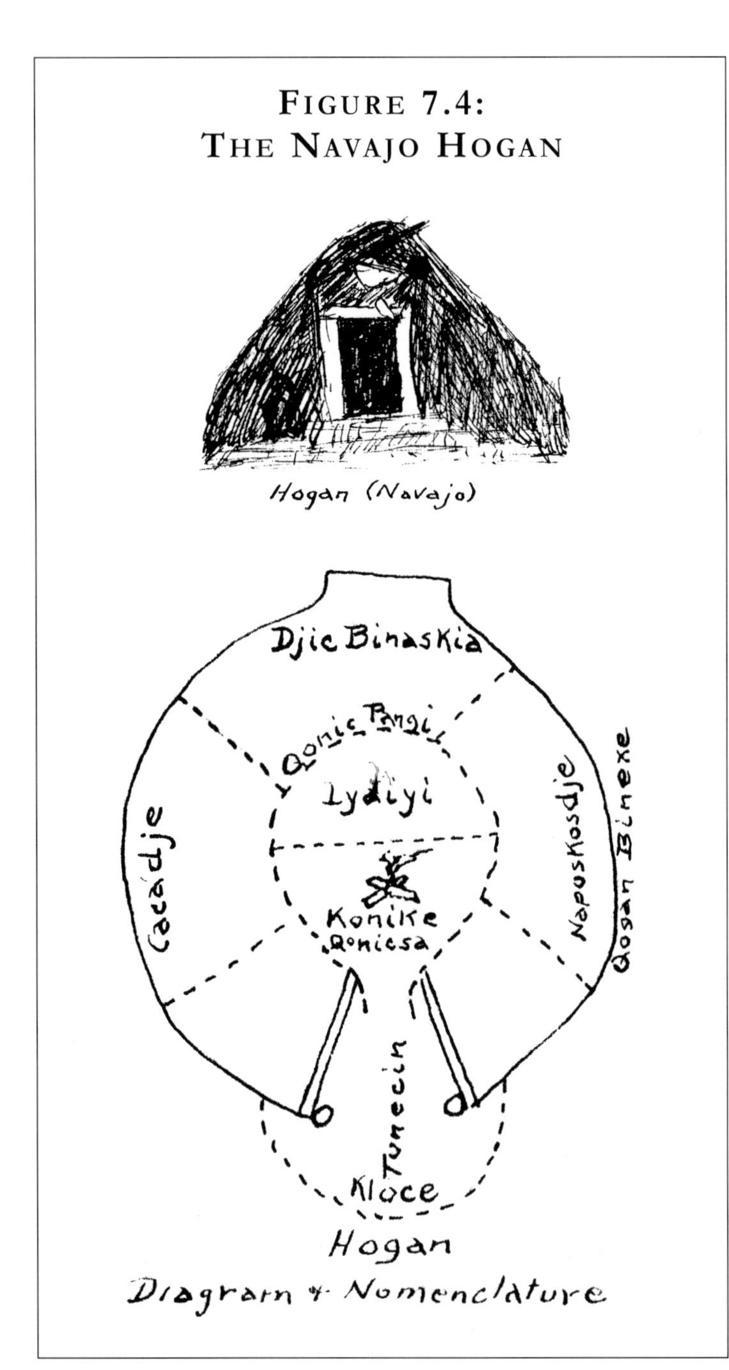

provided with a smoke hole. The single doorway on the east side also served as a smoke hole. For summer houses, they set four poles in the ground and put a brush and bark thatch on top, leaving the sides open. It was just a sunshade.

The Caddo built a grass house in a conical shape. Poles were set in the ground, forming a circle, and brought to the apex and tied. Horizontal poles were then lashed in place. Layers of long grass were then tied to the horizontal poles in overlapping layers. Starting at the bottom, the thatch was built up layer after layer until it reached the top. The thatching was similar to the roofs seen in Brittany even to this day.

In the Southwest, the early tendency was to gather together in communal houses. The cliff houses of the Mesa Verde were an interesting type of dwelling. These cliff palaces were built in various places, in caves, on the mesas, and in the valleys. The people built homes that rose several stories in height and contained a great number of cell-like rooms. The buildings grew smaller toward the top, and the floors of the lower level had the larger areas.

The walls were built of stone set in adobe mortar. The lower story walls had no openings, but the upper stories, which were reached by ladders from terrace to terrace, had square openings. The doors were small and sometimes "T" shaped, and all were closed, either with stone slabs or with skins.

The lower story was used for storage, while the upper rooms were for living quarters. The rooms varied from 4 x 6 to 10 x 20 feet. Sometimes a ceremonial room was even larger. The average ceiling was around seven feet high. The walls were often plastered with adobe, and sometimes colored and painted with designs. The roof was constructed by laying poles close together, over which fine brushwood, matting and finally a

Above: One of Johnston's colleagues with a Navajo hogan in Arizona.

layer of well-packed earth was placed. During hostilities, the ladders normally used to gain access to their houses were drawn up out of the reach of the invaders. Entrance to the storage rooms was achieved by ladders down through some of the living rooms or from a terrace.

The American Indian of Puget Sound—an area where there was an abundance of timber—built great houses of spruce and cedar. Buildings were 500 to 700 feet in length, and 40 to 90 feet in width, though the average house was about 20 x 75 feet. These houses were built in a lean-to style, with the roof sloping one way, while supporting posts divided the inside. Different portions were allotted to different families. Houses were built of plank which had been split from felled trees by using stone and antler wedges. In this way, and with wood so readily worked, they could rive out planks from two to three feet wide and usually six to eight inches thick. At times in river travel, they used plank to make platforms across two large canoes for transporting goods.

The Klamath tribe of the Pacific Northwest had a different house for summer and winter use. In winter, their dwellings were generally located along the shores of streams, lakes or ocean bays, where fish were obtainable year-round.

For the winter home, a large pit was dug to a depth of approximately half the desired height of the house. This was rectangular in shape. Posts were set at the corners and at intervals along the sides. By lashing light poles to these posts, a framework was made. Against this, rived timber was slanted, projecting far above, but not meeting at the top. This lumber was very rough, but these were the only dwellings in which the American Indian ever approximated the use of boards in building houses. Over the planking, layers of bark mats and earth were laid, forming a heavy roof over the pit. For the most part, the entrance was through the top opening, which also served as a smoke hole. A few, however, achieved doorways.

In summer, the individual dwellings were more widely scattered. They were generally located near hunting grounds and where wild berries and fruit were gathered. These were simple structures. Many of the Northwest tribes, especially the Chinook, used a simple brush

FIGURE 7.5: PIMA HOGAN

FIGURE 7.6: CLIFF DWELLING DETAILS

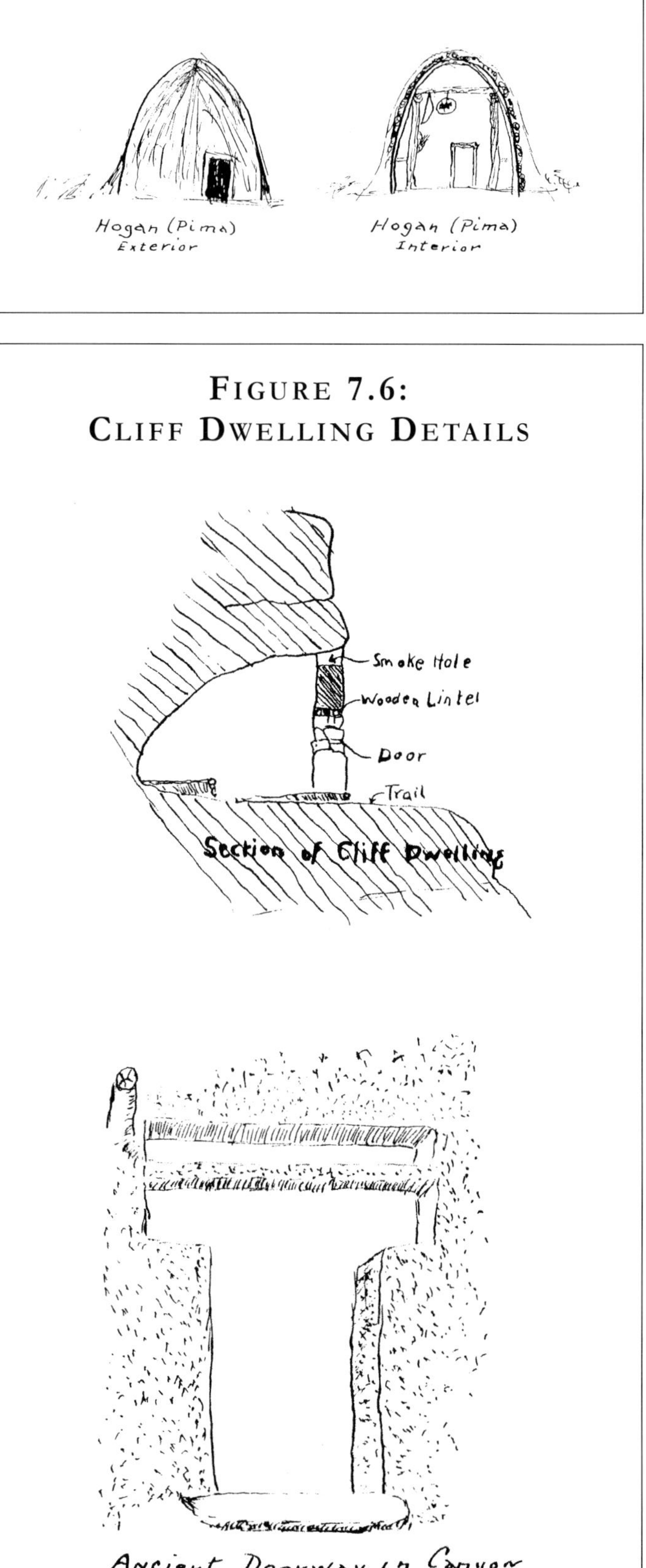

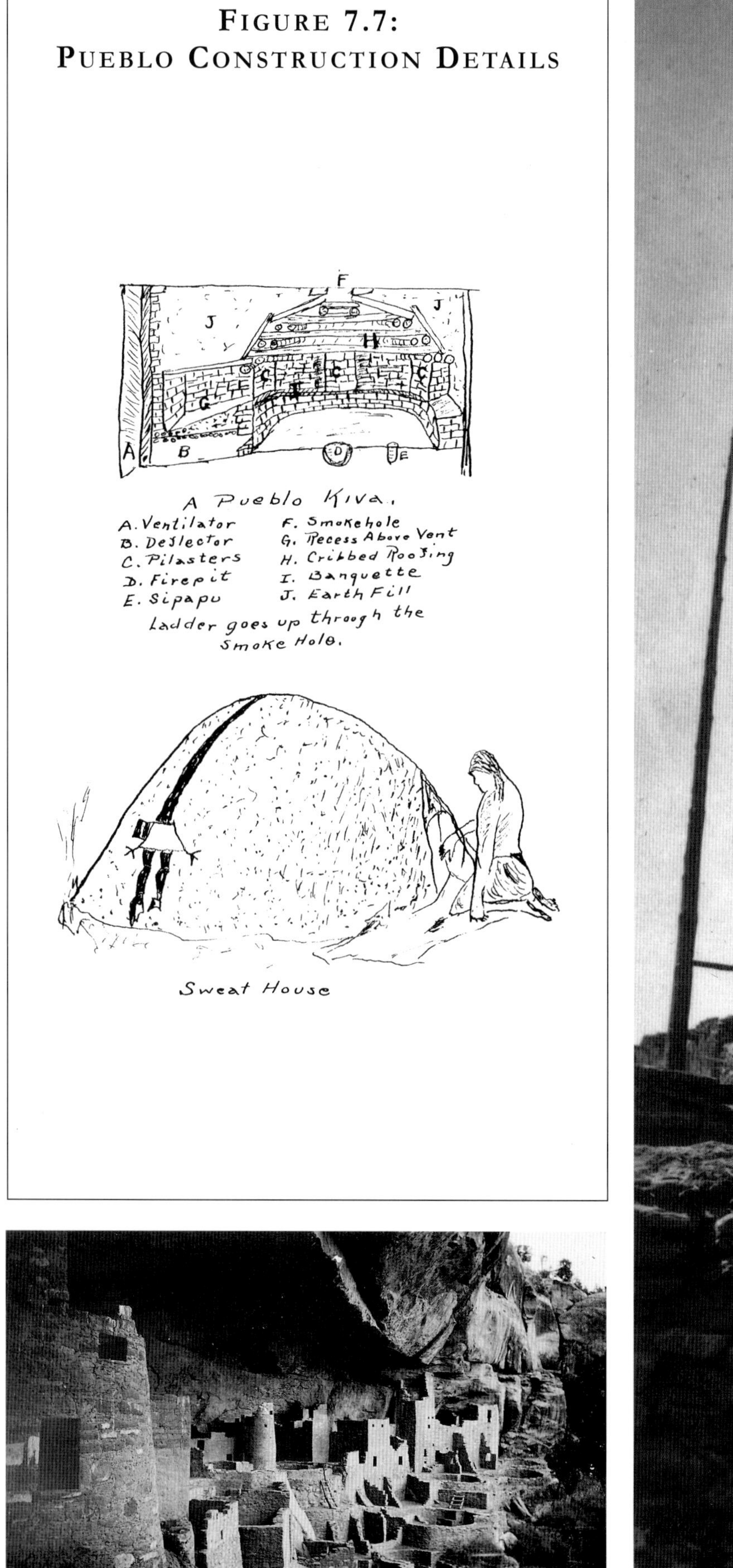

Above: Johnston's photograph of the Mesa Verde Pueblo ruins.

Above: The terraced houses at the Hopi Pueblo at Walpi, Arizona, photographed by John Hillers in 1879.

FIGURE 7.8: ESKIMO (INUIT) DWELLINGS

lean-to, or occasionally a brush "V" shaped wickiup, for summer use.

The Chinook winter dwelling was constructed from poles with a cedar bark covering and was quite substantial. The Haida tribes represented two strange extremes of dwelling construction, showing definite association with the Klamath, and also with the Eskimo. Their permanent houses were substantial and well built. Frequently they were sufficiently large to shelter 500 to 700 people. They excavated to a depth of approximately six feet. The walls projected above the ground four or five feet, with an opening for both entrance and exit, as well as smoke. The earth walls were lined with split logs. All were secured to upright poles, and the crossbeams lashed together. The whole was then thatched with bark and matting.

Another permanent residence was constructed on an elevated platform, some as high as 30 feet. They were well built structures, consisting of substantial scaffolding, and the house was constructed of planking and cedar bark mats lashed together. Cedar bark mats were used on the floors. A notched pole served as a ladder. The front of the houses were frequently decorated with figures of men and animals. This was one of the few instances where the American Indian attempted to decorate their permanent dwellings, either inside or outside.

The igloo was the more permanent winter dwelling of the Eskimo. Because of their experience in building ice houses, the Eskimo developed a more dome-shaped roof.

Due to the cold climate, they constructed a passageway to an entrance located some distance from the house. When not in use, the opening at the top of the house for smoke was covered with a sheet made from the intestine of a whale. Frequently, the upright supports and other portions of the framework were made from whalebone instead of wood, which was scarce in some localities.

The "ice houses," though occasionally used for an entire winter, were more commonly used only during sealing expeditions. On the frozen surface of the sea a circle about 15 feet in diameter was drawn. The frozen snow within the circle was cut into slabs three to five inches thick, their length depending upon the depth of the snow on the ice. These blocks of snow were placed one upon the other (as if brick), with the ascending circular layers growing smaller until a dome was achieved. The door was cut in the side and an entry passage constructed. Heat from the use of oil lamps inside soon scalded all joints and turned the entire building into a single frozen piece of ice. Later, snow was banked around the outside. Seats were built of blocks of ice and covered with skins, which also covered the doorway.

The American Indian also had some good means of purifying the air in their houses. Cedar and balsam boughs were burned in the lodge to purify the air, though maybe not so much for their own benefit as to please the Great Spirit. Likewise, many similar plants were burned, and all had a purifying effect. Some sort of brush or broom was found around all lodges for cleaning.

The sweat house, or temescal, was almost universal among the Indian tribes. For some, its construction was a great ceremony, while for others it was just another necessity. They built a small, dome-shaped structure, with a rough frame of boughs, and thoroughly coated it with mud. Often it was built near a stream.

The entrance was quite small, and through this the occupant crawled. Heated stones were placed inside and water poured on them to produce steam, or sometimes a small fire was used; in either case, the small area and the ventless structure caused a good perspiration to break out, and after it had lasted long enough to suit the occupant (quite often all night) he would dash out and plunge into the nearest stream for a cold bath. This was universally used as a cure for many ailments.

With many tribes it was a custom to go into the water at sunrise. Wherever there was a stream, there could be found some of the tribe, especially the children, playing in the water. All enjoyed its cleansing effect. The desert Indians cleansed themselves and their hair by using yucca suds as a soap. Other Indians cleansed their hair by plastering it with mud and grease. This also had a cleansing effect.

Each tribe made their beds of the material which was most suitable and obtainable—generally skins and mats. A few made a pretense of a framework or ledge in the side of the dwelling. The Mandan Indian was the only one who covered his bed with an enclosed canopy to keep out the draft.

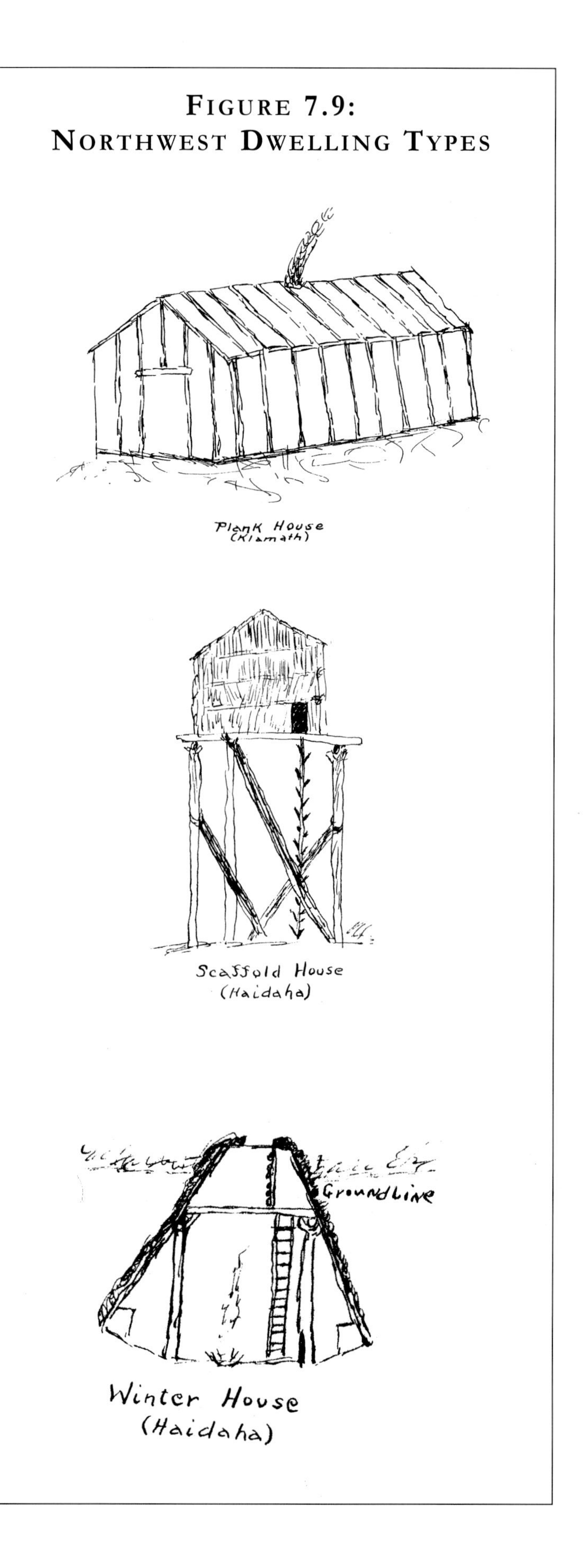

FIGURE 7.9: NORTHWEST DWELLING TYPES

CHAPTER 8

THE USE OF FIRE

The Indians have a legend explaining the origin of fire on Earth. According to this Indian myth, the gods always had fire, just as they had everything else. The animals, in going to pay homage to the gods, tried to steal the fire and bring it back to the Earth with them. The opossum tried by thrusting his tail into the fire, but his only luck was to have the hair all burned off his tail, and it has never grown since.

The buzzard tried by sticking his crested topknot in the fire as he made his formal bow to the gods. His head and neck burned bare, and this is the way they have always remained. The fox also tried. He tied bundles of resin soaked withe rod to his tail, and this touched the fire as he made his bow to the gods. He ran for the Earth, and by keeping the fire behind him, he was not burned. He succeeded in reaching the Earth, but his coat was turned ruddy by the glow of the fire, and ever since we have had the red fox.

The production and keeping of a constantly smoldering sacred fire was a custom with the Indians from the beginning, according to legends. They usually produced a new fire at the green corn festive season, or when enemies destroyed the house in which the sacred fire was kept.

The following rites were observed in preparing the new fire: A conical mound of fresh earth was made, the top marked with a square. On this was placed the inner bark from seven different kinds of trees, all taken from the east side of the tree, and all being free of any blemish. On an appointed morning after many ceremonies during a particular gathering, the official fire maker and six assistants assembled. A block of dry, hard wood with a small hole started in the surface was placed on the ground. Another piece of wood in the shape of a shaft with a pointed end was fitted into the hole of the first piece. Around this was laid the dry goldenrod, to act as tinder. The official fire maker then took the shaft. Spinning it rapidly in the hole of the other piece of wood ignited a spark that was taken up by the goldenrod tinder and, in turn, transferred to the heap of dry bark of seven trees.

After the fire was started, all the women of the village came for new fire, as the old fires had been extinguished on the preceding day. The new fire was kept for a year and was not allowed to go out. It was kept smoldering, and remained in constant attention by the fire maker or his assistants during that time.

Certain tribes made the drill used for starting fire by binding together with sinew a number of the hard, sharp, pointed blades of the yucca. The stem, once peeled and dried, was used as the hearth of the fire making apparatus, just as punk was used in the timber regions. The

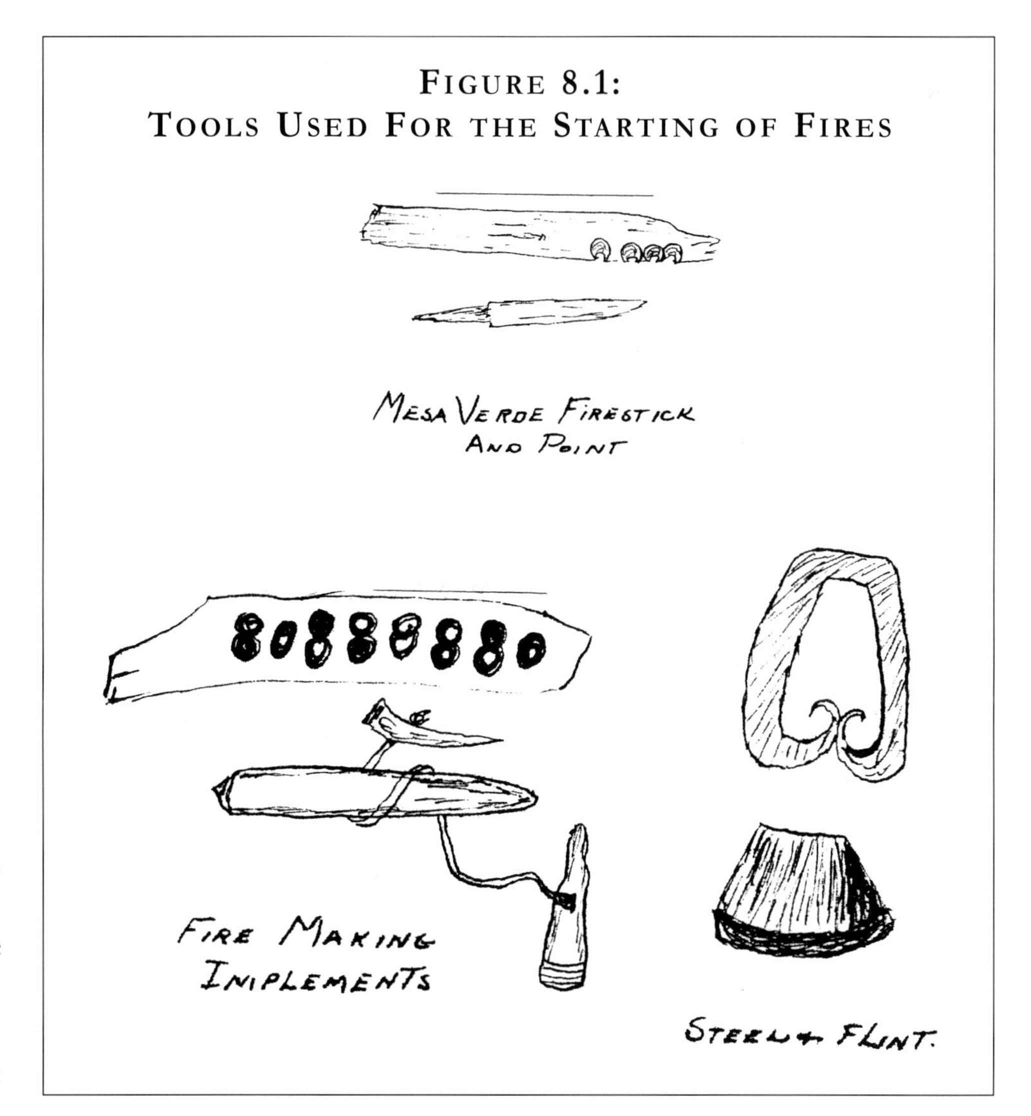

Figure 8.1:
Tools Used For the Starting of Fires

arrow weed was desired more than anything else as a drill and hearth in making fire, as the pith from the center acted as tinder and would readily take up the spark.

To keep a fire or to prevent it from smoking when on the march (which would give their position away), the American Indian used a fairly dry fuel and banked it with earth. A man on a journey in the coldest of weather could make such a small fire, and at night would sit hunched with his skin robe over his shoulders. The fire would be under the arch of his knees, and thus he slept in comfort. In the huts all fires were banked to keep them from drying out.

Working Wood

In general, the stone axes were really not suitable for felling timber. To assist the work, they would chop or bruise the tree near to the ground with their stone ax and then, by carefully controlling a fire started there, fell the tree with little labor, since the fire would take hold of the bruised part quite readily. At other times and with different tribes, after the groove had been hacked the tree might be bent over, and the tensed fibers in the groove sawed with a flaked stone.

The butts were usually trimmed to a conical shape, and were sometimes rubbed down to a flat surface. Shaping of implements seemed to have been done by whittling or scraping with stone knives or flakes. The finish was put on with a coarse sandstone, after which a closer grained stone was used. In splitting logs, wedges of antlers, or sometimes large bones, were used.

The Eskimo was usually thought of as occupying a treeless country, although he really had as much wood as is necessary from the driftwood deposited on the shores of the country. From the driftwood, he split out thin pieces; and after soaking them, he bent the wood and sewed the sides with sealskin sinew. In this manner, he made many boxes, both round and square, for the storage of his possessions. Shallow dishes and bowls were usually made of driftwood, as were as many ladles and spoons.

CHAPTER 9

MARRIAGE AND FAMILY LIFE

Nowhere in the life of the American Indian is there a wider variation of codes and standards than in marriage. Neighboring tribes had opposite regulations regarding the chastity of women. For example, one tribe demanded chastity only before marriage, another only after marriage. Some tribes, regardless of their separate codes, would meet at stated seasons each year when promiscuous relations were freely indulged in by all.

Among most tribes, however, the acquisition of a wife was a simple process: If you had the price, you could have the wife, as it was purely a business transaction. The girl's parents were paid for her and, in most cases, if she were not satisfactory she could be returned and the payment refunded.

A man's wealth was judged not only by his goods, but also by the number of his wives. There was always a favorite wife who directed the work of the others. As there were usually several, the burden was light enough to prevent rebelling.

The richest man naturally had the best wives, while the poorer had to be satisfied with what was left. Youth, comeliness and ability to work were the main requisites for a wife, although the latter was by far the most important. Among some of the Pueblo, the courtship was reversed: The girl chose her mate. Her father had to go to the prospective groom's father and make her choice known. The groom's father had to pay the purchase price to recompense for the loss of a daughter who was the laborer in the home.

In some tribes women had two husbands, in which case the second functioned only while the first was away. The rest of the time he acted as a servant in a little better capacity than a slave. Although marriage was contracted at an early age among the Chichimec of Mexico, legitimate intercourse could not be had until the wife was 40 years old.

The children of female slaves often became slaves themselves, but occasionally the female slaves were made additional wives. Another practice involved male concubines. Regardless of the variation of the moral standards, the enforcement was universally rigid. Infringements were punishable by death or mutilation. However, the standard sometimes varied as to the quality of the blame. With the Cree both sexes were equally punishable for transgression, both parties being severely chastised before the tribal group. If the offenses of adultery were repeated, they were often mutilated and driven away from the tribe.

Some tribes held adultery a sin for a woman but not for her husband. If a man were unfaithful, his wife was compelled, on each occasion, to supply a blanket or its

Above: The young Crow woman known as Ida Wrinkle Face, or Ida Day Light. Her dress is decorated with elk teeth.

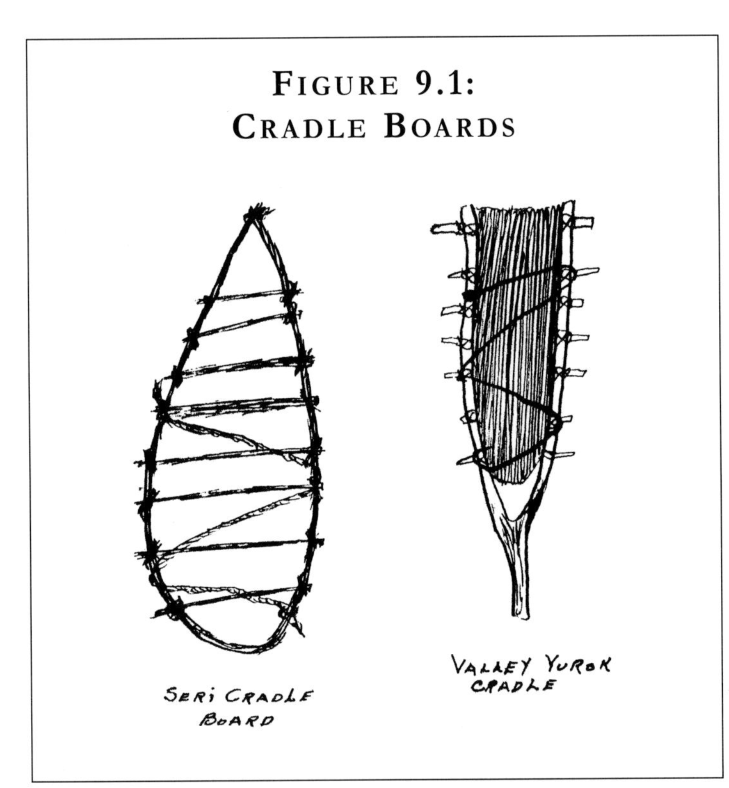

Above: A cradle board of a type used by the Pomo.

equivalent to the woman, even to the point of losing all her possessions, so that the tribe might know that for some reason she had not fulfilled her wifely duties, or her husband would not have sought another. Whereas the price of adultery was a blanket, as in this case, she who gathered the greatest number of blankets won admiration from her mate.

Among the Chipa, adultery was punishable by death for the man, although the husband of the woman could have the adulterer delivered to him, and he could then kill or pardon at his own pleasure. The woman was disgraced. Rape of a virgin was punishable by stoning to death. Among some tribes, a woman's nose was cut off, marking her lastingly and conspicuously for having committed adultery.

CHILDREN

It seems to have been a rather universal practice throughout all Indian tribes that, after the birth of a child, certain foods were taboo and the husband and wife lived apart for a period of time. Different ceremonies, however, were observed in the various tribes upon the birth of the first child. Among some, the father was intoxicated and surrounded by dancing groups who scored his body until he was bleeding from head to foot. In another tribe, a few days after the birth, if the child was a boy, all the warriors would visit the house and each, in turn, pick up the child, feel his limbs, and exhort him to be brave, finally naming him. If the child was a girl the women would go through a similar ceremony.

With the Lagunero Indians, the husband remained in bed for six or seven days, and could eat neither fish nor meat.

Some tribes had midwives, who would assist the mother in giving birth, and then would chant and, in some cases, pretend to pick the newly-born child out of the air. It has been observed that, after the the child was born, the midwife would go outdoors, covering her face with her hands. She would then walk once around the house. At that point, she would uncover her face, and the first object she saw would be chosen to inspire the choice of a name for the child.

Above: An eight-year-old Cheyenne girl with her doll, photographed in Montana by L.A. Huffman in about 1880.

FIGURE 9.2: BASKET CRADLE

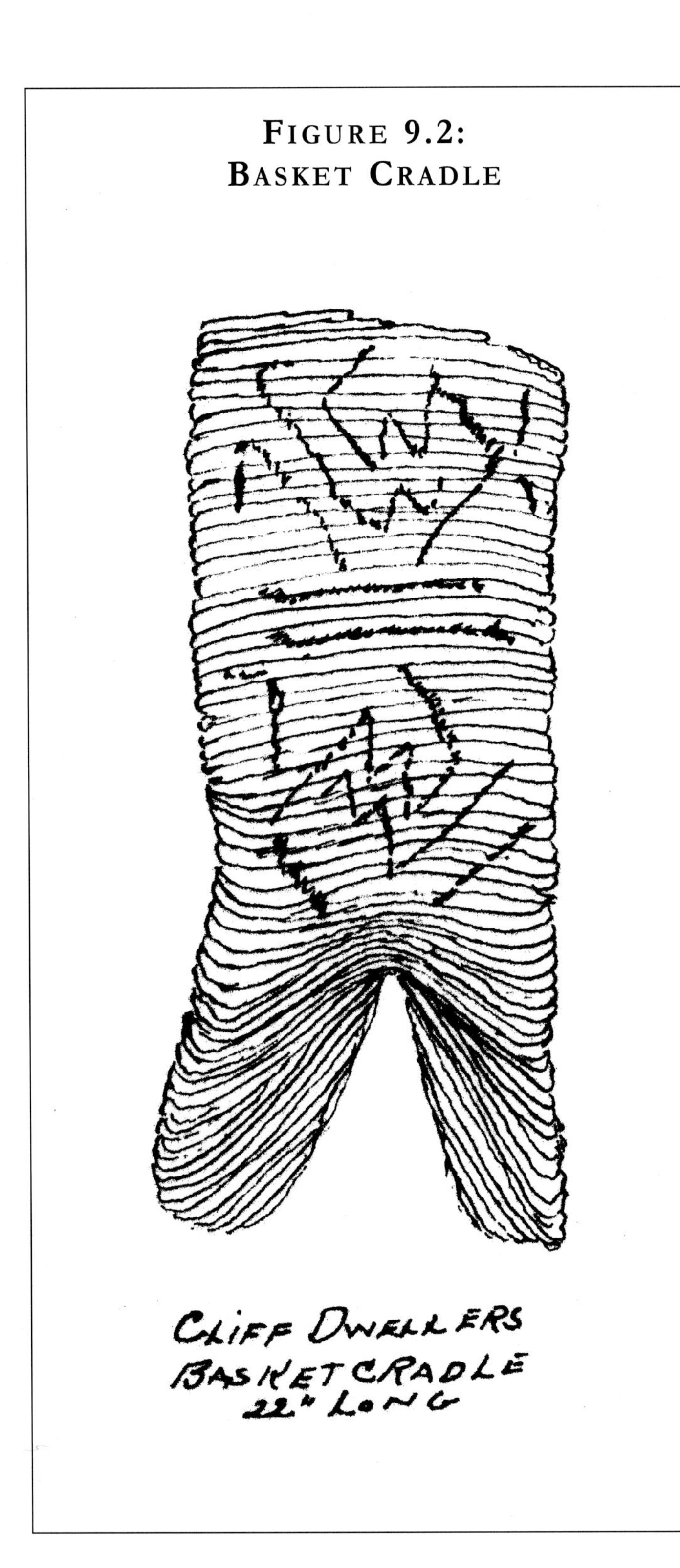

Another method of naming a child was during confinement, when the relatives had assembled in the hut, and all had begun to draw figures of different animals on the floor, and then rubbed them out as soon as they were drawn. This continued until the child was born, and the figure that was then sketched on the ground would be called the child's tone, or second self. As the child grew up, the animal became its protector.

An infusion of young pine cones, or the inside scrapings of a human skull, were supposed to prevent too rapid a family increase, while certain plants facilitated abortion.

The children of the Korak were not named for several years. If they died young they would not then be thought of by their name. The Yulis named their children when they first began to talk, and the name was usually given by some relative. It usually had something to do with the child — "Sore Eyes" or "Afraid of Shadow," for instance—or referred to some incident, such as "Handle Comes Off." With some tribes, the birth of twins was a great tribal event, even to the extent that neither the father nor the mother were obliged to do any work, sometimes for as long as three or four years. The children were also treated with reverence, and were kept painted and adorned. On the other hand, in some tribes, in the advent of twins the mother and children were put to death, even if she were of the chief's family.

A burial urn was found on the Pacific Coast recently that contained the remains of a mother and twins. The artifacts in the burial showed plainly that she was the chieftain's daughter.

With the Yurok, if twins of the opposite sex were born, the girl child was smothered. They had a dread of such births, as they believed if the children lived they might be incestuous. Boy twins were believed to quarrel all their lives, but were usually spared. Triplets were held in even greater dread, as they were believed to mean calamity. With the Mojave, twins were thought to have come from the sky, and were believed to be clairvoyants who possessed supernatural knowledge. Their dreams were thought to be different from those of other people. These children were always treated alike, for fear one would become angry and return from whence they came.

The Maidu people feared the birth of twins, and they were instantly destroyed. Very often the mother was killed with the children. With the Seri Indians, triplets were regarded as evil monsters, and their birth was considered a crime punishable by immediate death. In many cases, the birth of twins was similarly treated.

The cradle boards of some of the American Indians had a head board which projected down at an angle of about 45 degrees. The padding was of deer skin, which was laced to the sides of the cradle board. Fine shredded bark was placed underneath. The child was then placed inside, the front laced up and the straps tied around the bundle. The child was placed so that the front of its head rested against the head board. A little pad of hair or bark was placed there to prevent chafing. In time, this produced a sloping forehead, and the tribes who practiced this treatment were often referred to as "the flat head people."

Many of the children were nursed until another child was born. Some tribes held ceremonies for the child at its first year, when it was given salt for the first time. When it had cut all of its teeth it was given its first meat. One early authority insisted that certain tribes scorched the faces of young boys to prevent the growth of beards, but this seems inconsistent, due to the fact that in tribes where this was not practiced the men had little or no beards.

In many tribes the children were under the control of the parents until puberty, at which time they were made subjects of the chief. In some tribes a youth, on reaching manhood, went alone into the hills and remained there until he had had a dream of some bird or animal or fish. From then on that creature was his medicine; its teeth, claws, bones and skin his charm.

Another custom was for the young boy to go without food for three days. During this time he was kept intoxicated and beaten with nettles until he had a vision of some animal. When he told of this, a figure of the animal was molded of paste made out of herbs and roots. This was plastered on his breast and arms, then ignited and allowed to burn until consumed. The divine protective figure was tattooed on his body.

Among some tribes, in a practice known as kashim, the girls were closely guarded. At puberty they were placed in a small enclosure for a six month period, seeing no one except the woman who brought them their meals. In some cases it was observed that the daughters

FIGURE 9.3: CRADLE BOARDS

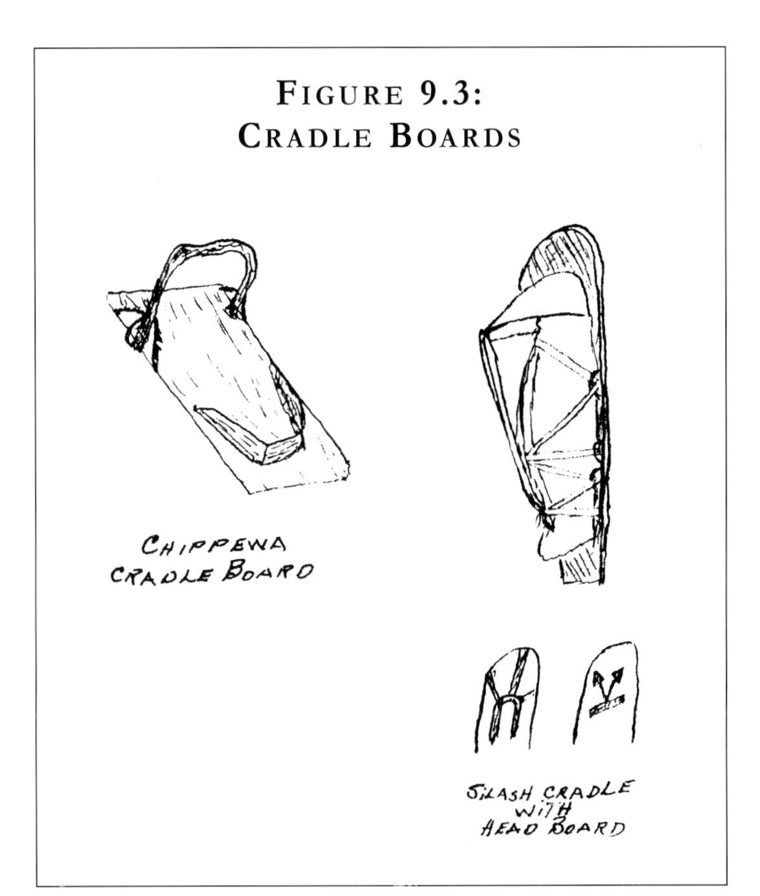

Above: A young Hopi woman with the "squash blossom" hair style.

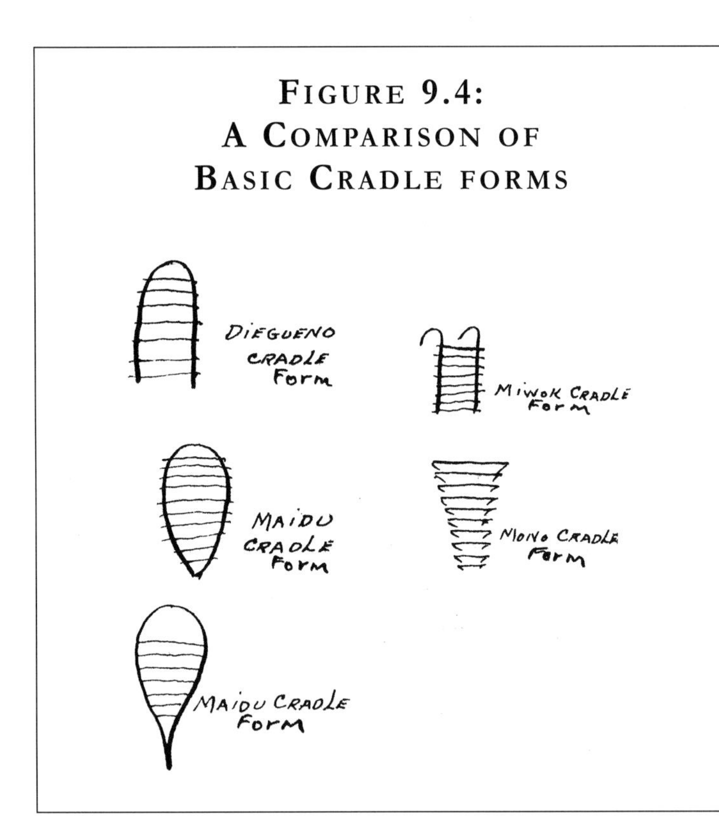

FIGURE 9.4: A COMPARISON OF BASIC CRADLE FORMS

Above: A Salish (Flathead) woman and her daughter, dressed in their ceremonial finery, photographed in Montana in about 1900.

of high-ranking persons could escape this practice through the payment of a bribe, usually to the village's shaman.

Among all the tribes, women were shunned during the period of their menstruation, and usually were compelled to live apart for 10 days. This was quite universal. For a woman to come into the presence of the sick during this period was courting disaster, and she was liable to be held responsible for any fatality to that sick person.

Above: Lizzie Yellowtail and her sister Mary with Lizzie's son Robert, photographed in about 1895. Lizzie died in 1969, at the age of 103.

Among the Otomi, the girls usually married young. When she had not found a mate by the time puberty was reached, her parents or guardian selected one for her. A man could take her on trial for an indefinite period. If afterwards both parties were satisfied, there was a marriage ceremony.

If, however, the man was not pleased, he returned her to her parents. This proceeding did not place any obstacle in her way of obtaining another suitor.

CHAPTER 10

CLOTHING

The clothing of the American Indian before contact with Europeans was very simple. If it was necessary for warmth, they put in on; otherwise, they often wore nothing. The breechcloth seen on many of the American Indians was not as much a covering for modesty's sake as it was for a belt, in which he might carry his knife or implements. In the same way, a woman might wear a girdle with a grass apron attached, and here also the belt was the thing of most value.

Some of the tribes used only skins as wraps in the coldest part of the year, while others wove skirts and mats to throw over the shoulders. The weaving was of grasses, bark fiber, strips of rabbit skin or yarn, depending on the tribe and the industrial habits they had learned and the material available.

Many of the more advanced tribes wove very striking robes, but would also use buffalo and deer skins, even taking the trouble to sew the skins of many small animals or birds together to make a covering. The Seri people made a robe from the feathered breasts of the pelican. The Navajo wove wondrous blankets of native wool, and also made a semblance of a garment. Another group made blankets which were very thick and extremely warm, by using strips of twisted rabbit skin with the fur on as the woof in the blanket. A robe of buffalo or bear skin was certainly warm, whether cut and fitted into a garment or thrown over the shoulders and tied around the waist. The Eastern tribes made more of a semblance of a garment than did many of the Western tribes.

All garments were profusely decorated. Porcupine quill work was usually the finest type of decoration, although the bead work, feathers and fur decorations were very beautiful. Shells, seed beads and bones were also attached for adornment. The wild fancy of the American Indian manifested itself in his dress and ornamentation. From native pigments and herbs, many fine dyes were made and used to great advantage. Unique patterns were dyed on their garments.

Tanning of skins was a very important part of the daily life of the Indian women, since hides made clothes, shelters and articles to trade with other tribes, and later with the whites. The dressing of the skins was usually the work of the women and the same procedure was followed by all tribes. Different pelts were treated differently. If the hair was to be left on, the skin was fleshed and then rubbed, usually with the brains of the animal, or with roots and ashes. By dint of continued working, pulling, massaging and smoking, the hide was dried out and left soft and pliable.

Sometimes a small hole was dug in the ground and the hide made into a sort of funnel. It was suspended above the hole in which a fire of green sticks was pre-

Above: An ethnographer of Johnston's era conferring with Blackfeet men in traditional fringed buckskin clothing.

FIGURE 10.1: HATS USED BY CALIFORNIA TRIBES

pared, and slowly smoked and cured this way with slow, continuous working. This was done to to make the hide pliable. These hides, however, had a tan color and not the white surface that resulted when using the former method.

The scrapers used in fleshing the hides were of many varieties, most of flint and stone, some hafted and others not. Some used crude chunks of flint, and others worked with finer tools. Some tribes made scrapers from pieces of elk antler. After they secured metal, they attached blades to these old implements in order to improve them. Some of the scrapers of the Eskimo had very finely wrought handles of bone, wood and ivory. Blades were made of flint and slate before metal was substituted.

If the hair was to be removed from the hide, the pelt was allowed to remain in a stream of water for a certain number of days until the hair would slip off, or by placing the skin in wood ashes which were kept wet; the lye would loosen the hair. By first fleshing and then continuous rubbing over a log, in a few hours the skin would be dry, white, soft and pliable.

Bone awls and needles were used in sewing skins for all purposes, and were also used for opening shellfish and nuts. The many varieties of awls found tell of the different types of bone used—rabbit and bird bones, and even the splintered bone of larger animals.

According to their method of clothing their bodies, there are really three groups of American Indians: First, those who were fully clothed at all times by completely made garments, such as the Eskimo and others of the Northwestern group (to a certain extent). These people were completely clothed in tailored costumes cut from

Above: Several Paiute children playing the game "wolf and deer," as photographed in Arizona in 1871.

Above: An Omaha woman, photographed in 1868, wearing her native attire and beads, and carrying a bird's wing as a fan.

FIGURE 10.2: SOUTHWEST DECORATION AND FOOTWEAR

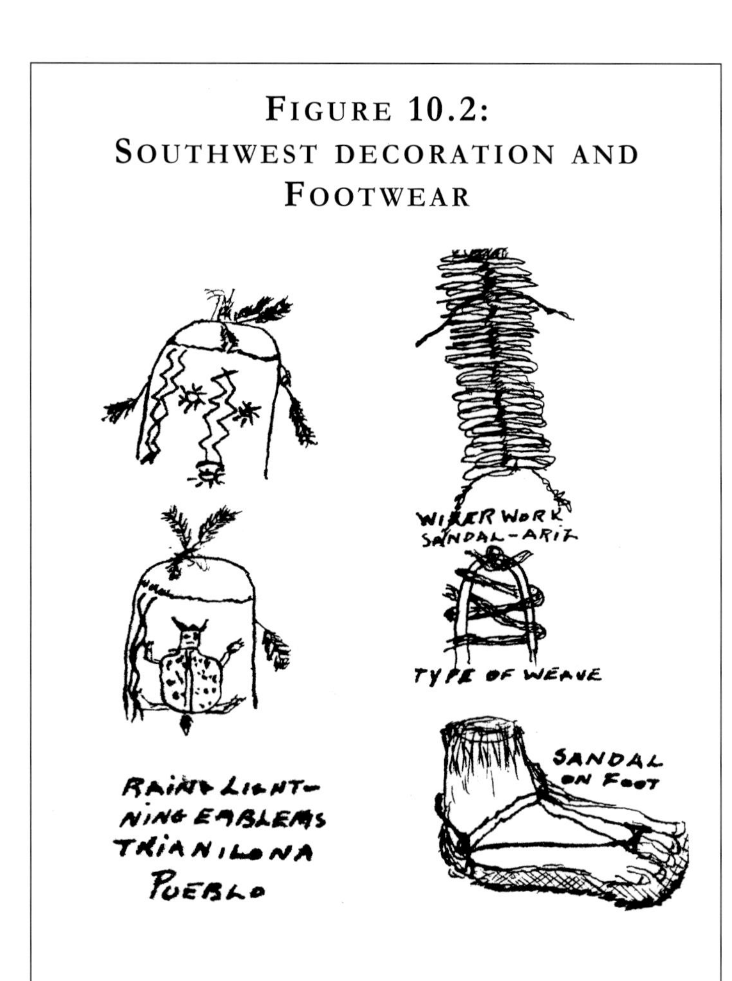

patterns and sewn together. During the winter months the Eskimo wore an inner and outer suit.

The inner suit was made from the skins of the smaller animals, with the hair next to the body. The outer garment was made up with the hair on the outside of the garment, reindeer skin as a rule, and had a hood attached. Both men and women wore breeches, completing their costume with mittens and heavy boots. They fared quite well in the cold. At night in the igloo they stripped for sleep, allowing their garments to dry.

Second, the tribes a little further south and in the Northeastern and central group also had to go fairly well clothed. They used cloth and skins combined, made into a semblance of clothing, but without any particular attempt at tailoring and fitting.

Third was the group which occupied a territory where the weather was such that a breechcloth was all that was necessary. These tribes used sandals only when they were on journeys over ground that was most severe. Otherwise, they usually went barefooted. The sandals were made of leather or some fiber braided together, willow withe rod or bark held on by toe loops and a cord around the ankle. Moccasins were made of skins, palm leaves, yucca fiber or any material the country supplied. Some of the above were made very plain, others profusely ornamented, especially after the white traders introduced beads. The variety of patterns was limited only to the variety of beads. I believe that the customs and government of the Natchez made them one of the most forward and outstanding groups. However, neither the men nor the women wore an excess of clothing. The costume of the men consisted of a breechcloth some of the time, and the girls and women wore a sort of apron in front only. During the winter months, they threw a robe or skin over their shoulders, as did all of the pre-Columbian people.

Above: An Eskimo group in traditional cold-weather clothing, photographed in Alaska in 1894.

Above: Kiowa chiefs sketched by George Catlin in the 1830s are Little Bluff in a buffalo robe, Bon'son'gee in a European blanket.

Above: Also sketched by Catlin and dressed in traditional buckskin, are the Kiowas Quay'ham'kay, Wun'pan'to'mee and Tunk'aht'oh'ye.

CHAPTER 11

BEADS AND ADORNMENT

Beads owe their existence to the desire of the early people for adornment. They were of all shapes and materials, shell, turquoise, stone, bone or horn and ivory. Regardless of the material, the bead making process was similar. They were rubbed down smooth and the holes were drilled with a drill of flint or stone, or occasionally a reed was used with sand as an abrasive. As each bead was drilled, it was placed on a cord until the desired amount was made. Then the edges of the entire string were reworked to make them more uniform.

The smaller the bead and the harder the material it was made of, the more valuable the bead. The long, slender beads of any material were much more difficult to make than the round bead, as they were usually of harder material and required more skilled labor. Some stones were used for beads, especially if they had fine coloring. The work required to drill them was a tribute to their determination and patience, as well as to their skill, considering the rude tools with which they worked. Many wonderful strings of turquoise, shell and coral beads have been found.

It is difficult to describe the beauty of many of the beads in drawings. Some were made with bone and had shell attached with pitch or asphalt. Shell beads had grooves filled with tar. Beads not an eighth of an inch across were worked with such fine lines that it takes a magnifying glass to see the incising. The American Indians were craftsmen of great skill. In some of the curved beads of both shell and stone, the drilling was remarkable, considering that they had to drill from both ends to make the hole in the center. The small size of the bead would puzzle a workman of today if he were using only modern hand tools, much less the hand or bow drill the American Indian used.

Some used a bow drill with a stone drill top which was held in the hand; others had a stick top. The Eskimo usually used a mouthpiece top, giving a free hand, which the other American Indians did not have. Some tribes used the pump drill, which left one hand free.

Runtees were shell discs with two lateral perforations. They could be strung with beads or used as a pendant at the end of a string. Many elaborately incised runtees have been found.

The dentalium shell of the Pacific Coast has been widely distributed. These peculiar, elongated marine shells resemble the hollowed fang of a large animal. Each shell is wound spirally with snake skin or fish skin, and at its end is a tuft of red feathers from the crested woodpecker. The individual shells are measured and their value determined by the creases in the left hand. The largest ones are valued at about $5.00. The next smaller

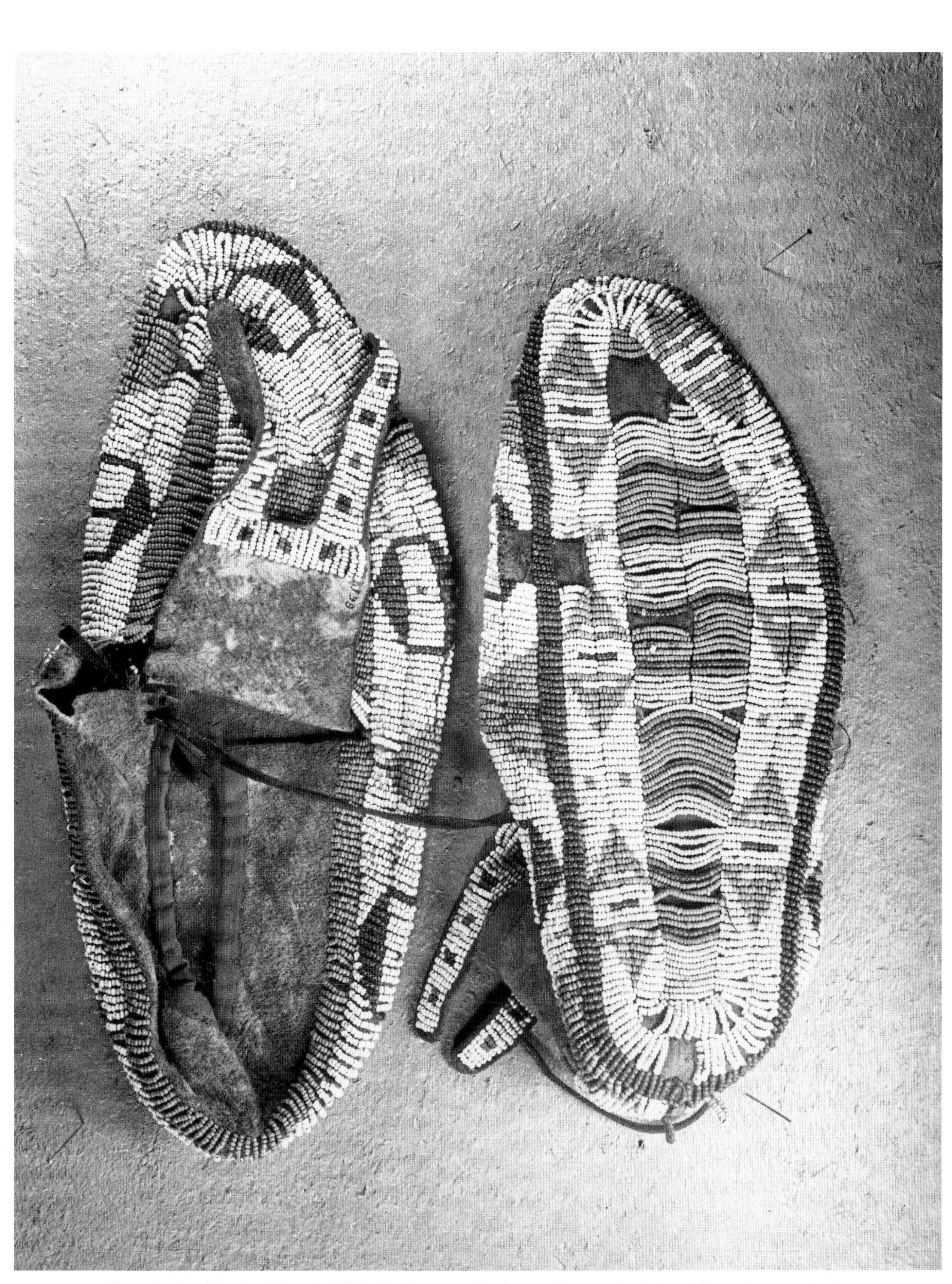

Above: A pair of intricately-beaded Plains Indian moccasins (top and bottom view) from Johnston's own collection.

FIGURE 11.1: BEAD MAKING TOOLS

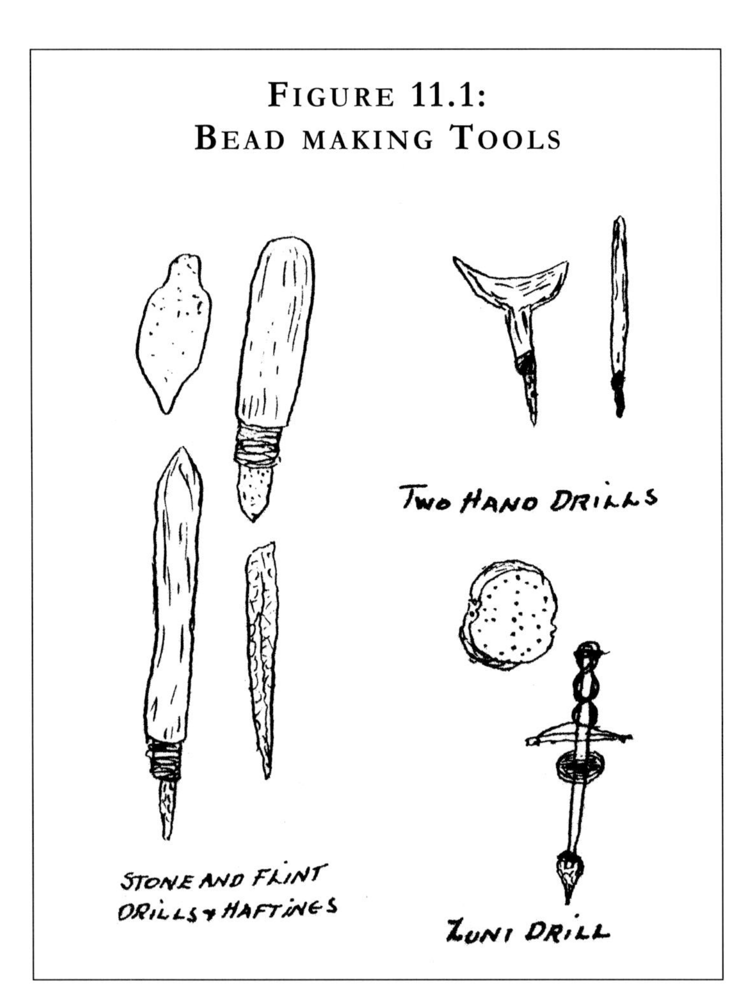

shells, measuring about 2 3/8ths inches, are worth about $1.50 each. A shell which is 1 1/8th inches long is valued at $1.00, while the smallest used as money, 7/8ths inch long, are worth from 50 to 75 cents. [*Editor's note: These prices are in 1937 dollars.*]

Bone beads were made by scoring the bone with stone or shell and breaking it off in sections, and then polishing the ends. Some have been found incised, and others stained. Human finger bones were used more as charms than as adornment.

Freshwater pearls were also used as beads. The majority were used by piercing, although a few have been found that were held in strings by tying five cords in a knot and bringing the cords up so as to form ribs about the pearl and again make a knot, and so on, forming the strand. No doubt a little dried fish oil or resin was used to help hold the string in place.

Sections of snake and fish vertebrae were strung with little effort. Some were worked extremely fine and were strung as bead runtees, some being pierced one way and some another. Many kinds of teeth and claws were used, the bear teeth and eagle claws being not only adornment, but badges of valor. The elk tooth was also prized and was sewed onto clothing.

Above: Chee'ah'ka'tchee in face paint with complex beaded earrings and necklace.

Stone of many kinds was used. Some show fine workmanship, being inlaid with silver, which brings them to a time after the advent of the white people.

Wampum, the most incorrectly used word pertaining to any one American Indian item, is the term correctly applied to a distinct type of bead of a certain shape and made of clamshell.

Two types were made, one of the white and one of the purple part of the clamshell. The true money wampum was about a 1/2 inch to 7/8ths of an inch long, and about 3/16ths of an inch in diameter. The center and all the shell was used for the white beads. The hinge furnished the purple material for the latter. They were harder to make and were scarcer, one purple shell being worth five of the white ones. Those used in the early

Above: George Catlin's 1832 portrait of Mint, a Mandan woman with beaded necklaces and a buckskin dress covered with elk teeth.

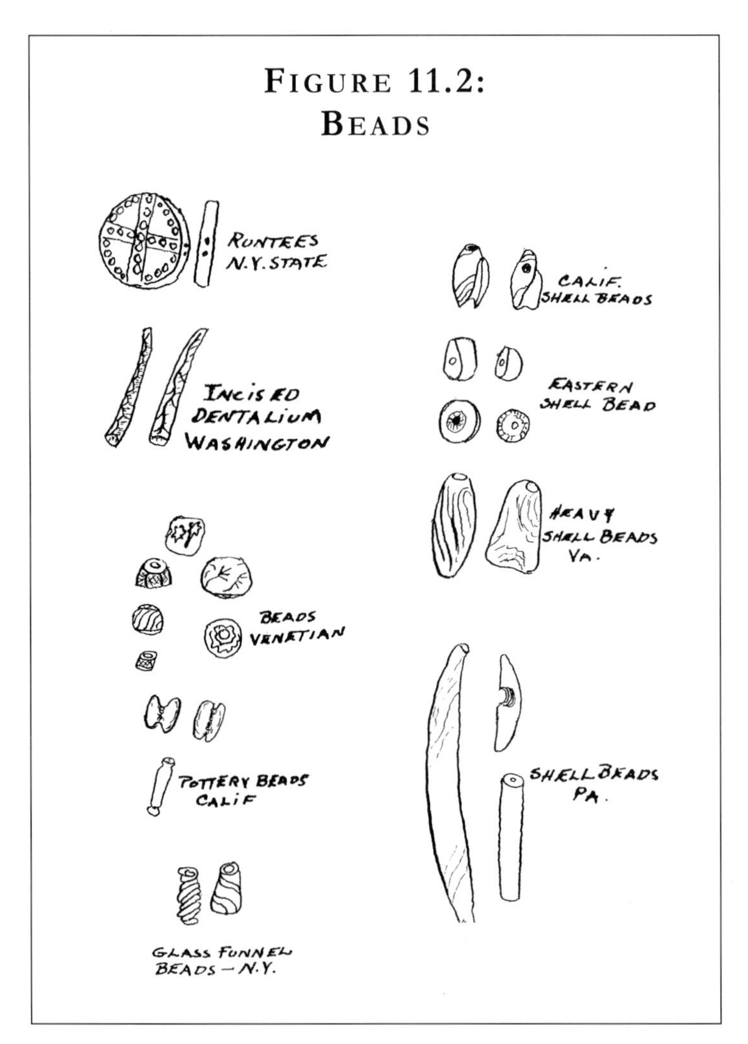

FIGURE 11.2: BEADS

Above: A grizzly claw necklace from Johnston's own collection.

treaty belts were about half the length of the money wampum. Seeds of many sorts were used; wild plum stones, pumpkin seeds and all the other varieties with which the American Indians came in contact.

Wooden beads, stained with the dyes they knew, were also used. Beads made of pitch and asphalt have been found in many graves, usually intermitting with some lighter colored beads.

Narrow strips of palm leaf woven into small beads have been found in many Latin countries, while pottery beads are frequent finds in parts of our country, some well colored and fired.

Trade beads were any type of beads brought in by the early traders, and they vary more than anyone might imagine possible. Some were very fragile and scarce. The majority of the early trade beads were of Venetian make. Regardless of who distributed them to the Indians; the Russian traders, the Hudson's Bay Company or French traders, they came from the same source. DeSoto left some fine types along the Southern coast which come to light from time to time. Early Moorish types are found on the islands bordering on the coast of California.

The star or chevron is a beautiful bead, and one difficult to make compared with other trade beads. The American Indians would pay several skins for one of them.

One collection features a pottery bead from the San Joaquin Valley. It was found with one metal and two clear glass beads of queer make. A glass cylinder 3/8ths of an inch in diameter was formed into a bead an inch in diameter, and the end of the cylinder butt was joined. One edge of the glass was fused together. In the same area other beads of Venetian type were found.

Beads were woven in belts and headbands in a specially made bow loom for this purpose, the warp being tied to each end of the bow, and held apart by passing the strands through a board or piece of skin with as many holes as number of cords. In some work the beads were held by using two strands in the weaving, and in others only one string was used; the two strands of the warp were then given a twist over and under.

The drilling of beads no doubt took much time, especially the long ones and those that were curved, as they had to drill from both ends to make the holes meet. Many specimens have been X-rayed to show the drilling

Above: Mountain Chief of the Blackfeet wore adornment of beaded necklaces and weasel pelts, and his clothing was elaborately beaded.

FIGURE 11.3: VARIOUS JEWELRY ITEMS

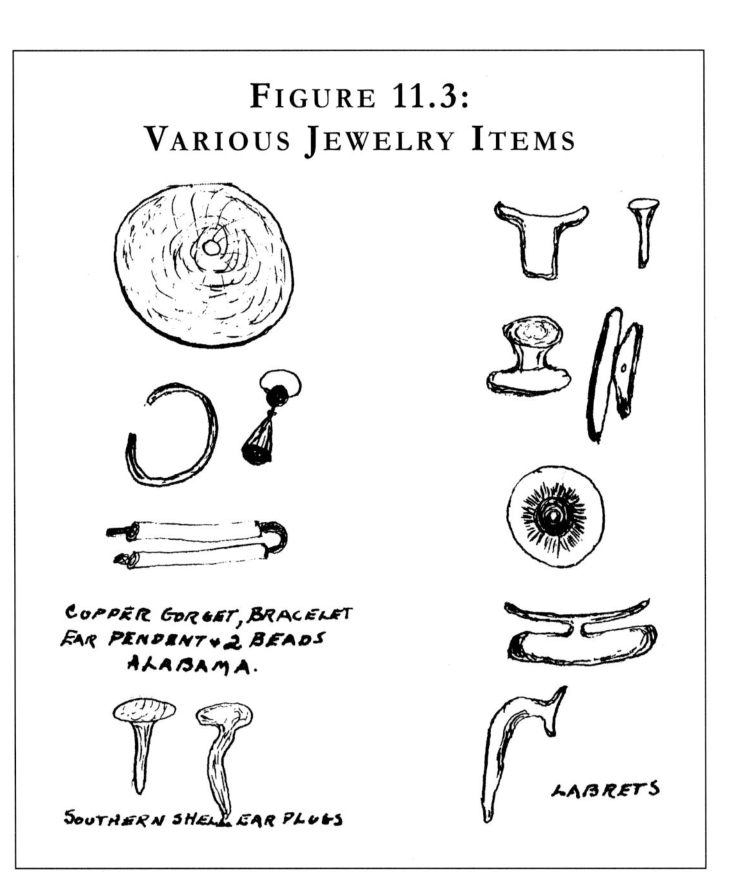

Above: Oto man No'way'ke'sug'ga wore grizzly claws and scalp locks.

and how the holes met. Some were split open direct, and grooved and glued, although many of the long ones were drilled the entire length, the hole being very small. Great patience was required for this work.

GOLD, SILVER, COPPER

Gold was used a little, but in general the American Indians had nothing to do with it. The few gold pieces found in the United States have been in Florida, although in Mexico and further south gold was used extensively and wrought into many wonderful shapes.

The silversmiths of the Navajo country of Arizona were remarkable for their crafts, although they did none of this work until after contact with the Europeans. They preferred the Mexican dollar to the American because it was softer. At one time, the Denver mint made silver slugs that were used by traders who traded them to the Indians for their finished work. The American Indians in the Southwest, notably the Hopi, made round and squash blossom beads mainly for their own adornment.

In the districts where copper was obtained they hammered it thin and then rolled it into small cylinders. Others drilled small lumps or nuggets and made natural beads that way.

SHELL PINS

Shell pins were made of the central column of some of the larger shells, such as the busycon, *Strombus gigas* and others. The method was to break the outer part of the shell away and rub down the central portion to the required size and smoothness. Some of these were up to eight inches in length. Pins were also made of bone. Determining the use of these objects is problematical, although they were no doubt used as both hair and nose ornaments. Some think they were used as blood pins to place in the wound of an animal made by the arrow. This prevented the blood from escaping. Some, no doubt, were used in games, and others used as pendants. Bracelets cut from shell have been

Above: George Catlin's 1832 portrait of Little Bluff of the Kiowa shows an abundance of silver gorgets, beads and multiple earrings.

FIGURE 11.4: PENDANTS AND OTHER JEWELRY

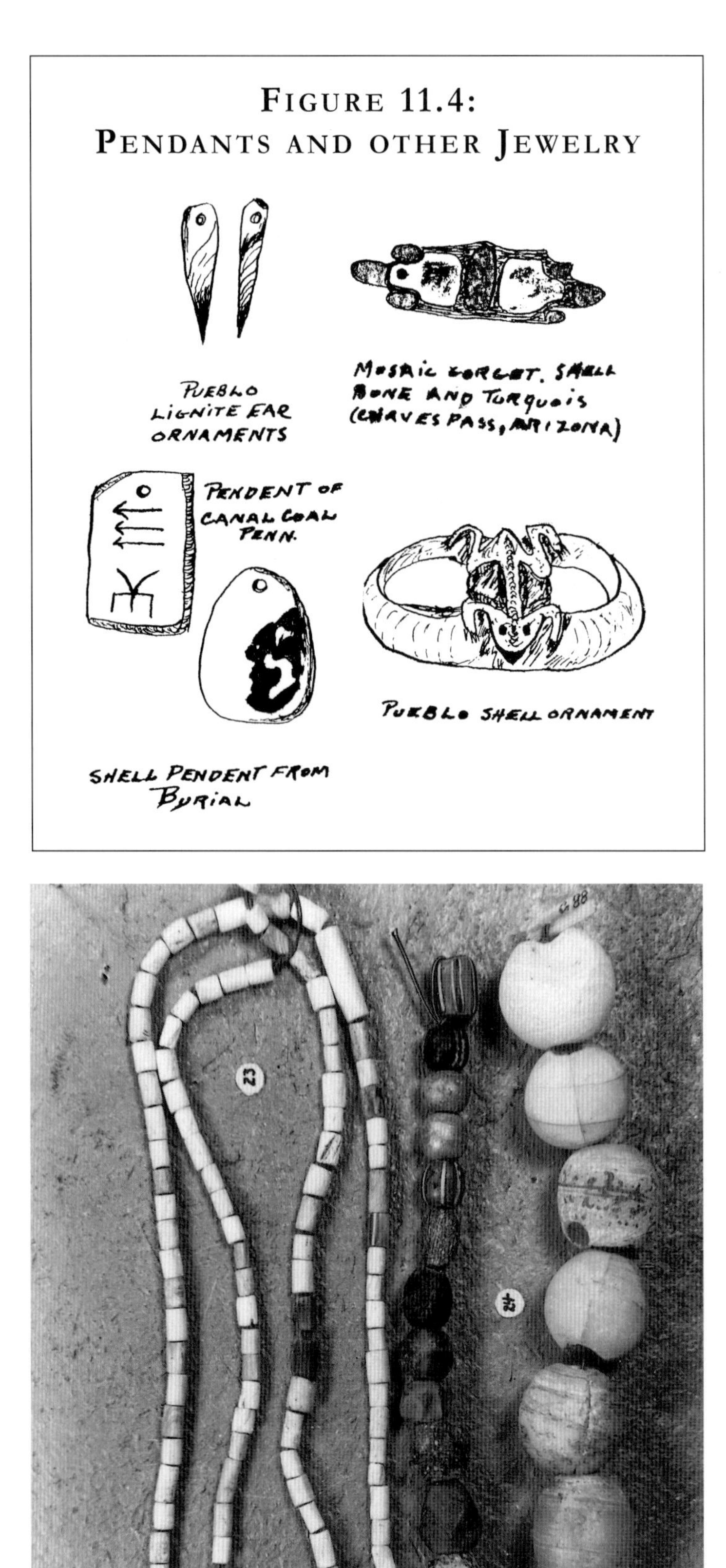

Above: Two beaded necklaces from Johnston's own collection.

found with burials of many tribes. Whether far inland or on the coast, they had shells for their personal adornment. The traffic and exchange of shells with coastal Indians was extremely popular.

PENDANTS AND GORGETS

The pendants were finely worked and made of as many materials as the beads. They were no doubt used as charms, which added value to their owners. One very fine pearl — pear shaped and as large as a hen egg — was found on the breast of a young girl, who was no doubt the daughter of a chief, judging from other items found in the burial, on San Nicolas Island off the coast of California.

The gorgets were like pendants, although larger and usually more finely worked. They were badges of authority and honor, and the characters incised on the gorget in picture form were, no doubt, the conditions by which the owner had a right to possess such a piece. Some may have been the result of a dream or personal fancy the owner had.

In the South, the gorgets were of a general type, with the designs being of the spider, human face, bird or serpent. Throughout the Southwest, where rain played an important part in the lives of the people, the frog, tadpole, lightning and serpent were the main characters. Throughout the country, the deities of greatest importance to the people were shown on their gorgets.

MOSAICS

Some of the Arizona tribes did beautiful mosaics, using turquoise which was set either on wood or shell. Some of these specimens rival similar work from old Mexico. The mosaics on wood are not well preserved, as the wood has rotted and some of the turquoise has shattered off. A few are intact, and the majority of those on shell remain in good condition.

Lignite was also used as a base for mosaics, although never carried to the extent of complete covering, probably due to the fact that lignite took a beautiful polish in itself.

Above: Red Cloud, the great Sioux chief, wore a feathered headdress, as well as a quill breastplate, both common to Plains tribes.

FIGURE 11.5: ADORNMENT AND JEWELRY

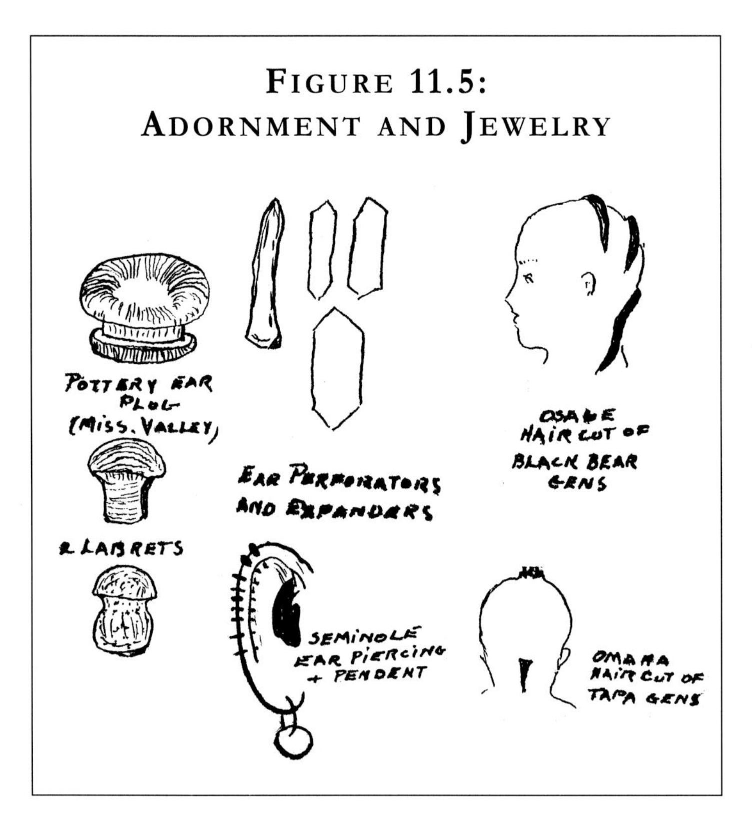

Above: Raw'no'way'woh'krah of the Oto wore a grizzly skin.

PAINTING AND TATTOOING

Painting was the most universal of all types of adornment among the American Indians. Tattooing was practiced almost as much as painting, although in some tribes only the women were tattooed, while in others only the men. The Eskimo did his tattooing with ivory needles and pigments. The desert Indians used several cacti thorns tied together, using charcoal of the mesquite and willow as pigment. This was prepared beforehand and kept in balls.

Until recently, all Eskimo did tattooing on both men and women, with different patterns for different district groups. Some of the tribes in the south and east used the locust thorn similarly, the work being done by both men and women, although the women were preferred. The fee was uncertain, although the effect of the tattooing was supposed to make the heart expand, and the one tattooed would usually pay generously.

In the majority of cases, the age for tattooing was between 15 and 20, and often a couple would both be tattooed after being married. Some of the tribes thought that tattooing prevented wrinkles and that by tattooing they always retained their youth.

Nose piercing in some tribes was a sign of courage and bravery, and it was quite generally practiced. Many groups also pierced their lips, the Eskimo being the most adept. The use of the labret was prevalent there until recently, the largest labret obtainable constituting a certain beauty among them. Bone, stone and ivory were all employed, and these substances were used for earrings also. Earrings, plugs and pendants were worn.

FEATHER OBJECTS

Feathers played an important part in adornment. The wearing of the eagle feather was a badge of distinction or a mark of achievement. Different markings on the feather, or the cut and the way it was worn, told the story of the accomplishment. The American Indians used the feathers of many bright hued small birds to bedeck themselves. Feathers were even used in basketry. With some of the Northwestern tribes, the

Above: A Comanche warrior wore a breechcloth and high-topped moccasins. His adornment included body paint, denoting rank.

Above: Two young Shoshone men, circa 1880, in beads and feathers with carefully-styled hair.

FIGURE 11.6: TATTOOING

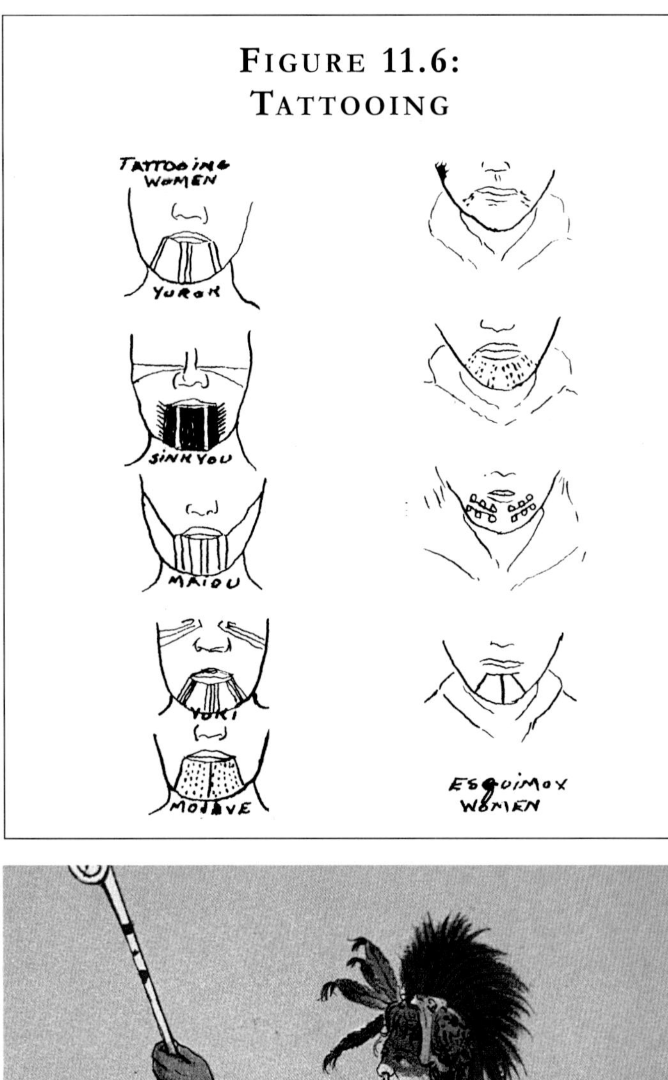

Above: We'chush'ta'doo'ta, painted and dressed for lacrosse.

topknot of the mountain quail was woven in with an artistic effect.

Small pouches and trinket bags were made of the skins of birds. Many fine robes were made in which feathers were woven in a manner similar to the rabbit robes of the Hopis, the skins being cut in long strips and twisted and used as the wool in weaving. The large feathers of the eagle and hawk were especially for the hair and headdresses, and also were used on the arrows and darts.

TREATING THE HAIR

In some tribes the hair of the men might be cut short and the women's hair left long, or vice versa, and in other tribes both might have their hair the same length. The majority of the Eastern tribes had some special haircut that identified the men and the station to which they belonged. The central scalp lock of the Dakota would be trimmed out and two, three or four tufts left on the side, according to one's classification. The hair could be braided or hang loose. Many wore bangs, while others would smear their hair with grease or earth and plaster it back.

The maiden of the Hopi tribes wore her hair in whorls over her ears before marriage; after that time she wore it in two coils falling on the breast. Her hair was dressed by a sister or mother, and was stiffened by the oil from the squash seed.

Wearing the hair in whorls was adopted after the puberty ceremony. The whorls represented the squash blossom and symbolized the power of being fruitful. This mode of dressing the hair is a very old, sacred rite.

The men of the Natchez tribe, which I believe to have been the most forward American Indian group, plucked all the hair from the body except a small spot on the head. As they kept at this from childhood on, their bodies were usually free of hair. The women, however, let their hair grow and braided it with strands of beads or porcupine quills. The men plucked the beard with shell pinchers until, in time, very little growth appeared; later, after the settlers came, they secured small coil springs which they used as tweezers and prized very highly.

Above: Curley of the Crow tribe scouted for Custer in 1876. Photographed in 1883, Curley wore greased and braided hair.

CHAPTER 12

EFFIGY AND CEREMONIAL PIECES

Slate pieces have always caused much speculation among archaeologists. They have advanced many theories as to the use of slate; however, it is more than likely they were used for ceremonial purposes only. Every item that American Indians used in their daily life can be found in replica in slate; in a varied form no doubt, but there, nevertheless.

The Indians in California used shell and steatite for making the same sort of item, and in the South shell, soapstone or wood were used. The American Indian used materials which were easily worked for fashioning objects to be used in their dances or at the altars in worship of the deities.

Occasionally these pieces were made of stone, in which case they were classified as purely ceremonial. The speculation arises when they were made of some less durable material.

The ceremonial items were all worked with greater care than everyday items, and they have a finer finish than anything ever found on a utilitarian object of daily use. They are found in various colors: black, green and red, which is the rarest.

The little boat found in the child's grave was to convey him to the beyond, since he had not learned to travel alone and find his way. There were fanciful ax forms known as banners, forms of birds, turtles and frogs. When we find these objects made of lignite, stone and in mosaic of turquoise, as in designs on their pottery, there is no doubt these pieces are ceremonial—all to some deity.

Many theories have been advanced as to the use to which the bird pieces may have been put and what they symbolize. Some of the older Indians have given their versions, and no doubt each version is correct as applied to the individual tribe.

One Indian with whom I spoke said that they were used as gaming stones. In this context, a number of them were placed in a basket and shaken, the object being to see who could shake the basket and still have the most sitting upright. A variation on the use of the so-called popeyed bird was that pregnant women wore them in their hair. Most of these birds were drilled on the bottom so that securing them to a stick would be an easy task; and since these drill holes show no wear, this version is plausible.

The majority of the slate items are found in what is known as "the Heart Belt" — Ohio, Indiana, Illinois, Michigan and Wisconsin — though like all other pieces they may be found far out of their territory due to exchange and raids. For example, a small turtle shell with incising that had originally come from Florida was found in the state of Washington.

Right: Fetishes in human form, male, female and neutral.
Below right: A pair of frog fetishes.

Plummets

The plummets — made of a variety of forms and materials — filled both a utilitarian and ceremonial purpose. They are found in the true 10 pin shape, with either a groove one way or another, and either bead shaped, drilled or grooved, cigar shaped or egg shaped. Some have no means of fastening at all. It is possible they may have been used as line sinkers, but if this was the case they would have holes or grooves.

At other times several of the smaller plummets were tied together and used on short thongs as throw or bolo stones for ducks and other water birds as they would rise from the water. The Eskimo used five or six small chunks of ivory this way. Since the thongs measured some 30 inches, the spread would be sure to entangle some bird and drag it down.

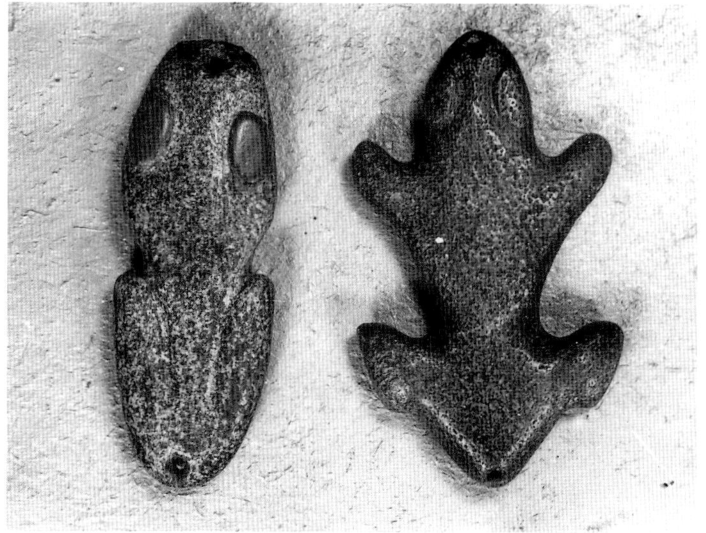

Flint

The chipping of flint into fanciful shapes has been practiced among the American Indians since the aborigine first learned to work flint. Animals, birds, dream versions and deities have all been worked out by some tribe at one time or another, although such items are rare and difficult to find. Few were made in comparison to the utilitarian chipped items, and were usually put into the grave of the owner; often in excavation only fragments are found. Flint pieces from Tennessee and Indiana in the form of a face are the rarest. The big obsidian blades of Northern California and Oregon are the largest pieces of chipped work found anywhere. They also had small pieces with unique chipping, which were used as a special knife to lacerate the flesh in some ceremonial dances. One, the Stockton Curve, was found near Stockton, California.

FIGURE 12.1: CEREMONIAL OBJECTS

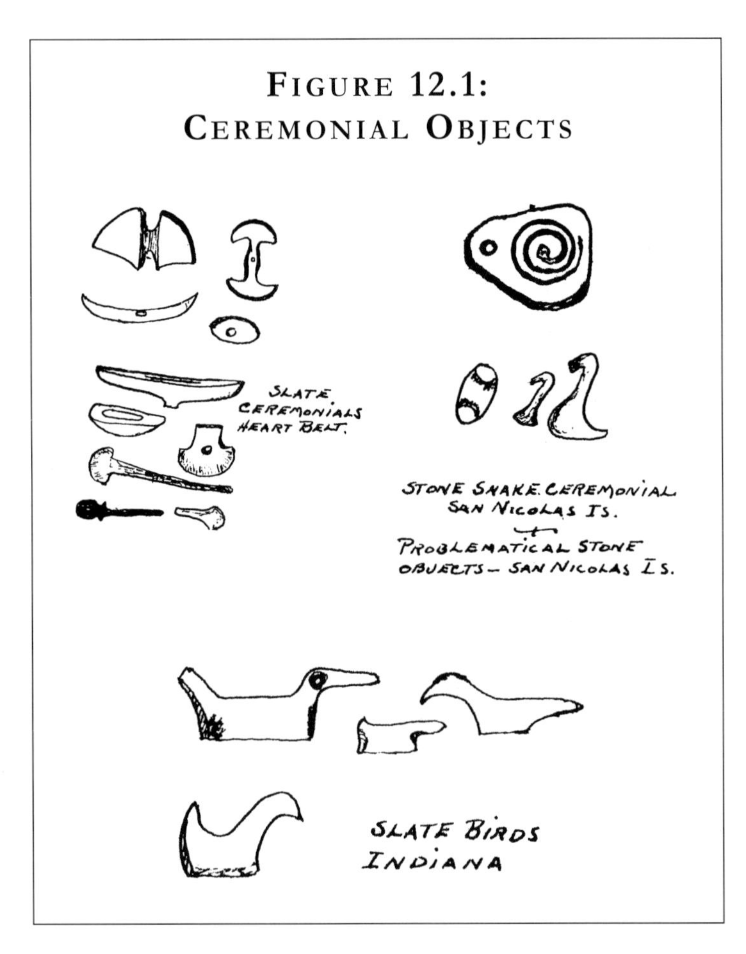

CEREMONIAL AXES

Fluted axes and other decorated ones may have been purely ceremonial, and may have been of some special service to their owners, who later embellished them. This seems quite plausible, since they are all of a serviceable form and not a purely ceremonial type, such as those made of softer stone and slate. In the latter case, it is evident by the small groove that they could not have been hafted for daily use. The five point ax would fall into this class, though they could readily have served as war axes; their hafting and strength made them suitable for such service. (The form would have served admirably for cracking skulls.)

STONE COGWHEELS

One artifact which has caused much speculation is the stone cogwheel. At first these were found only within a radius of 70 miles of Los Angeles, California; had they been confined to this area, matters would have been simplified. However, one was then discovered in Michigan. Following that, 25 more were found on a site in New Mexico, and two others on one of the Channel Islands.

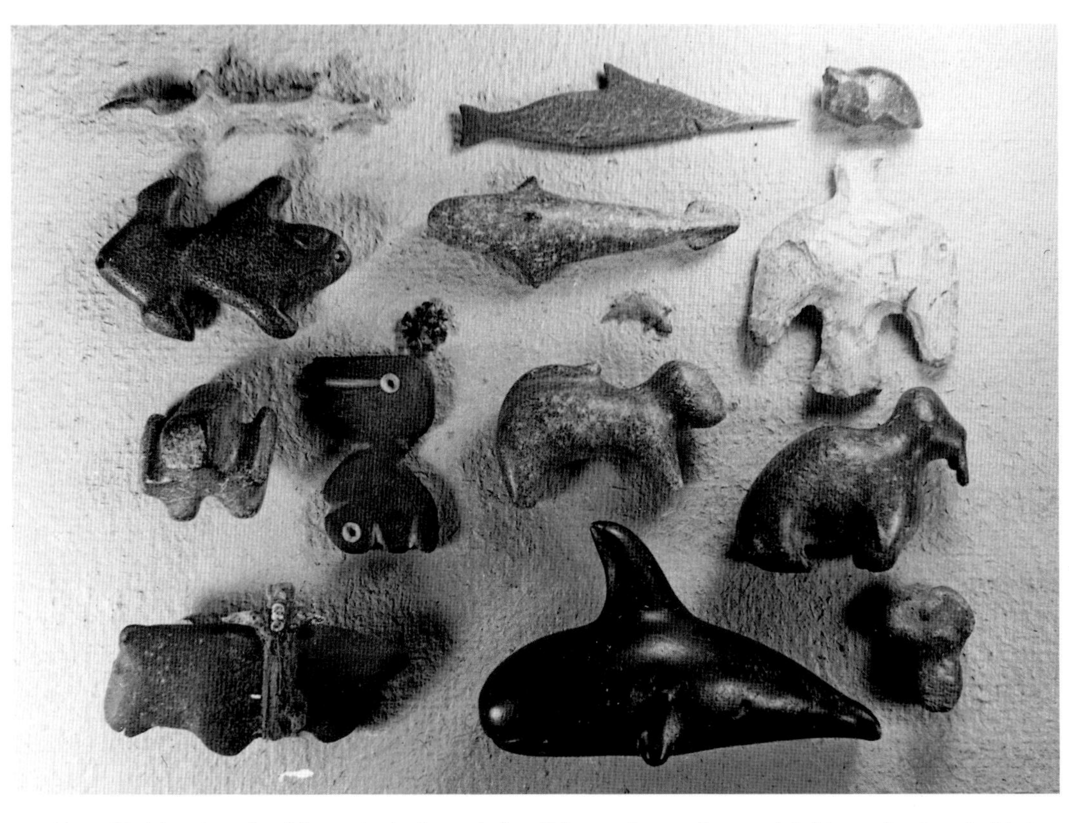

Above: Fetishes in animal form, including whales, fish, a walrus, a frog, a dolphin and a thunderbird.

No two wheels were identical; some had cogs indented, some had holes in the center, and some went without. The average Indian of recent years refers to them as having the same origin or use as the discoidal or chuckee stone, although he is very vague. The best authority that could be contacted, someone who for many years had dealings with the Indians and had secured these cogwheels and other items

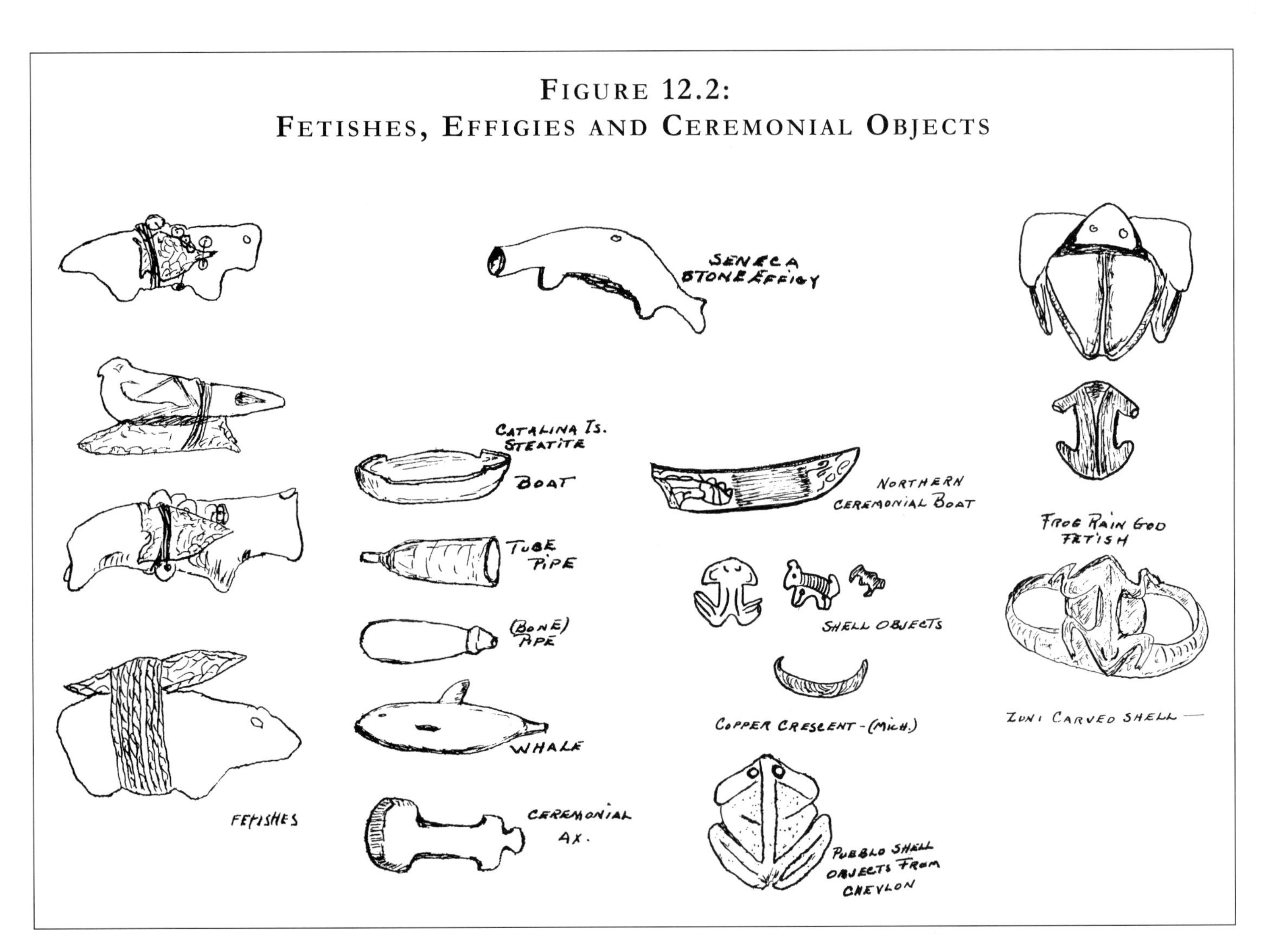

Figure 12.2: Fetishes, Effigies and Ceremonial Objects

from them, was told that cogwheels were used in the puberty ceremonial of the girls in the tribes of Central and Southern California. There are generally more than one of these wheels found in a place, and they are usually associated with discoidal stones, although not always. Some of the early writers have assigned these stones such purposes as arrow shaft straighteners, club heads, for making rope (each groove for a strand in the rope), medicine men's charms and other uses.

Ark of the First Man

The Mandan lived in large villages, and in the center of the group they set up "The Ark of the First Man." It was cylindrical, about five feet high, made of plank and bound around with withe rods and buffalo skulls, which were placed around the base of it. The ark had to do with the medicine men and the Great Spirit.

Above: A wooden Eskimo fetish in the shape of a snowshoe hare.

CHAPTER 13

INDUSTRY AND CRAFTS

SILVERSMITHING

Silversmithing was adapted by the American Indians after the coming of the early Mexicans, and it is one of the arts in which they excel today. Some of the most beautiful Indian artwork is found among their silver pieces.

With crude implements and homemade bellows they worked silver into beautiful ornaments, conchos, beads (of which the squash blossom excels), rings, badges, pendants and bracelets, as well as more unusual pieces which their fanciful minds devised. Turquoise was used in conjunction with their silversmithing and adds much to their work.

The Navajo gato, an armband of leather and silver, was as sacred to the Navajo as the rosary is to one of Catholic faith. The silverwork on many is exquisitely wrought. A few have heavier silver pieces, which are cast in sand molds.

They decorated their silver working with the symbols of their other arts, in addition to using Mexican and American forms that appealed to them. The Masonic emblem was copied in many variations, as was the old Scottish locked hearts.

The silversmith was the general utility man of the village. The American Indian never used native silver or copper for their artwork but rather relied mainly on the Mexican dollar and American coins. The Navajo was the best silversmith of any. The Eastern and Southern tribes did no silverwork at all. The ornaments found in excavations there consisted of trade items brought in by the fur traders and others.

WEAVING

The Navajo have a legend claiming the art of weaving to be of divine origin. The Spider Man drew some cotton from his side and instructed the Navajo to make a loom. The cotton warp was made of spider web. The upper pole was called the sky-cord, the lower pole the earth-cord. The warp-sticks were made of sun rays; the upper sticks, which fastened the warp to the pole, were made of lightning; the lower strings of sun-halo; and the heald of rock-crystal. The cord held a stick of sheet lightning, and was secured to the warp by means of cords.

The batten sticks were made of sun-halo, while the comb was of white shell. Four distaffs were added to this, the discs of which were of canal coal, turquoise, abalone and white bead, respectively. The spindle-sticks were of zigzag lightning, flash lightning, sheet lightning

Above: A Navajo woman working on a rug at her weaving loom, as photographed in about 1910.

FIGURE 13.1: NAVAJO SILVER BEADS IN THE FORM OF SQUASH BLOSSOMS (FROM A NECKLACE)

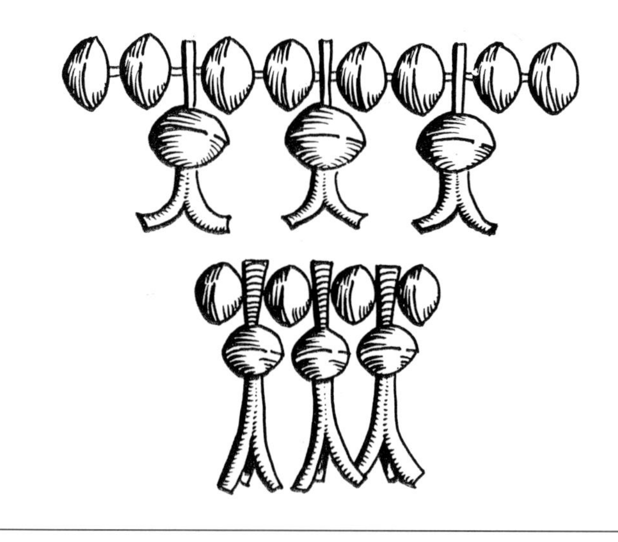

FIGURE 13.2: NAVAJO SILVER PENDANT (FROM A NECKLACE)

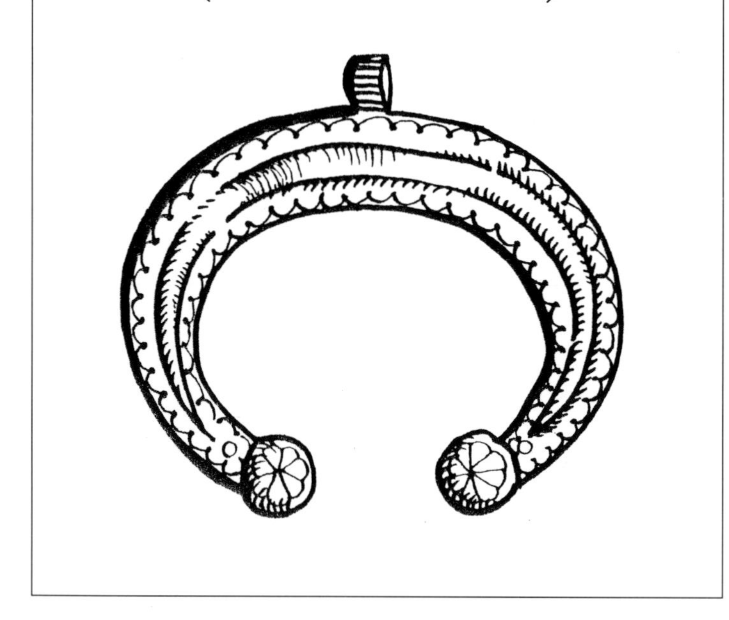

and rain-ray respectively. The dark blue, yellow and white winds quickened the spindles according to their color, and enabled them to travel around the world.

The art of weaving is of great interest to the archaeologist since it is of aboriginal origin. Weaving may be comprehended under two designations: loom weaving and finger weaving, or upward and downward weaving.

With a loom, the weaver begins at the bottom and builds the fabric upward; in the other method, the warp threads are hung loosely from a horizontal support and the fabric is built from the top downward, the weft being pushed upward into place with the fingers. Neither batten nor shedding device was used. Finger weaving is found in the Northwest area, the Chilkat blanket being the finest example of this type of work. Finger weaving extended throughout the eastern maize area.

Loom weaving began with the Pueblo people, and extended southward and also over the maize area. Nowhere has the art been carried so far as with the Navajo, who, in the beginning, no doubt learned it from the early Pueblo. With the Navajo it was the woman who did the weaving, and with the Pueblo it was the reverse; the men did the weaving; yet the two groups lived in the same proximity and with such varying habits.

In some tribes the maidens were not permitted to do any weaving before marriage, lest they overdo it; but in later years this practice disappeared.

The loom was a simple affair. Two main posts were set in the ground, and to this two main crosspieces were lashed. The support beam is attached to the upper cross piece. The length of the blanket or cloth decided the distance between the yard beams, the lower of which was at the bottom and lashed to the two upright posts. The upper one was suspended and tied to the support beam. Lying between the threads and the warp was the batten, which was made of a thin stick and used to strike down the course of the work as it progressed.

Two heald rods were passed through the warp and between alternating strands. Between these the yarn was passed in weaving, when, as usual, no shuttle was used. Sometimes, if the pattern was carried clear through, they wound the yarn on a small stick.

The warp was sometimes tied right in the loom and at other times it was set up in a frame and transferred to

the loom. The work, of course, depended on the weaver and the dexterity of the handling of the yarn. The art of weaving was no simple matter, since most of the patterns were in narrow lines, and the continual shifting of colors meant there was a continuation of counting threads and a constant use of the fingers in keeping the yarn in the proper place. The fingers were used more than the shuttle in placement of the yarn. In making the blanket, the weaver sat on the ground with her legs

Above: Navajo women working on a loom, probably in Canyon de Chelly, Arizona. Note the herd of sheep grazing in the background.

under her. The warp hung vertically before her and she weaved upward. As the blanket progressed, she could lower the support beam, and wind or roll the bottom crosspiece and re-lash it in place.

Sheep were probably the first animals domesticated. From these animals they cut the wool with all sorts of crude knives and spun it into yarn using the simplest means in the beginning.

The American Indian had cotton from a very early date. In 1538, Father Marcos de Niza made a reconnaissance of that country. "The natives were dressed in finely woven cotton garments," he said.

Bayeta is a term derived from the Spanish, which was applied to a certain kind of material, and which was a trade item to the early American Indian. In turn, they unraveled the cloth, and by respinning the yarn made fine, hard yarn which they used with striking effect in their work. In some instances they doubled or even quadrupled the yarn, to get a heavier weave. Bayeta blankets have been one of the finer types produced by the American Indian.

Many attribute the use of red by the American Indian as a desire for gay colors, while in reality it means sunshine to them; red meant light and life, one of the greatest gifts of God to man.

There is no doubt some mystery to the symbols in the early blankets. The story told in the characters or symbols had to be translated by the weaver, though in later times certain symbols were given a more universal meaning by all.

The first carding of wool was done by the use of teasels (thistles), which grow wild in many parts of the country. A group of the burs were held together on a frame.

The ease of purchase and the low cost of wool, cotton and dyes greatly deteriorated their art. The market has been flooded with imitations that have cheapened the Indian rugs and blankets. The American Indians have raised wool bearing animals and have cultivated cotton for a great period of time, and the working up of these materials was a part of their daily life. The original raw materials used and the dyes that they made were far superior to materials they now purchase and use.

Black dye was made from the twigs and leaves of the aromatic sumac. These were properly mixed and

FIGURE 13.3: BOW LOOM

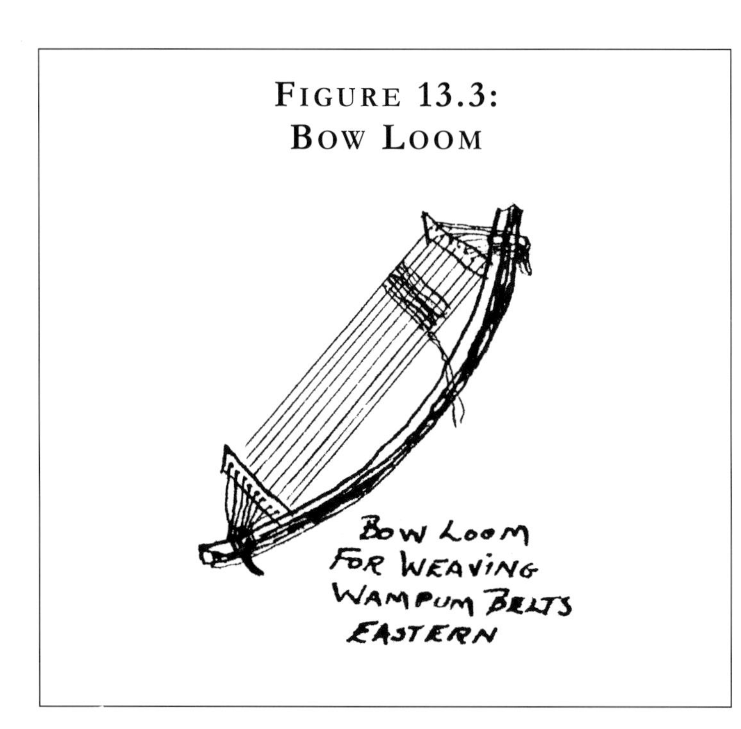

Above: A Navajo sand mold for the making of a silver ornament.

cooked for five or six hours. The mixture formed a fine dry, black powder.

Yellow was produced from the tops of herbs of the *gravenolens* type, which were cooked for hours. To this, some native powdered alum was added. After this had cooked sufficiently the wool was immersed and dyed a lemon yellow.

A reddish dye was produced by the use of the bark of the *Alnus incana* and the bark of the root of the *Cerocarpus pravifolius*. To this, fine juniper ashes were added. On buckskin this produced a brilliant tan, but on wool a lighter shade was achieved. The American Indian had other dyes as well, and by mixing their colors they produced shades of various hues.

Wool was never washed on the sheep, but rather after it had been shorn. The spinning of the wool was of the simplest form. A slender stick and a central wooden disc were used. By holding the carded wool in one hand and twirling the spindle with the other, a splendid quality of yarn was produced. The spinning of cotton and the spinning of wool were done by a very similar method.

In one of the excavations at Mesa Verde some fine samples of items woven of willow bark were found. In the headbands used for carrying loads, the weaving was exceptionally fine.

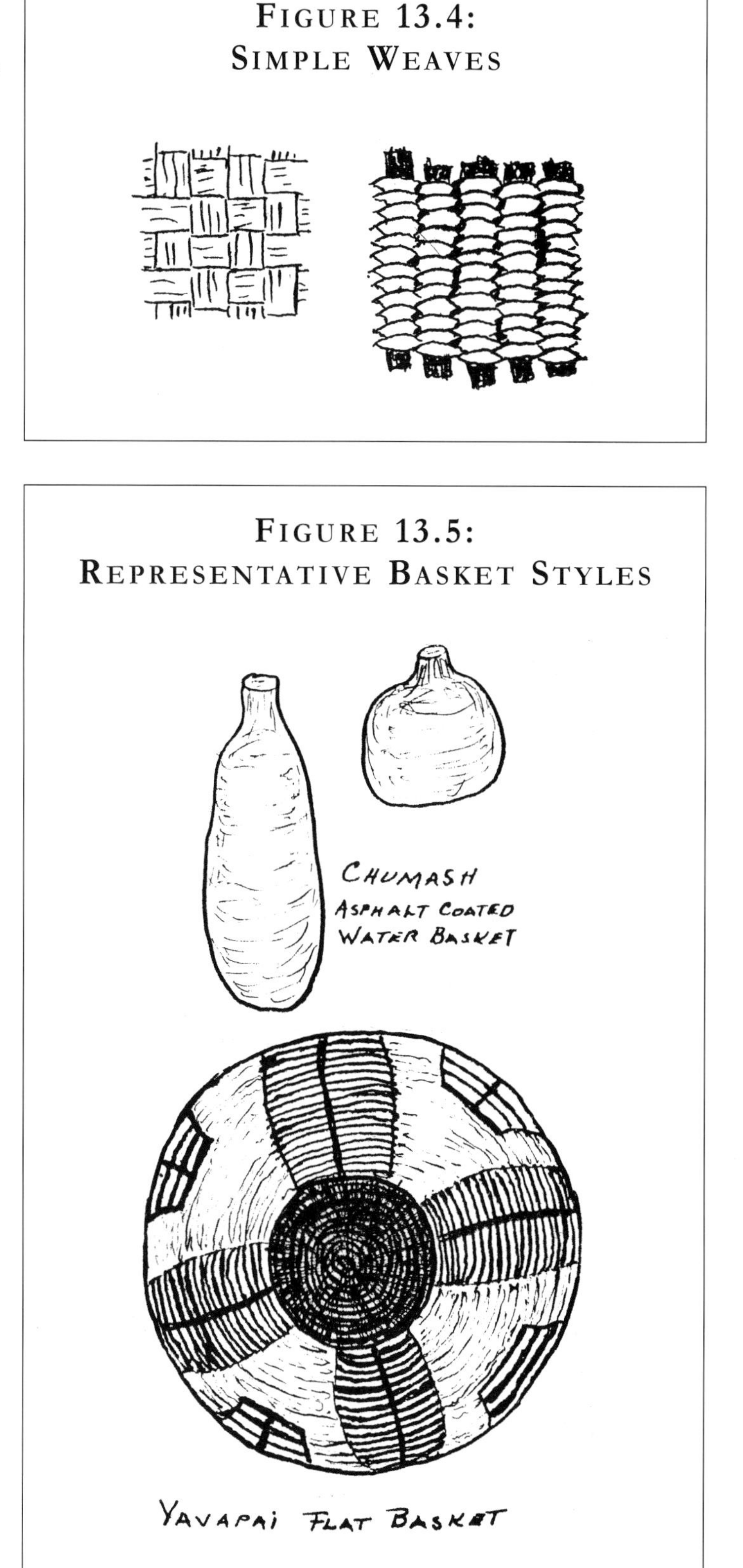

FIGURE 13.4: SIMPLE WEAVES

FIGURE 13.5: REPRESENTATIVE BASKET STYLES

BASKETRY

One of the most common and useful of the domestic arts of the American Indian was that of basketry. In the beginning, it was primitive; and though much finer work is done today, the method has not changed much since the day of introduction. The varieties of baskets made were almost as numerous as the Indians themselves, and were almost entirely the work of the Indian women.

The materials used depended on the locality. The desert Indians used yucca, wild grasses, willow, cottonwood, cattails and martynia. The Eastern Indians used splits of the ash, oak and other trees, which were woven with bark, grass and fiber. Some of the Pacific Coast Indians made a coarse basket and tarred the inside by placing lumps of tar and heated stones together in the basket. They would then roll the basket around until the

FIGURE 13.6: REPRESENTATIVE BASKET STYLES

stones had melted the tar. After that, they thoroughly coated the inside of the basket with the tar, making it watertight for use in cooking. Some of the Indians wove their baskets tight enough to hold water, while others coated them with pitch from the pine and pinon trees.

The Yurok used willow for the stays of the basket and tule grass weft for the balance. The Pima used the willow and the squaw weed; different materials were used among the different tribes.

The Zuni made a good coarse basket of the willow, dogwood and chrysanthemum. However, they were poor basket makers, and preferred to buy or barter goods from other tribes who were more proficient in basketry in order to obtain needed baskets. Perhaps the finest weaving done anywhere on the North American continent was crafted by the Aleuts of the Attu Islands.

The work of basket making comes under two heads, first the useful form that might have been ornamented, and second the aesthetic shapes, which were ornamented and might be useful. The introduction of extraneous substances, such as feathers and beads, belongs to a comparative late period in the history of basket making art. It is hard to fix time boundaries as to when one certain form came into existence, or when or how it originated. We do know, however, that basketry antedates pottery.

With the introduction of color and complex weaves, an added impetus was given to the art of basket making. Three evolutions also occurred: in the art itself; in the makers themselves, who went from being imitators to creators; and in an appreciation of art in general.

Baskets were used for everything: dishes, cooking vessels, storage bins, water containers, hats, fish traps, burden carriers, for burials, and by just a little changing in shape, for baby cradles, as well as for trays for winnowing seeds or for dice games.

Much research has been done to ascertain the symbolism in basketry. To the casual observer the designs and patterns are just pleasing, though in most instances the design has a definite meaning. Few can give the correct interpretation, yet if the maker can be prevailed upon to give an explanation, it is usually found to be a legend, story or some incident in the life of the tribe or the maker. The fallacy to think someone else could give an interpretation has been noted. With the Soboba people, a number of circles connected with lines meant connecting ties and blood relationship, while with the Thompson Indians the same design meant two lakes and a river. A cross to the Thompson Indians meant the crossing of trails, while to the Yokut it represented a battle, and to the Havasupai it was a phallic sign.

Above: At the time that Johnston interviewed this Pomo basket maker in the 1920s, she was 103.

POTTERY

Some pottery was found in practically every district where the American Indians have occupied the country. In many old campsites there was ample evidence of the abundance of the pottery industry. The fragments of crude, earlier types were found, as were intermediate grades, and finally some of the later and finer work that was eventually produced. Through sections of Arizona and New Mexico, as well as through the Mississippi Valley, the tribes excelled in the art of pottery making.

A classification of Indian pottery that would apply to almost any group is as follows: coarse unpolished ware, undecorated; coarse unpolished ware, decorated; polished ware, undecorated; and polished ware, decorated. The decorated pottery should additionally be sub-divided: white on black, black and red, polychrome and glazed polychrome. Each of these may be sub-classed according to finish and form.

The Indian pottery designs were as multifarious as were the shapes and pieces created. All the gods were represented in some form, as were serpents, birds, ani-

FIGURE 13.7: REPRESENTATIVE POTTERY STYLES

mals and dream animals. The various combinations of certain forms gave a new meaning. Certain symbols were used on food bowls, others on mortuary vessels, and still others for storage containers and water jars. The color often told the purpose for which the vessel was used.

The American Indian also made a variety of pottery forms. One tribe may have used a slipper-shaped vessel for cooking, while another used a pot with crude legs or knob-like feet, under which a fire could be built. Still another tribe would suspend their pots from a pole hung over the fire. Shape and finish of the pottery pieces would vary, even within the same tribe.

Each pottery group bespeaks a certain locality, because the materials used and the pigments available for coloring were diversified. The grade or clay found in one section would be unlike that found in another. Some clay was used nearly as it was found, but other clay was tempered with ground shell or certain kinds of ashes, or even bits of old pottery ground up. Some tribes used sand to temper the clay.

Above: A Pima pottery maker in Arizona, rolling her clay into a long strand in order to begin building up her pot with a coil of clay.

Some individuals in a tribe became quite noted for a certain type of pot or coloring, even in the present time. Food bowls to place on the graves were usually of very beautiful work, so as not to offend the spirits. One grave that was no doubt that of a pottery maker had the following items interned in it: two knives of rib bone, no doubt for cutting clay; rubbing stone, which was stained from use; lumps of clay in red, yellow and green, all in fair quantities; and micaceous hemetite.

The crudest type of pottery was probably the coiled ware, and from the methods later employed they gradually smoothed out the sides and made smooth ware. The art of the maker was a deciding factor in the work produced, both in molding and in design, and finally in the firing.

Never among any of the tribes was a wheel used in making pottery. The ware was built up coil after coil, with the exception of a district in the Great Lakes territory, where the vessel was worked into shape out of a single piece of clay.

FIGURE 13.8: TOOLS AND TECHNIQUE

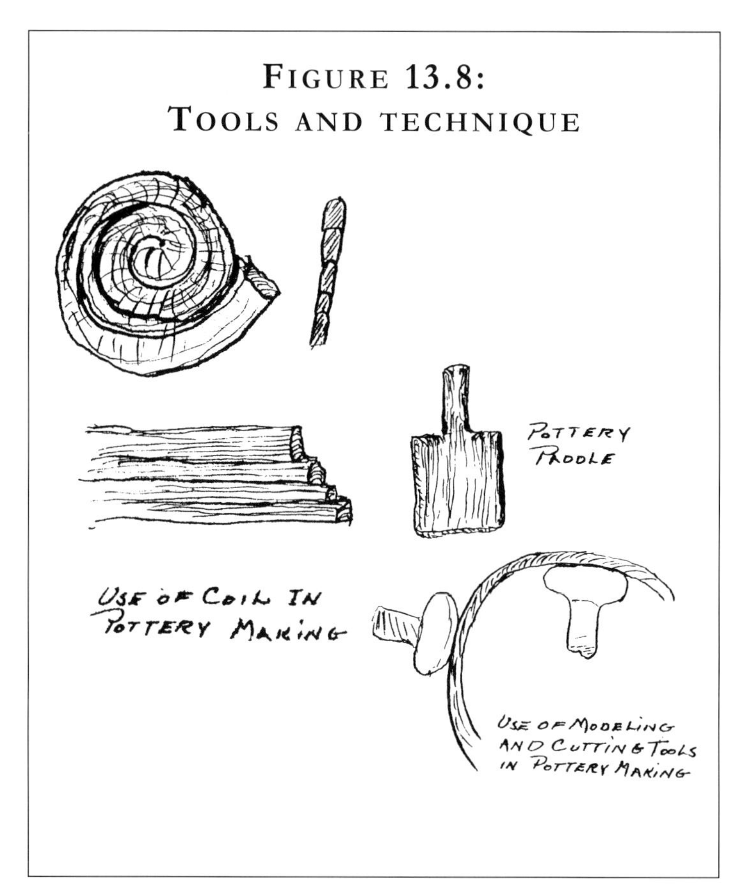

Above: After building up her pot with a coil of clay, the Pima pottery maker smoothes the surface with a spatula and water.

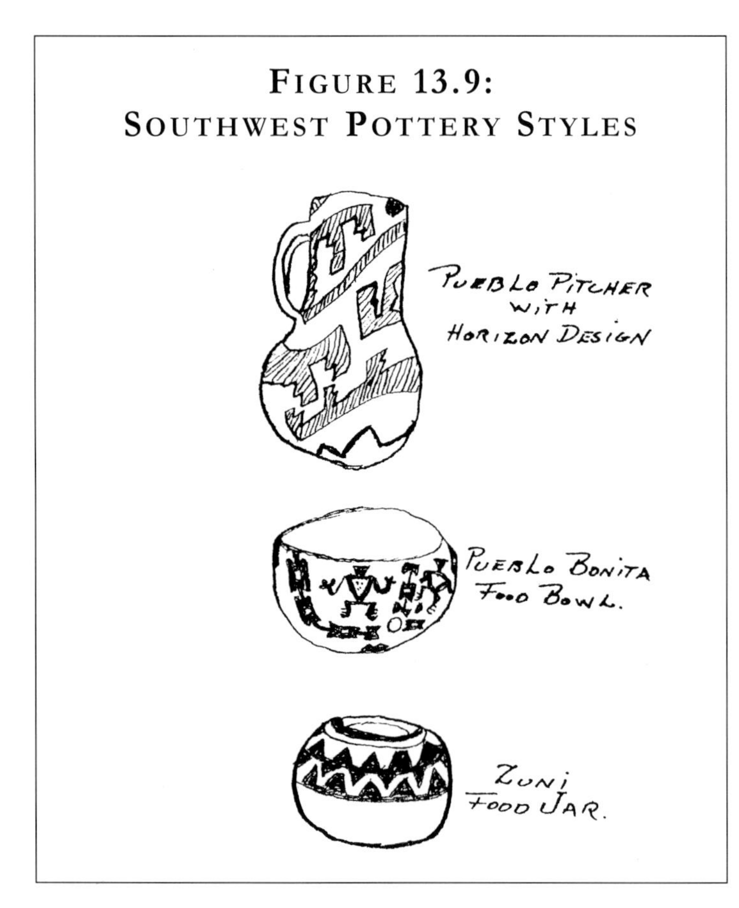

FIGURE 13.9: SOUTHWEST POTTERY STYLES

Before making a piece of pottery the preliminary tasks had to be performed. Securing the clay from whatever source they had at hand, it was then cleaned, and finally winnowed like wheat to remove all small pebbles and gravel, either of which would spoil a vessel.

Next came the kneading process and the adding of temper. The kneading was usually done on a skin prepared for this purpose. Into the center of a pile of clay a quantity of water was poured and worked in. Later, as more was needed, it was sprinkled on and work continued until the proper consistency was obtained. The temper was added in proportion to the density of the clay used, and a number of different materials could be used additionally. Ground up pieces of pottery were used, as well as shell, a certain kind of sand, some minerals and, in some cases, ashes. The purpose of the temper was to counter the cracking tendency of pure clay during the sun drying and firing process. If too much temper was added, the pot would probably not retain its shape and become a finely finished product.

Above: The Pima pottery maker seen on the previous pages applies decorative detailing to a pot that she has constructed.

The clay was then ready for use. The potter gathered her tools and started rolling the clay in small rolls, which were used to form the bowl. Coil after coil was built up until reaching the desired height and size. After molding and smoothing, either by hand or with a stone, wooden or pottery paddle, it was worked into final shape and allowed to dry for a time.

After baking in the sun, it was scraped lightly to remove any surface blemish; then it was ready for the slip. Thé slip was made of various colored clays or other pigments, and was about the consistency of milk.

This was applied with a piece of cloth to the tile surface of the vessel. The slip acted as a sizing mechanism, and also made the background upon which the design was painted.

There are many colors of slip—white, red, orange-red, and the various combinations and shadings made by applying one or many coats. After the slip was applied and allowed to dry a little, the vessel was rubbed with a stone or polishing tool. This was work done while

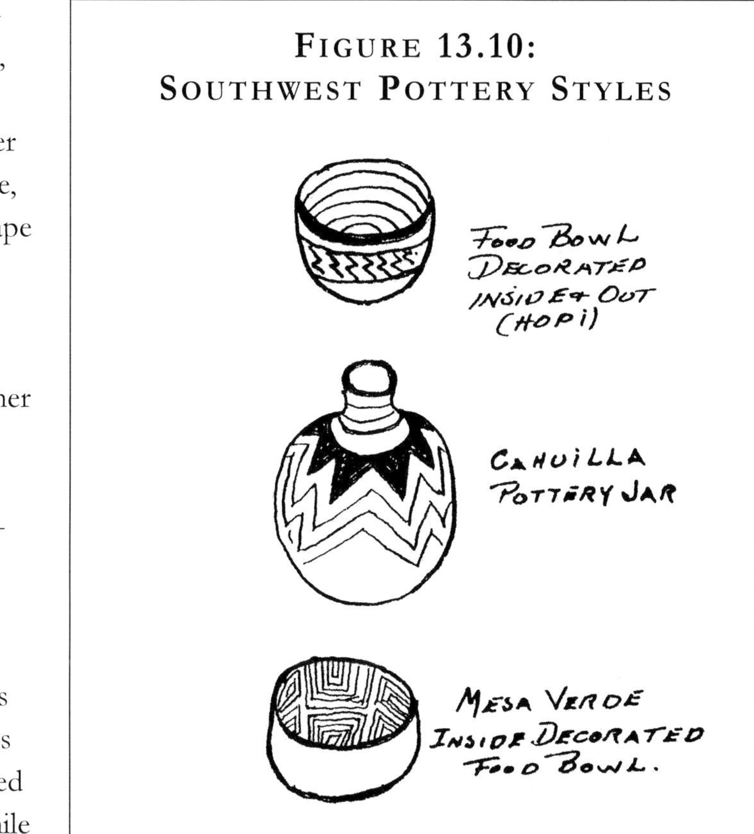

Figure 13.10: Southwest Pottery Styles

Above: A Hopi pottery maker constructing a pot by the coil method. The cottonwood to her right will fire the kiln.

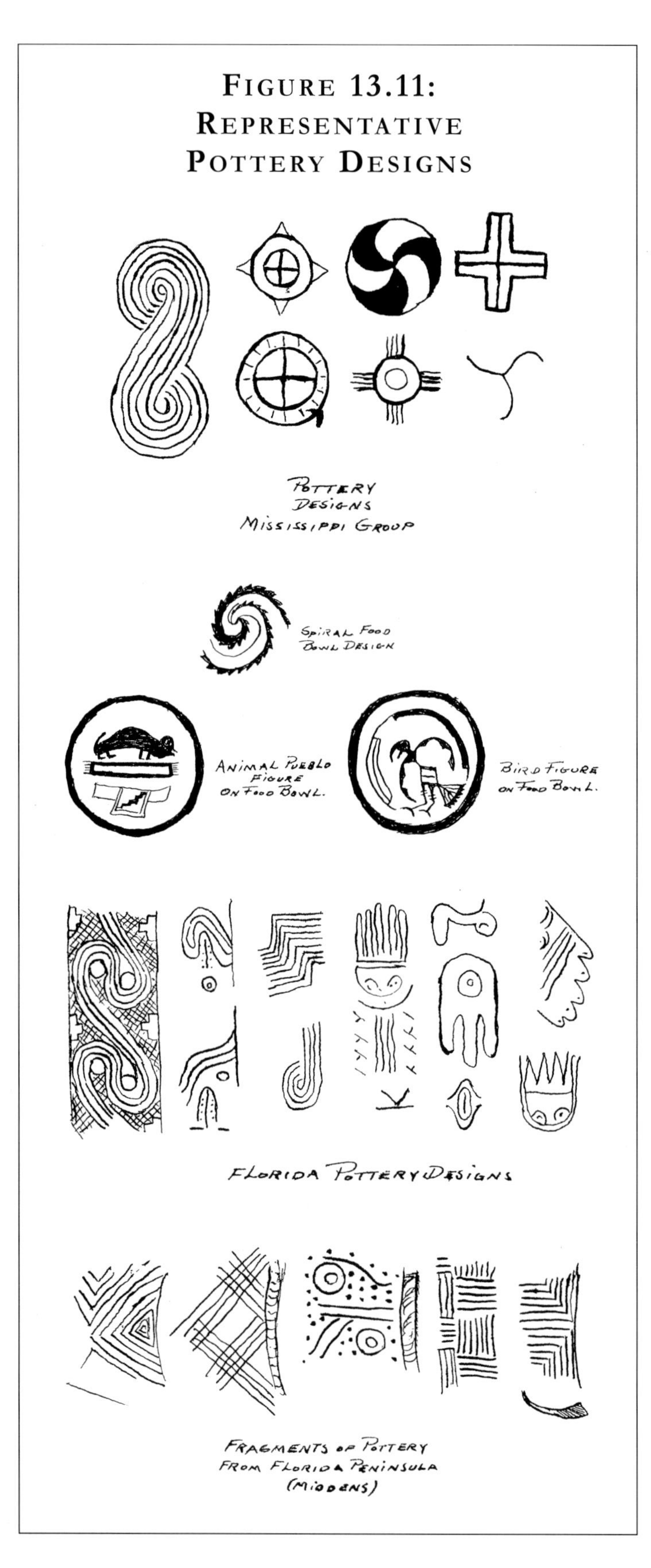

FIGURE 13.11: REPRESENTATIVE POTTERY DESIGNS

the slip was still damp. This polishing also removed any slight blemish; occasionally two or more women would work together, as it was tiring on the fingers.

Next was the painting. The potter had paints of the various colors, each in a small vessel, all about the consistency of milk or cream. The brush was usually made of some suitable local material. In the desert regions, a piece of yucca leaf with a shredded end was often used.

When the paint was first applied it appeared almost transparent, but as it dried it became more opaque. The painter guarded against flies and insects until the color was thoroughly set. When completed, it was covered with a cloth.

The method of holding the vessel or the brush in applying the design varied with each worker. Usually a long, sweeping stroke was used in applying the paint. The fineness of the line and the detail of the characters varied according to the proficiency of the worker. Some kept the vessel turning as they worked, while others worked one section at a time. A few of the better potters went directly through with their designs, while others made a layout to work from first.

In some cases the color was applied before firing. In other cases it was fired in part, and then the design and color were applied. Some tribes colored the piece, fired, then recolored and fired, thus producing what is known as slip-glaze. The firing was done by covering the vessel with fat and then baking. Dung fires were common, although each territory had its own process of firing and material used for the fire. Slow, steady, long-burning fires were necessary to produce the evenness of the temper of the pottery, and dung was considered the best fuel for such work.

The firing was one phase of the work that the men often took part in. This was not only the last step of the work, but was also the most critical. The oven was built as close to the house as possible, and where there was the least wind. The ground where the fire was to be placed had to be thoroughly dry, for moisture rising during the firing was fatal. Often a fire was built to dry the ground before the oven was set up.

Stones (in later days tin cans if available) or broken pieces of pottery were used to raise the vessel so that it could be fired off the ground. This way the firing would reach the bottom of the vessel. A small fire of cedar was started while the pieces of dung were placed around the oven. Again, cans or stones were so arranged to prevent the burning dung from touching the sides of the vessel during firing, if possible. If available, a grate was placed over the oven and dung piled on top so a uniform heat would be over the entire vessel during firing. In a way, the firing was done in a vault, since all the openings were chinked with smaller pieces of dung.

The firing was usually done in the morning, as it took several hours. The actual firing was accomplished in less than an hour, but the pottery pieces had to cool slowly. Some vessels took less time; cooking vessels required the shortest time; polychrome took the longest.

After coming from the oven the vessels were set near some building to cool. When sufficiently cooled to handle, they were wiped with a dry rag, after which they were gone over with a greasy cloth, and then later rubbed and given a final polish.

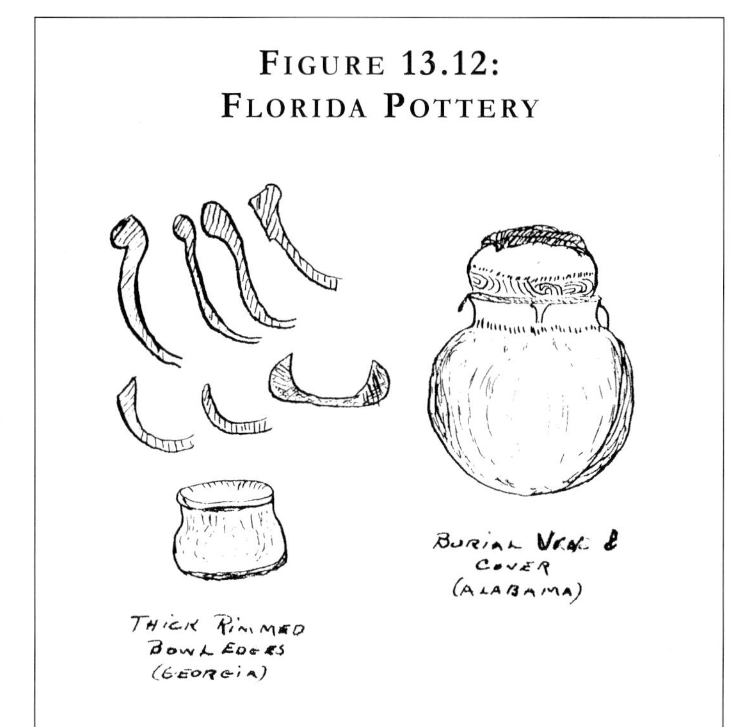

FIGURE 13.12: FLORIDA POTTERY

Among the Zuni, certain clay water bottles were made in imitation of "human mammae." The maker recognized a symbol in these imitative designs. They speak of water as the milk of adults. Earth is the mother of men, and with water she nourishes her children, just as the mother nourishes her young with milk of her own breasts.

In the Southwest, an almost unbroken lineage of development can be traced, from the earliest and crudest forms, through the intermediate stages, and on to the perfect styles of the nineteenth and twentieth centuries.

This gives rise to the theory that pottery making was of local origin from the beginning, though some ethnographers believe that it was brought from Mexico. Whether the crude, unbaked, heavy dishes are prior to or contemporary with the Basket Maker periods is not yet ascertained.

Above: The pottery maker worked quickly, supporting the vessel on a pile of loose sand.

CHAPTER 14

USING STONE, METAL AND BONE

Deposits of flint were found in widely separated areas. From coast to coast, different varieties of flint were found in many colors, the central states having the greatest deposits. It was seldom found on the surface, except for those nodules which had been loosened and carried out by glacial action or from flood waters at some early time. In excavation for flint, the top earth was first removed. Then, having exposed the flint stratum, they broke through this to the underlying formation. The flint layer was more readily broken down after the removal of the first stratum than by undercutting, as was done in some types of quarrying.

The quarrying of flint was of great importance to the life of the American Indian. It not only supplied him with points for his weapons of war and defense, but also for his projectiles of the chase and fishing — both important in supplying his food.

Obsidian was found most abundantly in Mexico and California; some was also found farther north. Obsidian had some of the properties of flint, although it was more readily worked into shape. It was black in color, while some was also red or mixed. Some of the blades were three feet or longer, but these were used for ceremonies only. Many fine knives, arrows and smaller ceremonial objects have been made of obsidian. At this time, much fraudulent work is done, since this substance is readily worked. An obsidian blade with a piece of pure gold swaged onto the point was found in a cache of about 300 obsidian pieces. It was buried three feet in the ground in the San Joaquin Valley, and found a few years ago by a man excavating for a pipeline. The blades ranged from a few inches to a foot in length, many just roughed out and not finished. The discoverer, having no interest in such things, gave the blades away before data pertaining to the find could be secured.

Steatite was quarried in New England and down the coast to Georgia. The North Pacific states had it, as did Canada, and there is some evidence of its having been mined in Alaska. Santa Catalina Island had a fine quarry, from which the Indians of Southern California secured their supply. The fine bowls and artifacts of that area were made from this material. There is no evidence of its having been found in the Central or Southern states. This stone made splendid cooking vessels and lent itself readily to this use, as it was easily worked. Many fine fetishes and ornaments were made from it and given a high polish. Cooking slabs (comals) were made of steatite, as were pipes, both tube shaped, "L" shaped and "T" shaped.

Mica was mined in North Carolina. It has been found in the graves of the Mound Builders in large sheets, 36 inches by 18 inches. It has also been discov-

Right: An Eskimo woman's flint cutting blade with bone handle.

ered in the graves of many of the Indians of the Central and Eastern states. It was probably not used for practical purposes, but rather for adornment and altar pieces.

Some tribes thought that mica was the scales of the "Mythical Horned Serpent," a rain deity. It was believed that if placed by a stream the scales' "rain medicine" would collect thunderclouds and plentiful rain.

Pipestone was quarried in Minnesota. It was found in a ledge. This was a rather hard red rock which lent itself to the making of pipes and ornaments. Until the government forbid the quarrying of pipestone, much material was used in manufacturing trade objects by the whites. The famous catlinite pipes were made of pipestone. The area around the pipestone deposits was sacred ground, as were a few of the Western salt deposits. If an enemy succeeded in arriving there, he was treated as a brother and permitted to depart at his convenience, but woe to him who ran into the enemy a few miles away. The quarrying of pipestone was similar to the working of flint deposits.

Hematite was used quite freely by the Indians in the territories where it was obtainable — Missouri, Arkansas, Ohio and Virginia. It was worked into implements which were quite serviceable, and it gave the Indian a commodity for exchange. Hematite made a fine, red paint that was greatly sought by other tribes where it was not to be found. In some of the ancient hematite quarries, the old workings look as if giant ground hogs had made burrows, bringing out the ore. At these spots great piles of the stone tools used in mining were found.

Turquoise was found in the vast region embracing our Southwest, and on down into Panama. These mines were operated long before the coming of the Spanish, as indicated by the extensive pittings and the many ancient tools found around the workings. The Spanish took over and operated many of these mines for years after their coming. Only meager details have been obtained as to how the American Indians worked these deposits, but the heavy stone hammers found nearby, and the evidence that many were hafted, show that they were used for heavy work.

FIGURE 14.1: CROSS SECTIONS OF QUARRIES

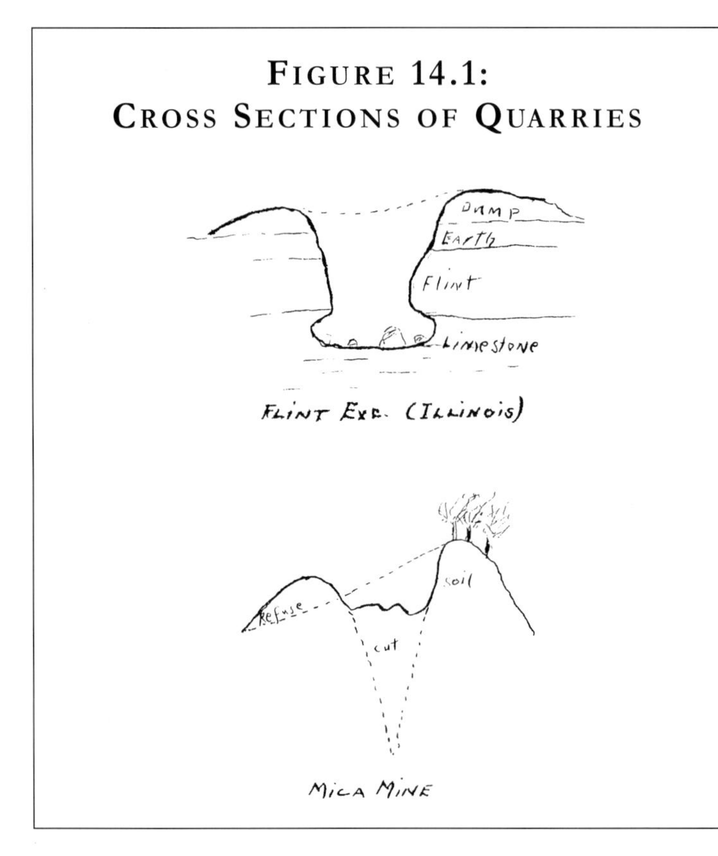

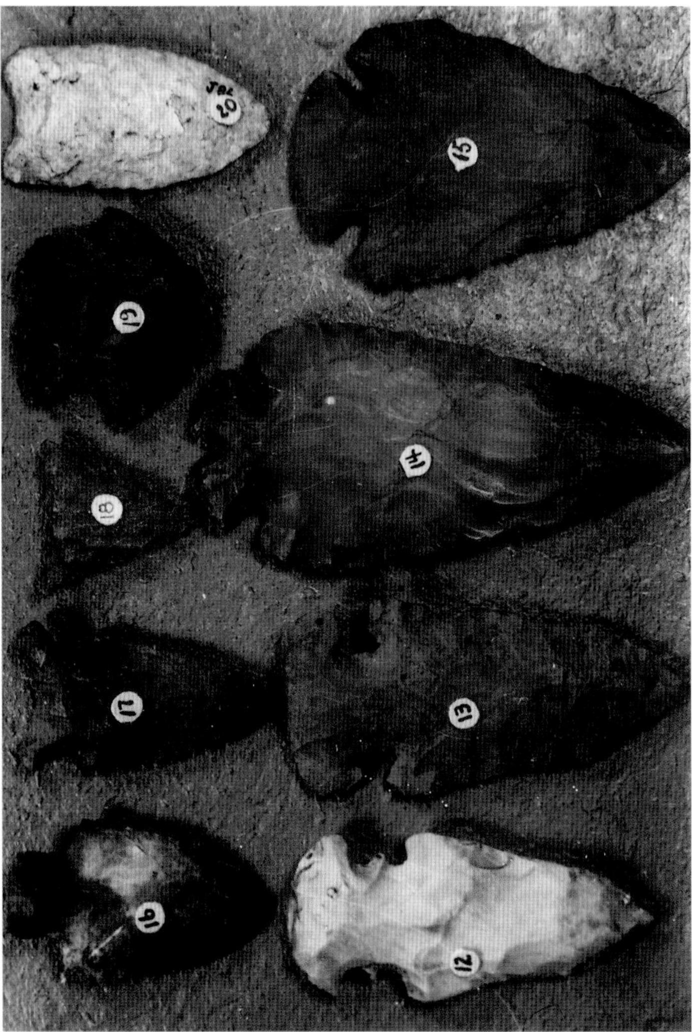

Above: A group of flint arrow points from Johnston's collection.

CHIPPING OF FLINT

Pages could be written on the chipping of flint. The methods used in different sections varied somewhat, though the final results were not altogether different. In the end, it was the result that mattered most, not how it was done.

After selecting a nodule or boulder from which to work, it was roughened out by striking with a stone or anything that was convenient to use in outlining the first rough shape. The Indian may then have kept on with a smaller hammerstone, or even a piece of antler hafted as a hammer to strike off the edges until nearly finished. The finishing was done with a piece of bone or antler by flaking. Whether held in the palm of one hand or the other, or whether the chips were from the upper- or underside, was of little consequence.

The general principle used in producing the finely worked specimens was important, for we find more chipped artifacts than all others combined. Many pieces show evidence of having been used, damaged, reworked and used again.

The chipping of flint is one of the moot questions for all who write of Indians. The theory that they heated the flint and dropped water on the heated portion was once advanced. However, this is now known to be wrong. This is not a practical method, as may be proven by demonstration. The use of bone pincers is another discarded theory. Neither did they break the edges with a stone hammer, except for the roughing out work. The finish was done with a flaking tool of bone, antler or ivory (if they could obtain it), and by pressure of the edge.

Finely worked flint objects were produced by much time and practice. They were first roughed out by stone hammers or percussion. The object was held with one hand and the tool with the other. The pressure may have been down toward the palm of the hand or on some object with a piece of skin laid over to absorb the shock and reduce the chance of fracturing. As arrows, spears and knives became damaged, they were often reworked, sometimes only slightly, and again, so they were smaller and different. The knives often had the edges finely re-chipped to roughen or sharpen them. This was truer of stone pieces than of flint objects, as the former wore smooth much faster.

Crumbling or Pecking

The working of stone into axes, celts and other objects, such as pestles and bowls, come under the process of crumbling or pecking. The boulder selected was first roughed out as well as possible by fracture; then the surface was worked into the desired form by slow and continuous pecking with a hammerstone, until the surface was worn down all over in the manner desired. An ax was shaped with the groove for hafting with a fairly decided edge, and then finished by lighter pecking, and finally by rutting and polishing with a stone of hard, fine texture.

In making mortars and pestles, the same procedure was followed. The center of the boulder was pecked until the entire inside of the boulder was worn out. With but one exception, they used only hammerstones and

Figure 14.2: Cross Sections of Quarries

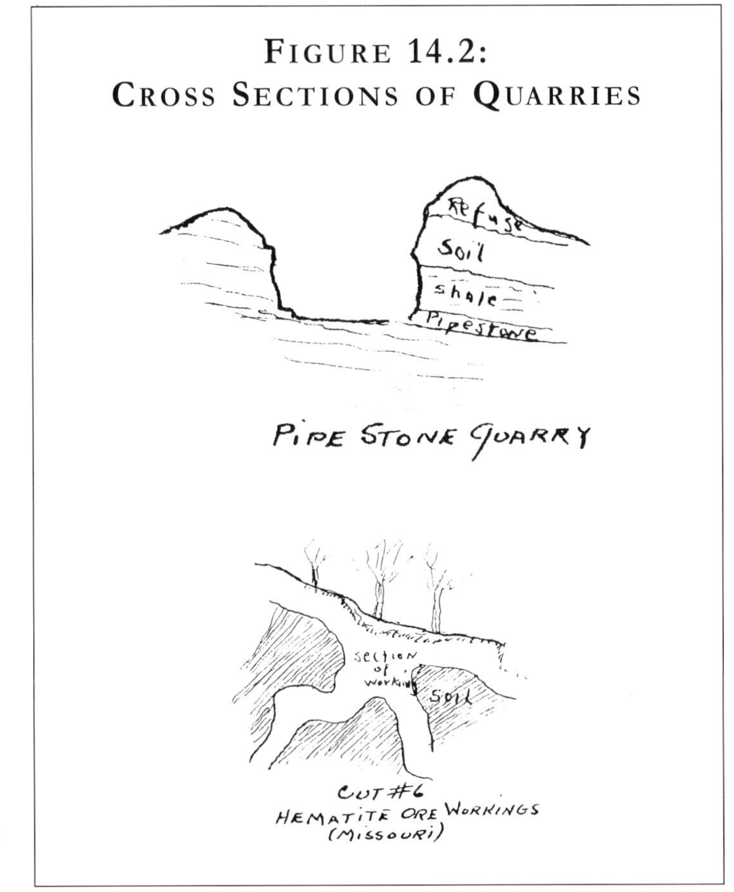

Above: This tray of artifacts from Johnston's collection includes pipestone pipe bowls, as well as other stone tools.

**FIGURE 14.3:
COPPER MINE CROSS SECTION**

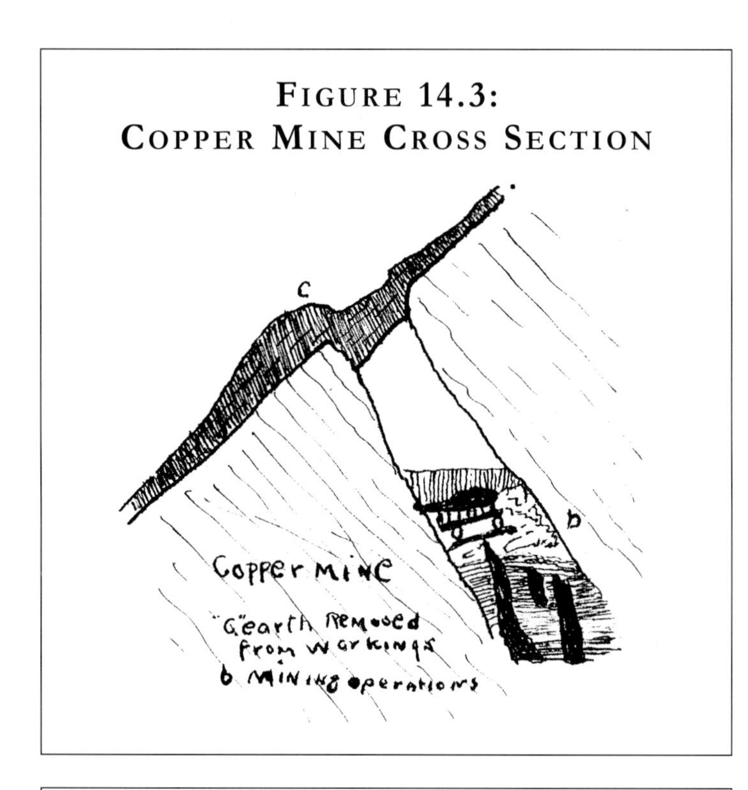

**FIGURE 14.4:
POINT-MAKING TOOLS**

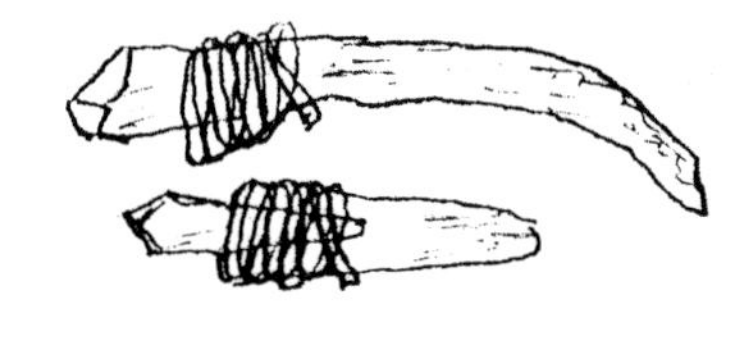

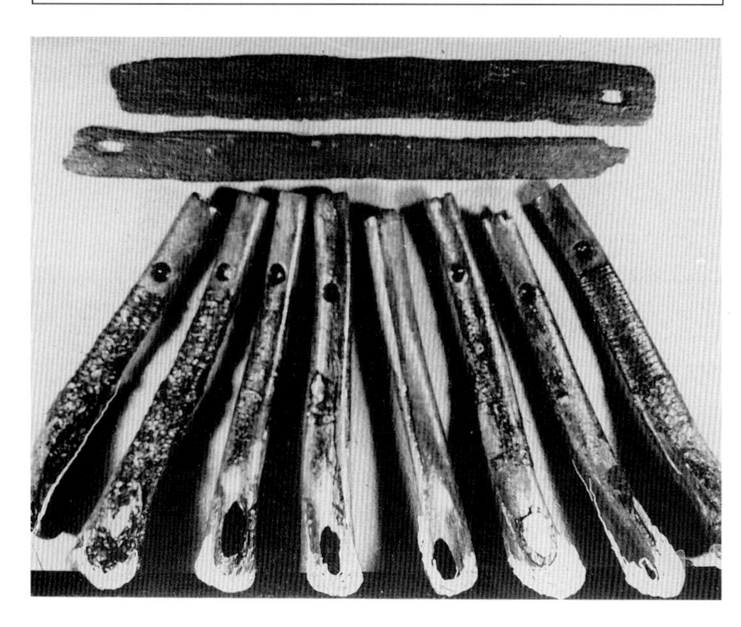

Above: Pit house bodkins made of bone.

such implements for their tools in this work. One assembled piece found in an excavation in Southern California would have been a very effective tool in this work. It was of stone, about three and a half inches in diameter and eight inches long, with three grooves pecked by the usual method around the center for hafting. In each end a hole had been made in which a chert piece was inserted and secured by asphalt. The advantage of this tool can readily be seen. Since the chert was so much harder than the stone, it was easy to replace a broken point in a tool that was already formed and hafted for use.

Rubbing was the method of finish for all items made by the Indians, whether by bone or stone. The finer the rubbing stone, the finer the finish. When a very fine finish was desired, certain kinds of earth were used on a piece of buckskin.

COPPER

The southern shores of Lake Superior were a great source of supply for copper, and this was where many early people mined their copper. Boulders of copper were found strewn over considerable territory, though not in abundance. The depressions left from their work were the first thing to call attention to the excavations.

At one place a piece of pure copper weighing over five tons was found 15 feet below the surface, under trees 10 feet in circumference and at least 400 years old. It had been raised on skids, bore marks of fire, and many stone implements were found there. In excavating, many stone hammers were found. In certain places the earth had been moved. The people found here by the first explorers had no knowledge of the origin of their copper working.

THE USE OF BONE

Bone was used by the various tribes at one time or another for almost every known type of implement or artifact — utilitarian, ceremonial and ornamental. They made knives, spearheads, agricultural implements and arrow points, all of which were necessary for the American Indian's very existence. More arrow points were made of wood and bone than flint, although the elements have disintegrated them. The flint arrow points which they lost are the ones we find.

Whistles and flutes, as well as other musical instruments, were made of bone. Also, objects of adornment and fetishes, while not absolutely essential to the American Indian, played an important part in his daily life.

The leg bone of the bear was used by some tribes to dispatch a deranged person — one of the few instances where such a treatment was applied. The blunt edge on some bone knives make it appear they were of little use in actual service, not even possessing the jagged cutting edge found on some of the stone knives.

Antler was worked into the same class of items as bone. The tips of the antler made admirable points for projectile shafts, requiring but little work in preparing them for use. The elk antler was made into hide dressing tools. Some had stone or flint blades lashed securely in place; later, pieces of steel replaced the stone and flint scraper blades.

Beads and gambling pieces were made of bone. Often just the bones of certain animals were used to make gambling pieces; for example, one of the Northern tribes used the leg bone of the wild cat. The leg bone of the pelican was used in making hair ornaments.

Handles of knives, drumsticks and war clubs were often made of bone. Some of the tribes had armor breast coverings made of bone strung close together.

Many of the bone objects were ornamented profusely, both by incising and with pieces of shell, which were held on with tar or pitch. Spoons and ladles were made of bone for daily use. From both whalebone and the leg bone of the deer fine fishhooks were fashioned.

The Eskimo would not have been able to exist without bone. He put it to many uses, using whalebone in the construction of his house as framework when he couldn't get wood, and often making a bone bow, which was lashed with sinew and backed up in a way that was very effective. He used it for harpoons and weapons of all sorts. Runners and even entire sleds and toboggans were made of bone. Shovels were made of the shoulder blade of the caribou for moving snow and other digging.

In general bone was as important to the American Indian as skin in their daily life.

Figure 14.5: Tools Made from Bone

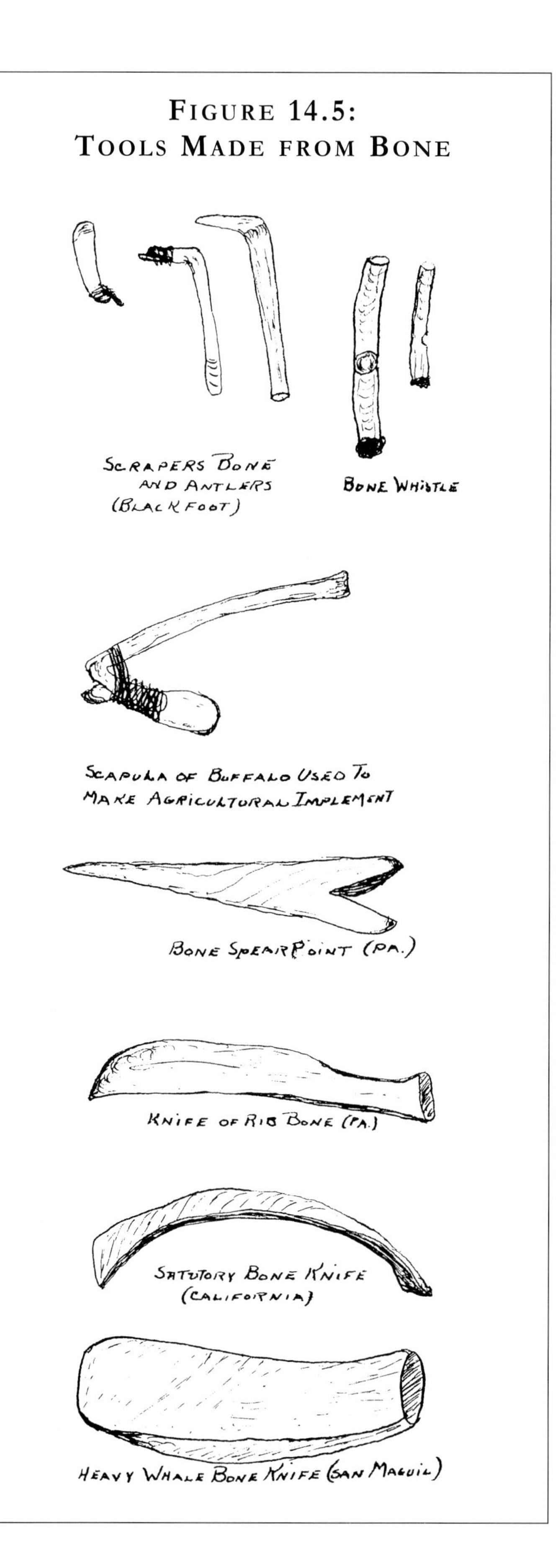

CHAPTER 15

THE SHAMAN

The American Indians almost universally attributed the cause of all sickness to the entrance of some evil spirit into the affected person. It was the duty of the shaman to combat these malignant spirits. The medicine men used some roots and herbs in their treatments, but for the most part they depended on exorcising the evil spirits by dances and other ritualistic performances.

The shamans were known as wizards, sorcerers and priests. Their place in Indian life was strongly based upon the belief in the ability of the shaman to communicate with supernatural beings by means of magic arts. The shaman attempted to control the evil spirits to whom death, sickness and all other misfortunes were ascribed by incantation and ceremonies. (*Note: The term shaman is similar to the Sanskrit root, indicating several forms of religious exercise.*)

Innumerable methods of treatment were used by the shamans, which grew out of the inventiveness of the medicine man, the credulity of the people and the steadily growing list of precedents and traditions. For example: biting the affected part and sucking until the blood flowed; applying plasters of eagle down or pine gum; and brewing unctions and administering them. Wasps' nest, when pulverized and mixed with water, was taken as a tonic. Rheumatism was sometimes treated by swallowing hot ashes, followed by hot and cold baths. Sage and rosemary were also used for treatment. Cases of paralysis were often treated by a beating with nettles. One interesting example of shaman healing was a method of curing a rattlesnake bite. The person affected, having seized the offending reptile and holding it firmly, would bite the snake repeatedly all along the body. It was asserted that the person bitten would not thereafter suffer, but the reptile would swell from its own poison, until it burst.

Arrow wounds were first sucked, then peyote powder was put in them, and later powdered lechuguilla root. These wounds would thoroughly heal unless the arrow was one of poison tip variety, which meant almost certain death. The tips of the arrows were sometimes poisoned by roots, but the usual method was to allow a rattlesnake to bite a piece of liver, which was then allowed to become putrid. The arrows were dipped into this mass.

The Acaxes employed a sucking process, or the blowing through a hollow tube, for the cure of diseases. The Yaqui had a primitive form of stomach pump; putting a stick into the patient's mouth, they drew the disease from the stomach. Bloodletting was a common practice among all tribes.

Among the Karok there were two kinds of doctors or sorcerers: root doctors and barking doctors. The latter

Above: The shaman would often appear to enter a trance-like state. Johnston took this amazing photograph in about 1929.

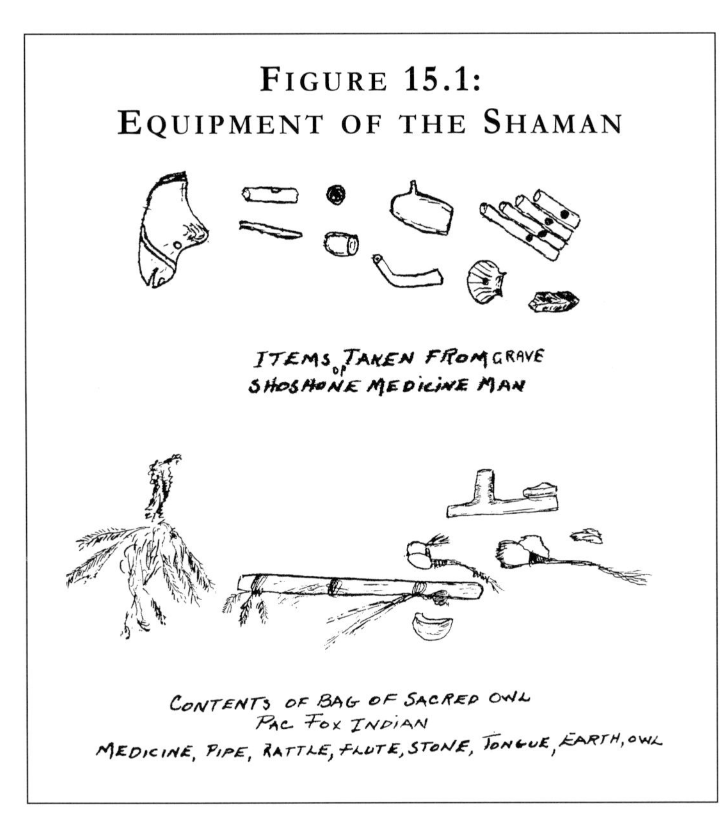

FIGURE 15.1: EQUIPMENT OF THE SHAMAN

Above: A shaman's talismans in the shapes of a cat and a human.

was the one who diagnosed all causes of sickness. He sat by the patient and barked like a dog, sometimes for hours. If it was a poison case or a malady he considered caused by some conjuror, he sucked it out through the skin or he administered emetics. If, however, the case was of a less serious nature, the root doctor then came, and with his herbs and a few minor incantations he proceeded to cure the patient.

If the patient died among the Karok, the doctor had to return the fee, and if he had refused to attend anyone and they died, then the relatives could collect from him the nominal fee he would have charged. With rare exceptions shaman's fees were extracted first or no services were rendered. In some tribes if the patient died the shaman paid with his life, or he was driven from the tribe. This no doubt gave rise to the practice of the shaman blaming some person or object with bewitching the patient, thus causing the illness. In such a case the blame of death was directed to another.

Among several tribes the medicine man administered antiseptics when practicing surgical operations. If they were to amputate a small member of the body they simply ran a sharp knife around the joint and snapped it off. This was done among a few of the tribes at the death of a relative. They never amputated a limb for any cause whatsoever. Narcotics were made from the jimsonweed. The root and the blossoms were dried and ground to a powder for external application to wounds.

One case observed by early pioneers in a Zuni camp was the illness of a woman with an ulcerated breast. After an herb narcotic was administered, the woman went to sleep while the breast was operated upon. She felt no pain, waking normally a little later, the sore having been successfully treated.

In the majority of the cases when the Indian doctor used herbs and roots to obtain a cure, he made no effort to determine the reason for his cures. He was satisfied to rest on experience. Massage, which was often quite violent, was used by many of the tribal doctors to relieve abdominal troubles, constipation and in the treatment of sprains.

Bleeding was commonly employed. Two different methods were most frequently used: the making of small incisions or gashes between the eyebrows with a flint knife, and the cupping on the back by the use of the tip of a buffalo horn. In the latter case, the vacuum is produced by suction with the mouth. The only time the doctors scarified before cupping was for snake bites. Cobweb, dried pulpy fungus and the inner bark of certain trees were used to stop bleeding. When bandages were used they were usually tied too tightly and left too long.

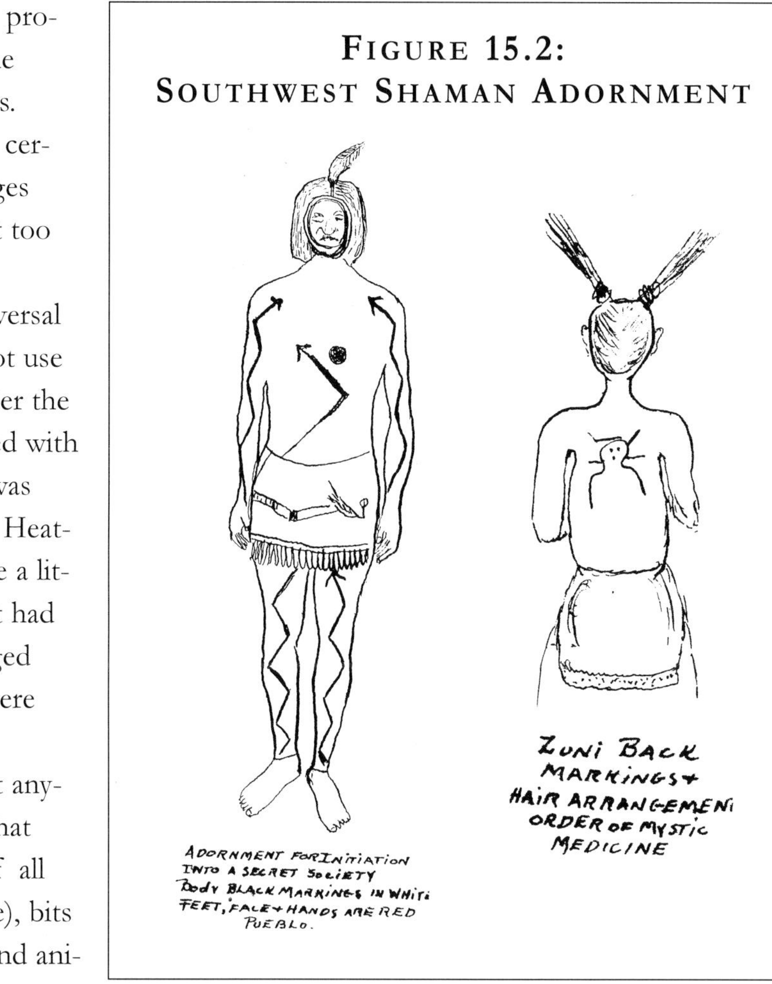

**FIGURE 15.2:
SOUTHWEST SHAMAN ADORNMENT**

The temescal, or sweat house, was almost universal with the American Indians; only a few tribes did not use it. The temescal consisted of a small hut, half under the ground, with a framework of sticks. It was plastered with mud and thatch until quite tight. A small opening was left at one side, through which the patient crawled. Heated stones were placed inside, and from time to time a little water was poured on the stones until the patient had sweated to exhaustion. He then emerged and plunged into a cold stream for a bath. In all cases women were barred from the temescal.

The kit of the shaman might have had almost anything in it. His pipe was always there, but beyond that there was a conglomeration of items — fetishes of all sorts (types of which were associated with his tribe), bits of bone and crystals, paints, dried parts of birds and animals, his medicine sticks and little bags of medicine. Each and every item was tied separately and was never avoidably shown to anyone.

Many people had the shaman make personal medicine bags or talismans for them by telling him of certain dreams, which he then depicted on the bag. In these bags the American Indian would carry sacred medicine that warded off the enemy's arrows, or produced such characteristics as invisibility, immunity from disease or having good luck on the hunt.

Above: Dolls, even commercially manufactured ones, were an important allegorical tool for a shaman.

Above: A rare 1888 photograph of a group of shamans treating a sick boy in the kiva of the Zia Pueblo in New Mexico.

CHAPTER 16

CEREMONIALS AND DANCES

As with all of the world's indigenous people, pre-Columbian American Indian ceremonials were largely religious and served as a focal point of tribal life. The religion of the American Indian was a pantheistic one with no theology (attempted explanation of supernatural phenomena) developed beyond the mythological stage. Climactic differences and environment greatly affected the extent of the religious impulse. Thus, the frequency of ceremonials and their importance varied among the widely scattered tribes.

It is a moot question whether or not the American Indians ever worshiped the sun. All tribes had more ceremonials pertaining to the sun than to the stars or planets, although falling stars or stars in unnatural positions were considered omens.

Some said that Honani (Badger) Chief came from the underworld to tell them these things. In each tribe the priest had certain sacerdotal kindred in the underworld, with whom they communicated and received their knowledge.

The Indian dance ceremonies were carried on at different seasons of the year in honor of the various animals they reverenced; they also honored the pets and animals of service to them, the rabbit, snake, coyote, elk, fish, eagle and buffalo. Each variation in this animal list signified a different clan with its sacred animal kinship.

Based upon their knowledge of the sun's movements, the priests determined the proper times of the year for religious and other ceremonials. As the sun traveled on its course, the priests made magic and communed with the spirits, from whom they obtained their instructions. When the sun rose in line with some familiar object on the horizon it was time to plant corn; when the sun appeared to the side of a mountain peak or directly over a certain spring it was time to plant melons, and so forth.

THE GHOST DANCE

The Ghost Dance was observed by more tribes than any other one dance. It has never been taken up by the Navajo or any of the Pueblo except at Taos, though it has been estimated that 146,000 Indians participated in the Ghost Dance, not counting any of those in Indian Territory [now eastern Oklahoma] who took part.

The participants were gaily dressed, red predominating. They gathered around the high priest or master of ceremonies who, after addressing them, gave them their songs and instructions. Forming a circle they stood with both hands on the shoulders of the one in front.

Right: The Corn Dance, as photographed at the Santa Clara Pueblo in New Mexico in 1911.

They started to chant "Father I come, mother I come, brother I come, father give us back our arrows." This was followed by shrieking, moaning, groaning and wailing. Between movements they took up great handfuls of dust and threw them up in the air. They kept up the wailing and implored the Great Spirit to allow them to see and talk with their people who had died. They kept up this chanting and circled around in different formations, sometimes hand in hand as children in their games, until one by one the weaker ones staggered away and fell. No attention was paid to those dropping out other than to see that they were not trampled upon. The American Indians believed the sick would be cured by participating in this dance.

Prior to the performance, the dance ring was consecrated by one of the leaders, who sprinkled sacred powder over the ground, praying all the while. At this time the feather, which was an official ordination, was conferred upon the seven leaders by the apostle who first brought the ceremony to the tribe. At times it was also given to seven women, as well as the seven men, although not in all tribes. The feather was of the crow, the sacred bird of the Ghost Dance, or of the eagle, sacred in all Indian religions. It was worn on the head during the dance. After the priests had consecrated the feathers and had given them to the chosen ones, the recipients, in turn, had to reciprocate with presents of ponies, blankets and other property.

The painting of the dancers was a special ceremony in itself, as each painting was an inspiration from a trance-vision. The dancer to be painted came before the painter and, laying his hands upon his head, said, "My father, I have come to be painted so that I may see my friends; have pity upon me and paint me."

The dance usually commenced about the middle of the afternoon or a little later, the announcement being made by criers, old men who went about the camp shouting in a loud voice to the people to prepare for the dance.

One of the peculiarities of the Ghost Dance was that no musical instrument was used at any time, and in

FIGURE 16.1: WOODEN DANCE MASKS

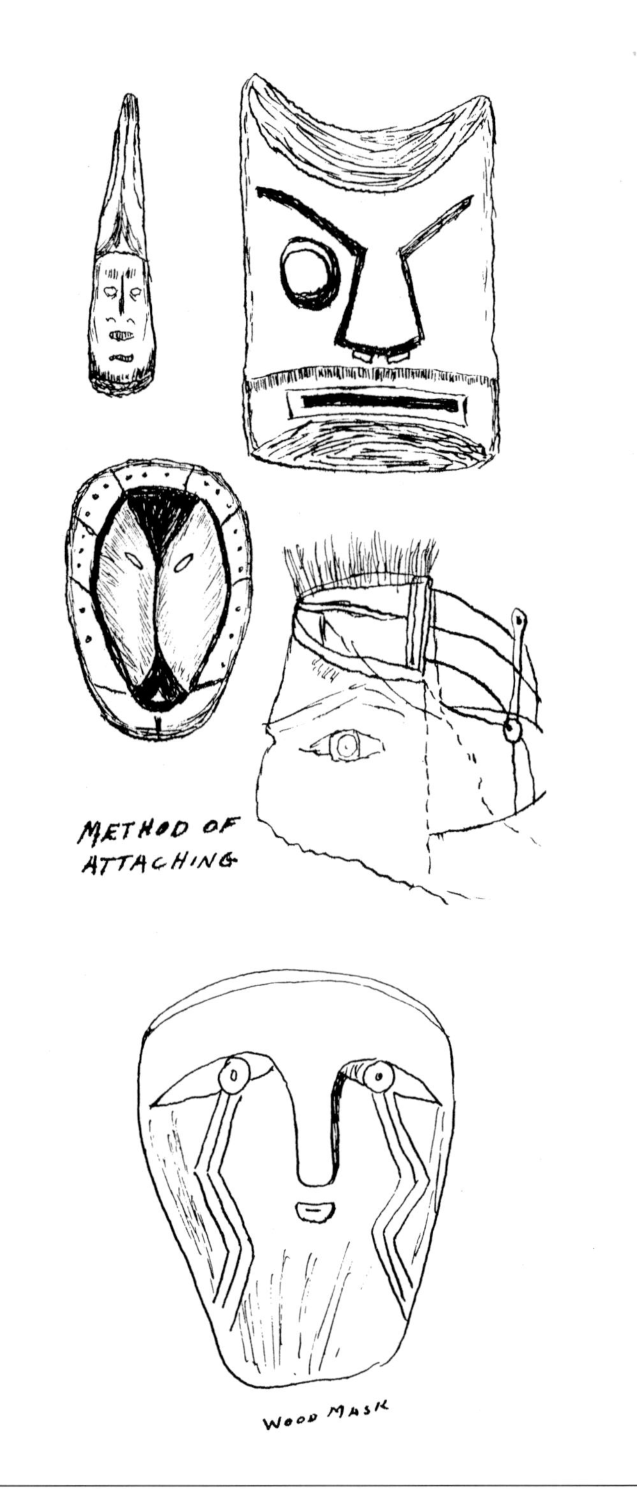

this it is different from every other Indian dance. There were no fires built within the circle by any of the tribes, with the exception of the Walpi.

On breaking away at the end of the dance the performers all shook their blankets with the idea of driving away any ill influences. Later, all went down to a stream to bathe, men and women separately.

THE SNAKE DANCE

The Hopi of Arizona are among the few surviving tribes still retaining an ancient ritual that has been unmodified by any other religion — the Snake Dance. The Snake Dance was not done for the purpose of curing the sick as so many ceremonials were. It was performed for the purpose of bringing rain to assure plentiful crops.

It was the most important observance of the Hopi, who lived in an extremely arid country. It has gained worldwide notice because of the fact that the participants carried venomous reptiles in their mouths. It was thought by many to be the most important ceremony on the calendar.

The Snake Dance covered a period of 16 days, nine of which are active ceremonies, some secret, some open. The ceremonial days were: Yunya, Custala, Luctala, Paictala, Naluctala, Sochahimu, Komokotokya, Totokya and Tihuni.

For four days the snakes were gathered from the mesa by the snake priests, who dug them from their holes with sticks or wherever else they could get them. During this time the implements were kept on the kiva roof and were not returned to the owner until the end of the fourth day.

The snakes were kept in pottery canteens, in either side of which were holes. These holes, as well as the neck, were plugged with corncobs.

On the morning of the ninth day the snake priests and all members of the snake clan bathed their heads to prepare for the ceremony; the reptiles were also washed, supposedly by the elder members of the clan. Since this was a rain ceremony the washing was logical.

All participants were naked and stained red with iron oxide. Each one wore a red feather in his hair. The priests seated themselves at one side of the kiva, with the snake priest in the center. Behind them were several novices who returned any reptiles that might escape.

Two snake kilts were spread at the end of the kiva, and against one leaned a row of the sacred snake whips. These kilts were decorated with a figure of The Great Snake. On some of the kilts, the head was omitted, but not always.

Prior to the releasing of the snakes, the chief drew with meal on the sand in front of him six short lines, representing the six cardinal points recognized by the Hopi. At the junction of these lines he placed an earthenware basin, similar to the ones in which they bathed their heads, and into this he poured liquid from six different gourds.

After pouring from each gourd, he made passes to the six cardinal points, and then placed some herb or root in the basin. Following this, there was a formal smoking ceremony, during which the terms of the relationship of the members was discussed. The ceremony closed with prayers led by the chief.

After this ceremony the snakemen took the snake whips and began a quick song. The priests took the snakes from the canteens and placed them three and

FIGURE 16.2: HOPI CEREMONIAL MASK

Above: Johnston took this photograph during a 1929 ceremony at precisely the moment that the Hopi dancer turned to face him.

FIGURE 16.3: REPRESENTATIVE DANCE MASKS

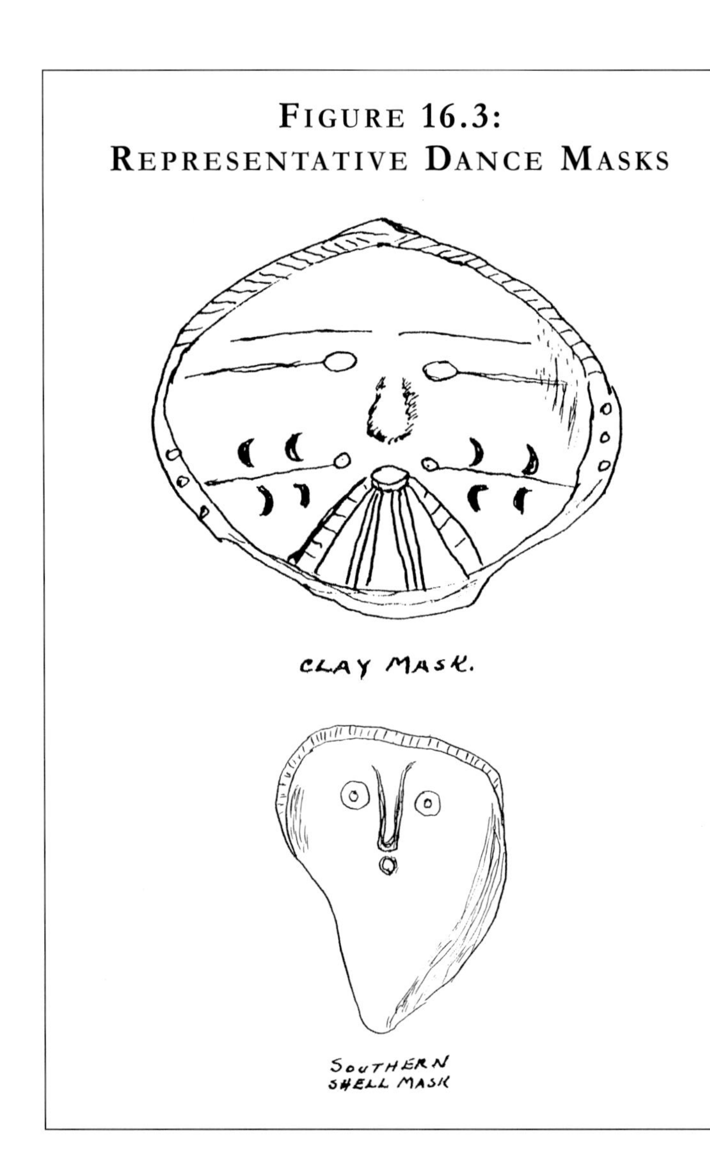

four at a time in the basin, after which they laid them on the sand to dry, where they were left for some time.

All being in readiness for the dance, a kiva was dug in the center of the snake pavilion, with cottonwood boughs placed about and partially covered with cloth. The covering being sufficient to conceal whatever was placed therein, the reptiles were now deposited there by two snake priests.

The antelope priests, headed by their chief with his tiponi on his left arm, started the dance. Each priest, except one, carried two rattles. The third priest in line carried a medicine bowl and an aspergill. Entering, he dipped the feathered aspergill into the medicine bowl and asperged the cardinal points. Before the dance actually started this priest called out an invocation to the warriors.

The antelope priests made four circuits of the plaza. In passing the shrine and before the kiva they stamped and dropped sacred meal, after which they formed at the kiva to await the coming of the snake priests, who now made the same circuits as the antelope priests had made.

The snake priests deposited their meal in the same manner and formed a line facing the antelope priests. The ceremony of the kiva now began. There was a sway-

Above: Johnston photographed this group of students and others observing a Havasupai dance in Arizona in about 1929.

ing motion in unison with songs, and the snake priests shook their whips and struck the ground as though striking a snake. This ceremony lasted about a quarter of an hour. From the line of snake priests one man, dressed as a kalektaka, entered the kiva, and as the snakes were needed he passed them out.

The snake priests now divided into groups of three: a carrier who held the reptile in his mouth, a hugger who placed his left hand on his shoulder and accompanied the carrier on his circuit around the plaza, and the gatherer, who collected the snakes which were dropped. The antelope people did not receive any reptiles, but continued to sing and shake their rattles. During the procession the women sprinkled the dancers and snakes with sacred cornmeal from trays which were held as prayer offerings. Anyone could offer a prayer by throwing sacred meal on the reptiles.

At the close of the ceremony the chief drew a ring on the ground and made six radial lines, corresponding to their cardinal points, and into this ring the reptiles were dropped. After a prayer the snake priests rushed in

Above (both): Johnston's own photographic documentation of a Hopi dance demonstration that took place in Arizona in about 1929.

FIGURE 16.4: SOUTHWEST HIEROGLYPHICS

and seized all the snakes they could and then rushed out onto the mesa to liberate them to their cardinal points. As the priests left, the spectators all spit on them. It was a disgrace if the priest failed to get a snake in this close of the ceremony.

After the reptiles were released, the snake men returned to the pueblo and took an emetic, followed by a great feast, which always closed the Snake Dance.

It has been noted that in the early Snake Dances some of the priests carried small frogs in their mouths, as the frog was also the rain symbol for many American Indians.

THE SCALP DANCE

The Scalp Dance was celebrated upon the return of a war party. The flesh side of the scalp was painted red, and the entire scalp was stretched in a small hoop, which was suspended from a pole and carried by the wife or sweetheart of the warrior. The dances usually took place at night. During the dance each warrior in turn would step into the center of the dancing group and, with improvised song, tell of his exploits. If his deeds merited it, he would be given a new war name. These dances were sometimes held for many nights or at short intervals for weeks.

When skins were to be used for anything pertaining to a ceremonial object, the animal whose skin was to be used could not be shot; instead, it was captured alive and then strangled to death, after which it was sprinkled with sacred meal and blessed.

In the arid regions where rainmaking ceremonials were predominant, water animals were adopted as their symbols, the tadpole being the foremost symbol. In most of the designs the head was just a globular form with a zigzag tail and was often colored black. In pottery design they were found in conjunction with lines representing falling rain.

The frog was used as a pottery symbol for the Rain God, and also made in the form of fetishes of stone, shell and pottery that were used in the rain ceremony. Rattles and drums were also decorated.

One excavation found altar pieces in a cache. They were probably used for a ceremony of planting or harvesting. Among the pieces there was a bird, highly decorated, and many wooden cones that represented acorns. There were a great number of sunflowers, a few of skin and others of wood. The center and the petals were all beautifully colored, well fitted together, and were held by a pitch on gum.

SOUTHERN CALIFORNIA

The first Europeans who came in contact with the Indians of Southern California were surprised at their seeming lack of initiative and advancement. They said the Californians had no houses as the Eastern Indians had, but they failed to take into consideration the fact that the California climate did not demand a house of the type the Indians in the colder and more severe climates needed.

A brush wickiup sufficed; when it became dirty or too disorderly it was burned and a new one made. In general, these were cleaner than the houses of their Eastern neighbors.

Their clothing was a similar case. Little was needed and it was easily attained. Because of these things, however, the California Indians have been wrongly classified by many of the early writers.

The Spanish fathers tried to bring the Indian into the Church, and some were slow in responding. Life was beautiful to them and they were loath to change.

The Hupa retains the religious beliefs of his ancestors. Most weird and colorful of all his native ceremonies was the White Deer Dance, in which they carried long obsidian ceremonial blades. The prime purpose of the dance was the purging of all individuals of iniquity, hatred and motives unworthy of good Indians. This rare spiritual quality has played a major part in the inevitable process of adaptation of the white man's way, which has awakened little of the hostility found in more aggressive tribes.

Their ceremonials were some of the finest and most beautiful any of the tribes performed. The clothes burning rites at the time of death, and later the image burning rites, convince the historian that this is a culture unlikely to be eradicated. These ceremonials are practiced even now, at intervals of about three years.

Above: The obsidian blade used in the Karok White Deer Dance.

FIGURE 16.5: YAQUI MUSICAL INSTRUMENTS

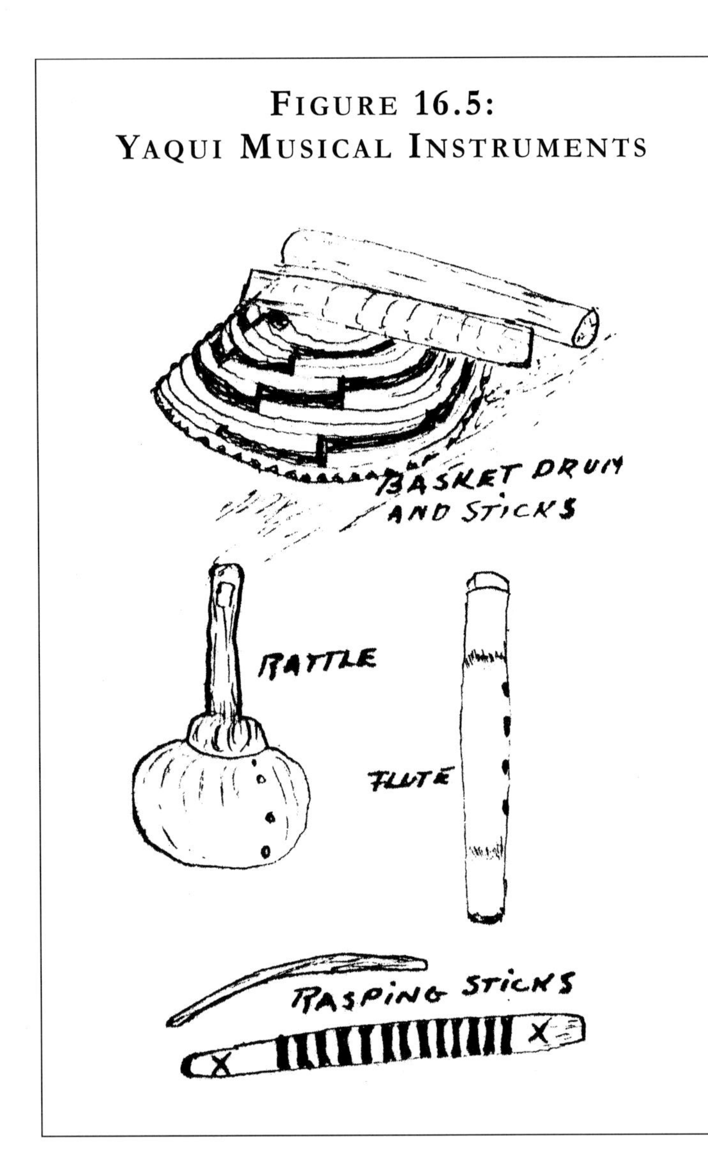

SONGS AND MUSICAL INSTRUMENTS

The American Indians had a myriad of musical instruments, which they fabricated from a wide variety of materials. Flutes were of bone and reed. Drums were made in many ways — skin stretched over an earthen vessel or the end of a hollow log, or the beating of the log itself. The Indians used many types and kinds of rattles, including those made of turtle shell, gourds, dried skins with pebbles inside, striking of stick against stick, or bone and stick.

A early sort of violin was imitated by using the yucca stick as the body. Scraping sticks were employed by many as musical instruments. A hardwood stick with notches cut in it was drawn over another stick or bone which was laying on an upturned basket or similar container, thus creating a rasping vibration.

The Papago used the basket drum considerably, sometimes striking the basket and again striking a stick resting on the basket. The Mandan used a hand drum similar to the tambourine for dances. The California Indians did not use drums. The flute, made in many forms of wood, reed and bone, was their main musical instrument.

Chippewa songs were always accompanied by either a drum or rattle or both. The drums were made by hollowing a basswood log and then charring and scraping it; an untanned deer skin was then stretched tight, while wet, over the ends. This was hung suspended between stakes. It was said these drums could be heard for a distance of 10 miles, and yet at close range they were not unpleasantly loud. Some of the rattles were in reality small drums; others were of birch bark. The tone varied by the number and size of pebbles in them. The courting flute was usually made of cedar and similar to those used by other Indians.

Above: A group of Hopi dancers in kachina costume at the Walpi Pueblo in Arizona in 1893.

Figure 16.6: Apache Stringed Instrument

APACHE YUCCA STALK
VIOLIN, HORSEHAIR STRINGS

Above: Johnston's photograph of Hopi dancers using rattles.

The love charm song was a popular form of magic with the Chippewa. The following is one of them:

A'ninajun': What are you saying to me?
Ogini'bagun': I am arrayed like a rose.
Ajina' gooyan: And beautiful they are.

Among the principal characters in folklore are We'nabo'jo and his grandmother. The following is a We'nabo'jo song for curing the sick:

We'nodikwe'biwug': They are in close consultation with their heads together.
We'nabo'jo: We'nabojo.
Okwosmisum': And his grandmother.

The Fox people of the upper Midwest told what they called the "Owl Sacred Pac" at their clan festivals and ceremonies. It went: "And you must think seriously of all songs. If anyone thinks seriously he (Manitou) will strengthen you. Moreover, he will make you warriors. If anyone keeps a secret in his body he weakens and he will die, that is the only evil in it. That is all. Are you listening? Now we will sing. As we sing the Manitou hears us. The Manitou will not fail us. That is why we sing, that he will know when we have celebrated the gens festival. You are to sing loudly."

The Ashes People

The story is told among the people of the Southwest that in "the old time," there was a flood which covered the Earth. The Elder Brother gathered gum from a certain bush and a big olla. When the coyote came and wanted in, the Elder Brother told him to get some bamboo growing in the west; when the coyote brought him this, the Elder Brother cut off the end and put the coyote in the bamboo; however, his tail hung out. The flood came and all were afloat.

When the water subsided they all got out, and the coyote and the Elder Brother met. The coyote's tail was all muddy from dragging and he could hardly walk, but he sang this song as he came toward Elder Brother: "I cannot walk, I am dragging along, I cry I Ah, Ah!"

The song goes on and on and gives versions of the various animals and the olla that carried them.

Above: Native American musical instruments from Johnston's collection, including some that are pictured on page 137.

Above: A group of American Indians in their ceremonial finery at a celebration on the Oregon coast in about 1910.

CHAPTER 17

THE IMPORTANCE OF MYTH

We have yet to find a people without language, and so too does every people have their mythology, that is, some form of preserving historical tradition and presenting ethical maxims. It is a recognized principle of philosophy that no religious belief, mythology or historic tradition can be held by the majority of the people for any considerable time as true, without first having some foundation of fact.

Some element of truth must have been in every legend, in every tradition, in every belief that has ever been entertained by the majority of the people. Without such a foundation, it would be difficult to recommend these beliefs to the minds of men in the first place.

We may conclude that the purpose for which these narratives were so carefully preserved and handed down to posterity was twofold: to keep alive certain facts and to inculcate certain doctrines.

As with many European cultures, and with aboriginal cultures around the world, Indians had many myths explaining natural phenomena which they did not understand. Just as Europeans had beliefs about black cats and salt thrown over the shoulder, Indians had some common superstitions, such as that one must never cut fish across the grain in the flesh or all the fish in the streams would die. The Moqui believed that at death they should be changed into animals — bear, deer and such beasts — which they believed to have been their original form. As with ancient people in Europe, an eclipse was an event of great importance, and may have been among the most feared of any phenomena among the Indians.

Certain fowl and squirrels were regarded with reverence, although the reason for this is hard to find. For some tribes a great bird was the chief deity — the thunder was a flap of his wings, and the lightning was the glance of his eyes, according to the Kenai.

Other animals also had significance. Chirping of tree frogs was a sign of damp weather. The whistling of a bobwhite meant more wetness. Locusts told of warm weather. After first hearing of the locust, it was to be a moon and a half till frost. A circle around the moon meant a storm was approaching. The flight of wildfowl had various significance. If a bird flew in the house it meant death to some member of the family.

The American Indians believed the Earth was round and that it floated in the sea. It was held in position by five ropes stretched by the Creator; when these ropes were shaken, earthquakes were caused. The Maidu recognized five cardinal points, whereas the Kushu recognized four, and some of the Pueblo recognized six.

To the Chippewa, dreams meant life. An aged Chippewa once said, "Our people had no education. Their wisdom came to them in dreams." To dream and

Right: The expression on the face of the storyteller embodies all the spirit and complexity of tribal mythology.

remember what you dreamed was always taught to young people — purity of thought being most essential. Some of their dream subjects were placed on bark. One ancient said, "A picture can be destroyed, but stone endures. It is well, therefore, to have your dream subject carved on your pipe so it can be buried with you and not be taken from you."

The one who in his youth had dreamt many times of the bear took the bear as his dream symbol and believed that he received his rugged strength from it.

Some Important Myths

The Creation of Light

In the beginning, thick darkness covered the Earth, man stumbled against man and animals and birds clashed together. Confusion was everywhere. The Hawk flew into the face of the Coyote; mutual apologies followed, and after a long discussion of the situation, they determined to make some effort toward abating the evil. The Coyote gathered a heap of tule reeds, rolled them into a ball, and gave it to the Hawk. He also gave the Hawk some pieces of flint. Gathering all together, the Hawk flew straight up into the sky, where he struck fire with the flints, lit his ball of reeds, left it there in a fierce red glow and it is now the sun.

The Origin of the Pheasant Dance

A pheasant once saw a woman beating corn in a mortar in front of her house. He said to her, "I can do that too," but the woman would not believe him. He then went into the woods and got a hollow log and drummed with his wings, and the woman, when hearing him, thought he was really beating corn. In the Pheasant Dance, the Green Corn Dance and others, the participants tried to imitate the drumming sound of the pheasant with the drum and the shuffling of their feet.

Rattlesnake Myths

The Indian word for rattlesnake, utsa'nati, can be interpreted as "He has a bell." The rattler was the chief of the Snake tribe and few Indians would venture to kill one, and then only in case of necessity, after which he would ask the pardon of the Snake Ghost, either in per-

FIGURE 17.1: DREAM SYMBOLS

Above: The thunderbird icon represented powerful natural forces.

son or through meditation of the priest. The Indians believed that *Silene stellata*, a plant known as rattlesnake master, was the only thing the snake was afraid of, and that he would flee in terror from a person carrying a piece of the root. It was this plant that the doctors use to counteract the effect of the rattler's bite. They sometimes applied chewed linn bark to a bite, perhaps from some occult connection between the thunder and lightning, since they think the linn tree is immune to lightning. Notwithstanding their fear of the rattlesnake, his rattles, teeth, vertebrae, flesh and oil were greatly prized for doctor medicine. The priests, however, killed the snakes, as they were the only ones who knew the formula of obtaining the Snake Ghost's pardon. The copperhead, wa'dige-aska'li, was hated and never worshiped because it was supposed to be a descendent of the mythical serpent with eyes of fire.

How the Buzzard's Head Became Bald

The buzzard formerly had a wonderful topknot and was very proud of it. He refused to eat carrion, however, and the other birds became infuriated with him. One day they pulled out all his topknot, and since then all buzzards have been bald. He lost his pride after this episode, and ever since has subsisted on carrion.

The Origin of Death (Cochiti Pueblo)

The Cochiti Indians were coming from Shipap (land from whence they came), and one of their children became ill. They did not know what to do for him, so they asked Shyoko, the curing society chief, what to do. He went back and asked the mother in Shipap what the trouble was and she said the child was dead. He returned and told them, "If you people did not die the world would fill up and there would be no place to live. When you die you come back to Shipap to live with me. Keep traveling and do not trouble when your people die." In those days they all treated one another as brothers.

The Origin of the Cat

All were at the cave and ready to go out to hunt for food, but before they left they said, "We have no cat, how can we get one?" The mountain lion stood in the middle of the circle and the other animals were all smoking around him. He said, "Now I'm ready," and he sneezed. A female cat came out of his right nostril. He sneezed again and a male cat came out of his left nostril. From these two, all cats came. The lion said, "Now you are the offspring of the mountain lion and have my face. When you have kittens people will want them so that they may not have mice and rats any more. You will be the goatcini (watchmen) and live in the house while the rest of the animals shall live in the mountains."

FIGURE 17.2: OBSERVATION OF THE NIGHT SKY

Above: The bison, or buffalo, was central to Plains Indian mythology.

THE ORIGIN OF THE FIRST SACRED PACT

When the first married couple made a sacred pact there was a great celebration with dancing. At that time they were merely given power to slay their enemies by the Manitou. When they made the pact they put in the spear head, the point of the arrow and the scalp, as these were all part of slaying the enemy. They fasted and the Manitou spoke to them. They had desired a lance and the Manitou told them to go to a stream and they would find one. He also told them to bless the stream and cast tobacco on it. They did as they were told and did get the lance. Then the Manitou blessed all and held a gens festival with the deer's head, which he boiled in a pot. Then he blessed the fire and he offered the fire tobacco. Then the Manitou blessed the lance, since it was to be his and he was to be the keeper of the sacred pact in the future, as well as the head of the village. Each item added to the pact was acquired through directions given by the Manitou, and he directed them to sing songs — a different song for each purpose. So as the directions were received they completed the pact, and each had its sacred duty and protection.

A green-striped snakeskin was used if an attack was to be made early in the morning. If you were to go spying, you would spray yourself with the sacred medicine from the bundle of the sacred humming bird, which would make you almost invisible and swift and so on, for all the different duties of life. When the man had grown old he went to the great Manitou and said, "Surely I will die someday, and what is to become of my pact?" The Manitou said, "Now you are to instruct someone to carry it as it shall last as long as the Earth, and he who carried it shall never fall in battle, but will carry on and live to old age and come to the one who blessed you." Many carried the pact in battle, but never did one fall, though shot at many times.

CHAPTER 18

USING TOBACCO

The use of tobacco in some form was a widespread practice among all tribes. Yet it seems probable that its initial use did not antedate the arrival of the white man by more than two or three centuries. While the use of a pipe for smoking was the most general method, a few of the tribes rolled cigarettes.

The tobacco was quite frequently mixed with other plants, and was undoubtedly very potent. By smoking only on certain occasions, the strong mixture produced a sort of intoxication. This pleasurable effect — which induced dreams and other reactions (somewhat similar to the results of opium smoking) — was unquestionably the strong factor in bringing about the widespread use of tobacco. The telling of legends connected with its use followed as an excuse or explanation.

A common American Indian myth explains the origin of tobacco. One day Manabush, a young brave, while passing a certain high mountain, detected a strange and delightful odor. Peering through a crevice in a rock, he discovered the mountain to be inhabited by a giant known as The Keeper of the Tobacco. Manabush located the mouth of the cavern leading into the heart of the mountain and entered it.

In a loud, stern voice the Giant called out, asking what he wanted. Manabush demanded some of the aromatic tobacco stored there. The Giant then informed him that there was a great ceremony required, with the smoking to be done only once a year. As this time had just passed, Manabush would have to return a year hence. Looking around, Manabush, very displeased, saw several sacks of tobacco. Snatching one of these, he ran, and was closely pursued by the Giant.

Manabush rushed to the top of the mountain and leaped from peak to peak; fearing he would be caught, he suddenly lay down on one of the mountaintops and allowed the Giant, who was coming at a great speed, to jump over him. The Giant fell into the chasm beyond and was so terribly bruised that Manabush was able to grab him by the back and throw him violently against the cliff. "Because you are so mean," Manabush reprimanded him, "you shall become Kaku'ene (the grasshopper), and you shall be known by the stain on your mouth. More than that, you shall always be a pest."

Manabush returned to his tribe and divided the tobacco among his brothers, giving to each some of the weed, that the tribe might always have some to plant for their use and enjoyment.

The Eskimo had no tobacco until it was imported from Russia in the early days. In order to stretch their somewhat scanty supply, they adopted the practice of burning a common fungus, and mixing these ashes with the tobacco.

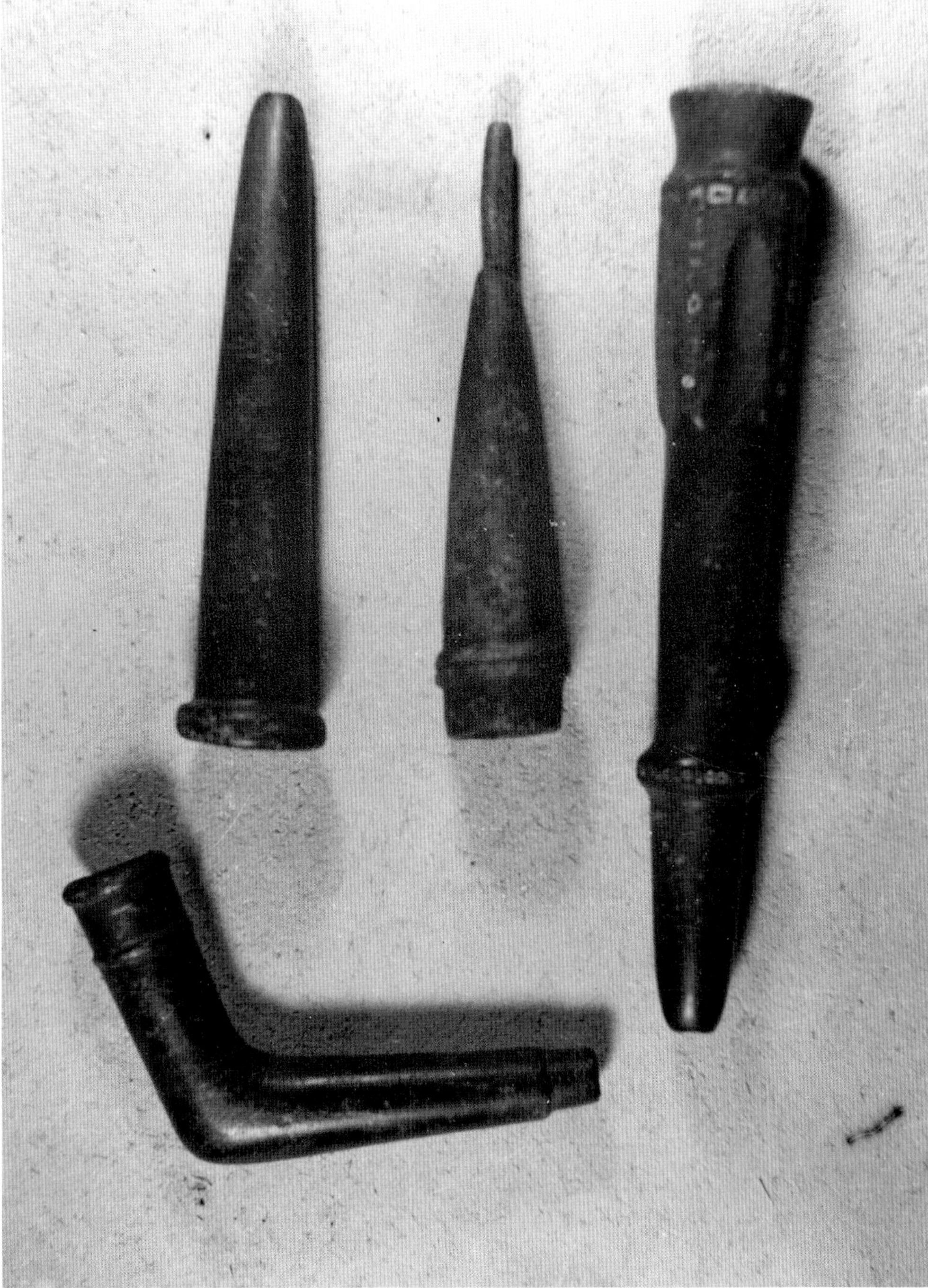

Right: A traditional pipe bowl and tube pipes from Johnston's collection.

To prepare the pipe for smoking, the Eskimo pulled a little tuft of fur from his garment and stuffed it down in the pipe bowl. On this he would place a pinch of tobacco, which he lit with tinder, flint and steel. The smoker would then give two or three strong puffs, which ignited the tobacco. Inhaling a few times, which would exhaust the tobacco, he would hold the smoke in as long as possible, then exhale and put his pipe away. The Indians never smoked while standing; they would either squat on the haunches or sit down.

The Eskimo pipe was probably the smallest bowl pipe used by any tribe. (This pipe has traces of Asiatic origin.)

Most of the time was spent in preparing the pipe for the three or four puffs obtainable. The cleanings of the bowl and stem were saved, and mixed with the tobacco quids or little pellets, which they placed inside their cheek, although they did not actually chew and did not expectorate. The Eskimo apparently suffered no ill effects from this terribly strong mixture. They also used snuff.

Isleta Indians used the cigarette as their sacred smoke to the gods. A native tobacco, of which the chief was the custodian, was made into the cigarettes with wrappers of corn husk. In their ceremonial smoke they puffed in all directions, five of them total, the four cardinal points of the compass and the vertical, or skyward, direction; and then they puffed toward the persons or gods being addressed. The smoking was called paki'mu, mist or fog. They believed the smoke produced clouds

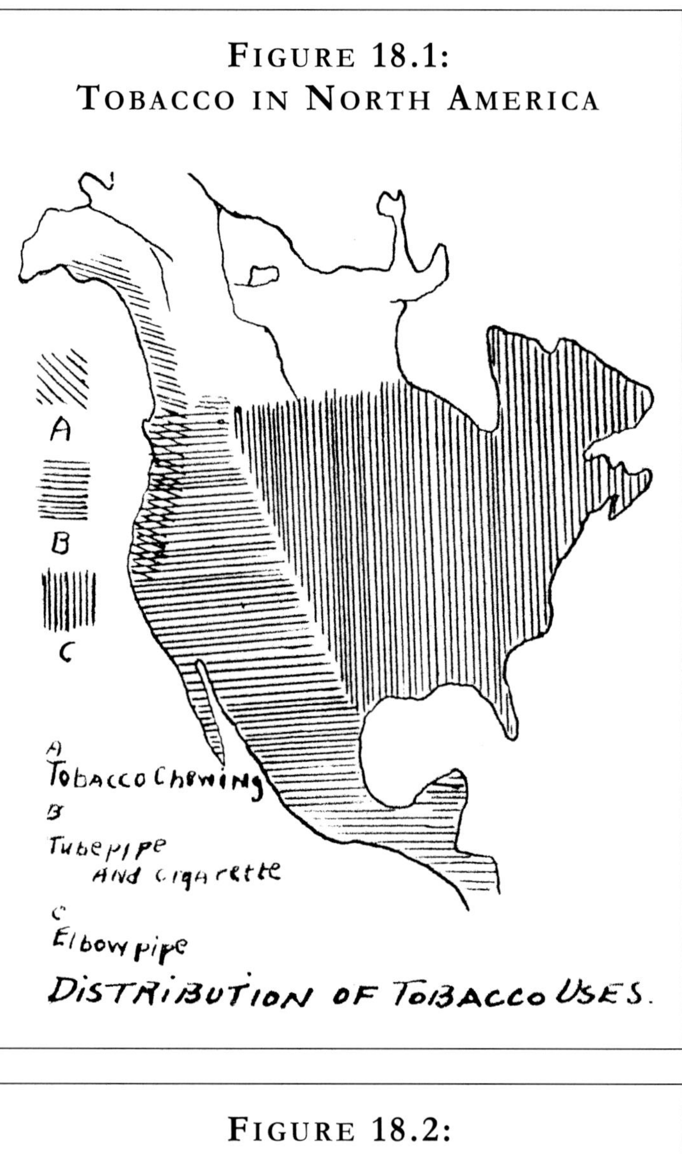

FIGURE 18.1: TOBACCO IN NORTH AMERICA

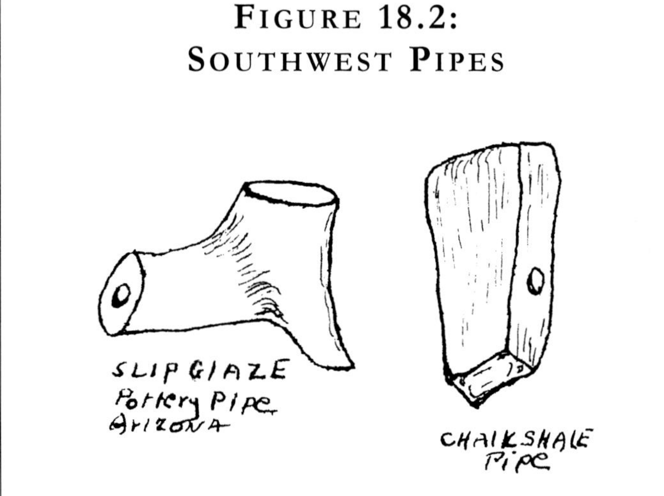

FIGURE 18.2: SOUTHWEST PIPES

and rain; they also believed that before a hunt the smoke got into the eyes of the game, thus blinding the animals so they could not so easily run away. At times the pipe, which was the most widely used smoking method among other tribes to create sacred smoke, was employed by some of the Isleta medicine societies.

The Thompson Indians had a genuine tobacco plant, *Nicotinana attenuata*, which grew wild in the warmest valleys of their district. The leaves of this plant were much narrower and had a finer stem than the *Nicotinana tobacum*, the common variety used and cultivated by most of the tribes. The preparation of this tobacco was simple: The leaves were gathered, dried, often greased, and usually mixed with the leaves of some other plant. In the Northwest was a plant called kinnikinnick and this was smoked extensively by the tribes there. It was either smoked as gathered or mixed with some of the plants used as adulterates, according to the supply they had. However, the word kinnikinnick was an Algonquin word, meaning, "that which is mixed by hand." In the East the bark of the dogwood and arrow-wood were used.

Among the American Indians a number of different plants were used in lieu of tobacco in different areas. With some plants it was the leaves, others the bark; and still with other plants it was the berry that was used. The bearberry, the mullen, the wild heather, valerian, and bald-hip rose, dogwood leaves, whorthleberry leaves, the bloom of life-everlasting and others were also used. The Wintu Indians smoked black manzanita, palosanto, creeping sage, wild sunflower, creeping mistletoe and black oak as readily as tobacco.

Chewing tobacco was a habit not widely practiced among the Indians, although some of the tribes along the Northwest coast used tobacco in this form. The taking of snuff was also indulged in this same territory. In preparing the tobacco for chewing, these tribes would mix the tobacco with pulverized ashes or shells which had been ground into a fine powder.

Further south, the Jibro Indians took a concoction of liquid tobacco through the nose; and to the south of them, and in the West Indies, the tribes used the cigar. The most popular form of smoking in Mexico was the cigarette. On the West Coast of North America the tube-type pipe was the most popular, except in the

FIGURE 18.3:
TYPES OF PIPES IN USE THROUGHOUT NORTH AMERICA

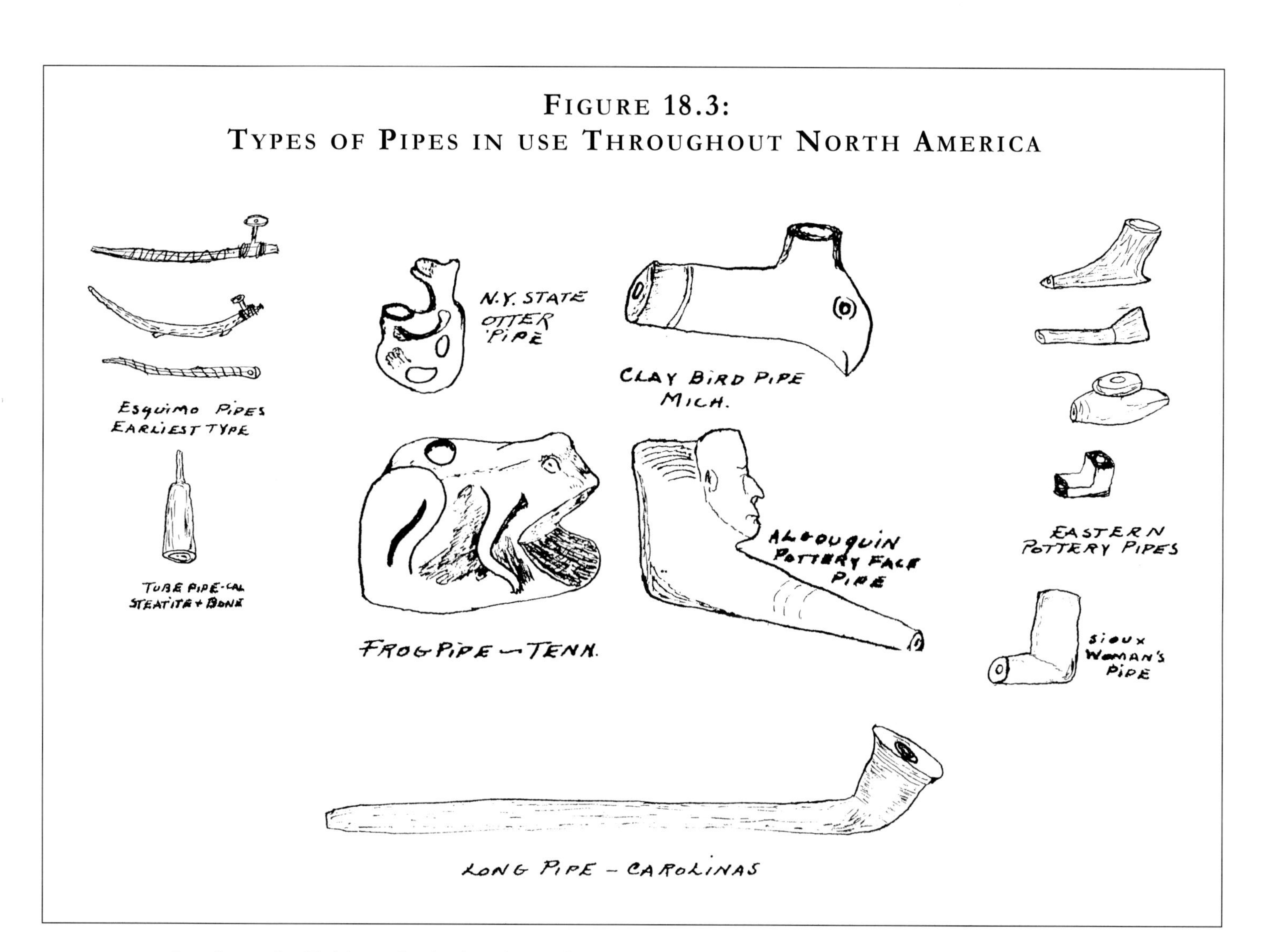

extreme north, where the Eskimos had a bowl peculiarly their own. Central and Eastern tribes adopted the elbow pipe of various forms and materials. The true catlinite pipe of the Dakotas was a work of art, rivaling even the fine greenstone pipes of the South and East. Other pipe shapes were also fashioned; many effigy pipes — made of clay and the hardest of stone — were also used.

Manzanita pipes were considered the best among the Northwest American Indians. The better ones had stone bowls and were rubbed and polished to a fine finish. The stone bowls lasted longer, and the additional work in fashioning them added to their value. The pipe smoked by the women was always much smaller than the one smoked by the men.

A hat full of tobacco was worth a third size dentalium bead or a full-sized, dressed woodpecker scalp. Among the Northwest tribes this was the exchange value of these commodities. On the Plains, where the bayberry was scarce, a pony could be had for the equivalent of a pint of leaves.

FIGURE 18.4:
SMOKING PARAPHERNALIA

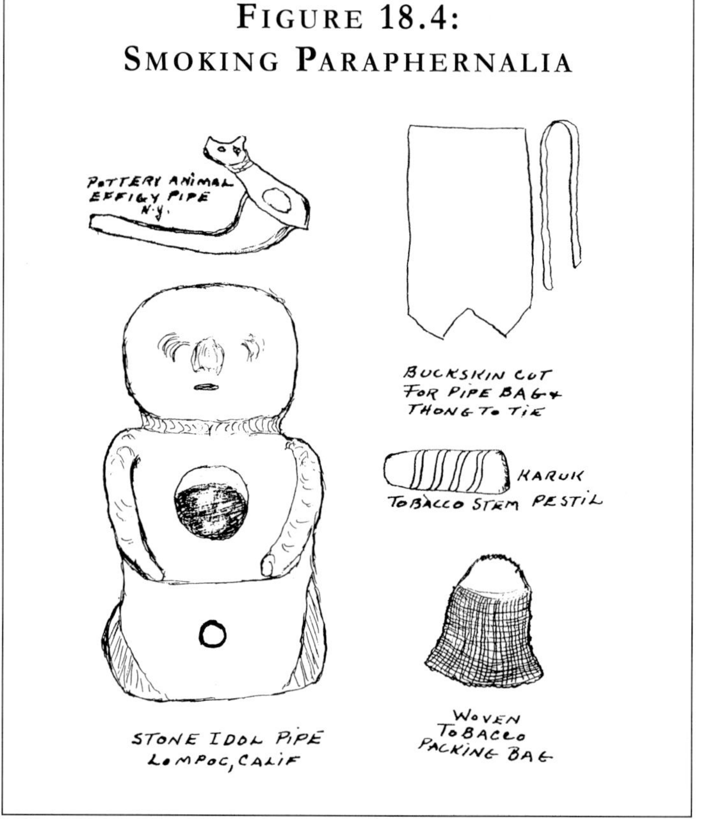

CHAPTER 19

GAMES AND THE RECORDING OF TIME

It has been said that the American Indian's principal source of amusement was their games of chance. Their great love of gaming and betting was evident in the number of games played and the skill with which they were developed. After they returned home from a hunt, having brought back two or three days' food supply, they would first work over their bows and arrows to see that all was in proper order. They would then spend much of their time gaming.

The most popular pastimes were played with gaming pieces similar to dice. They used beaver teeth, small ivory figures, wooden and bamboo pieces, dice of various shapes made of pottery, bone, ivory or wood, and the seeds of the plum and peach.

Ball games similar to our sports of soccer and lacrosse, and other games of skill played with darts and arrows, were also favorites. Racing and wrestling were enjoyed, but were usually engaged in when there were group gatherings, rather than in the everyday program of the men.

The ghost gamble was a game played after the death of a person to determine who would gain his goods. One contestant played the part of the ghost and gambled against all the rest. The gambling pieces were made of the wild plum stone. There were six of these in a set. Pieces were marked on both sides and were in a series of patterns. Plum or peach seeds were used by many tribes as dice, with anything from a pair to eight dice in the set. They were carved and colored according to the different tribes. Some played the game from baskets, and some by shaking in the hand.

Small bone dice have been found in a number of graves in Arizona, with different characters on each. They had a small bone or wooden cup accompanying them, and the game was no doubt similar to our modern dice games. Another set of bone dice was a different color on each side, with each player using a different color. These dice were thrown from a basket. Pottery dice were also used in many tribes. These pieces were round and had a varying number of spots.

A game was played with small ivory figures by tossing up the pieces from a basket. Those figures that face the player in falling are his, and those falling upright counted double. Each player had one toss of the basket.

Chair shaped ivory dice with different characters on all sides were also used. Each player named a character and played by tossing his lucky one up.

Stick dice were used in a game for two players. They tossed to get the dice in holes measuring 10 feet apart, and the player who succeeded in getting the greatest number in the hole with the marked side up scored the most points in a throw.

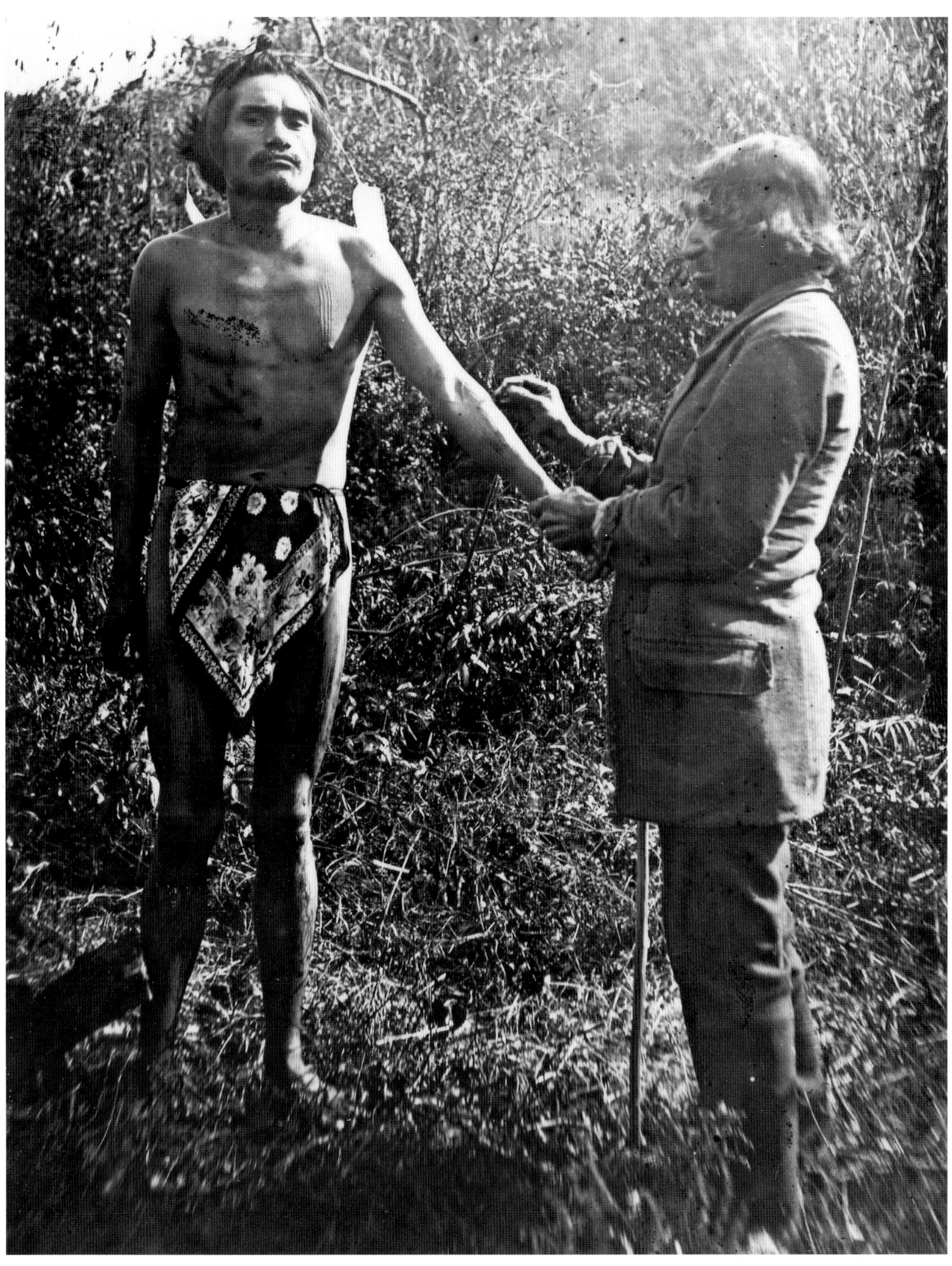

Above: This rare 1888 photograph shows a Cherokee ball player in North Carolina as he prepares for a game.

FIGURE 19.1: NATIVE AMERICAN GAMES

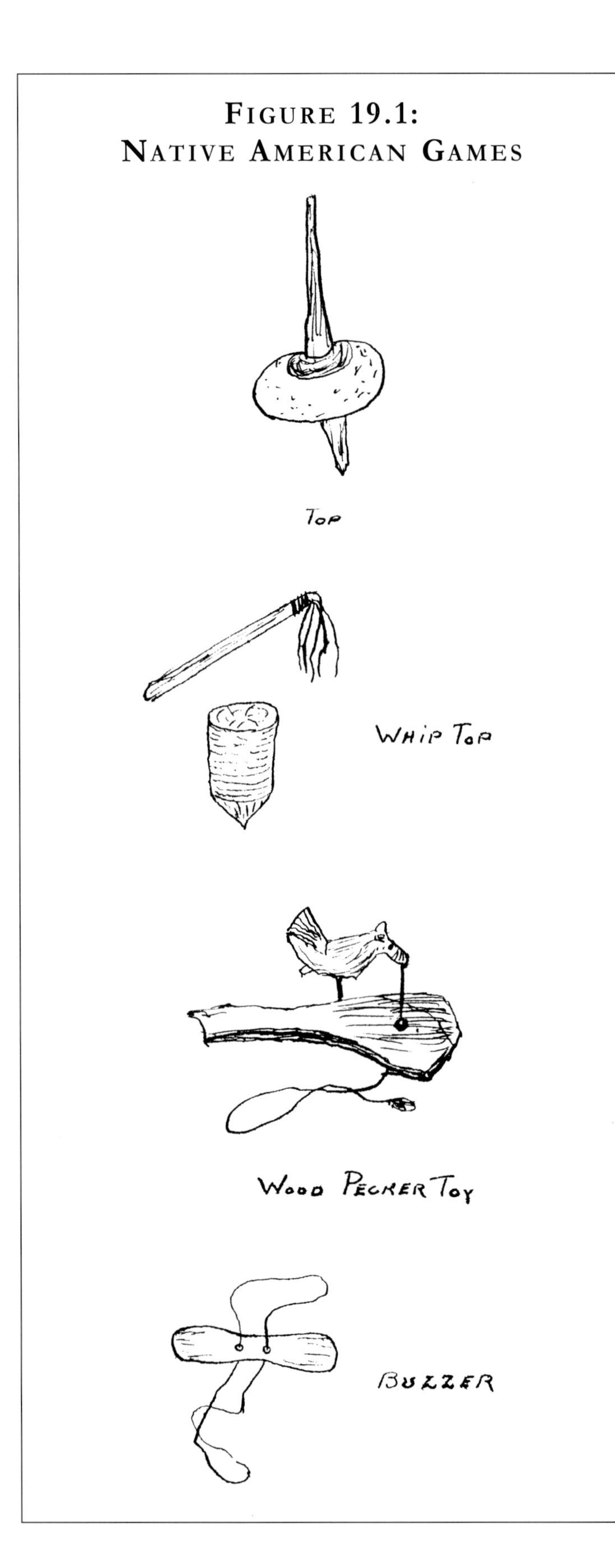

Whip tops were never thrown, but rather kept in motion by whipping with a top whip made by tying thongs to a stick. The whip top game was usually played on the ice. In the spring, all tops were thrown in the water as the ice broke up.

Other games were also played in this manner. There is a Blackfeet nursery tale saying that playing winter games in the summer made the hair grow all over the body, where it would have to be pulled out.

Top spinning was played by children of all tribes. In one game played with the top, the spinner had to run to a designated spot and return, or run through the hut and back; he who succeeded was the winner.

Beaver teeth were used in many games. A guessing game was played with just two of the teeth, which had different markings. They guessed as to which hand held which tooth.

In "smetale," four beaver teeth were used, two marked with dots (women) and two with lines (men). They were then thrown as dice. If all faces were up, it was two points. If two faces were up and two down, it was one point. If they came up blank, the count was nothing and the next player tried.

The women also played a game with beaver teeth, but their method of counting was quite a bit more intricate. Each combination was a different value. In their game, one of the teeth had a string wound about the center, which added to the play and made a difference in the count.

The cup game was played by many of the desert tribes. The wooden cups were hollowed out; a small object, such as a kernel of corn, a mesquite seed or a bean, was hidden under one of the cups. The opponent guessed which cup it was under.

The snow snake game was played in the winter on the snow by both men and boys. Each player made wooden snow snakes from a slender shaft five or six feet long. These were then well polished and decorated according to individual taste. The object of the play in this game was to see who could propel his snake the farthest by grasping it by the tail and thrusting it forward. Whomever sent his snake the farthest in a given number of plays won.

Some of the tribes played a game of football. The ball itself was a leather ball stuffed with deer hair. The players were in pairs, two on each side, and two balls were used. The balls were driven back and forth to goal lines, and those who had the least number of misses in a given number of passes were the winners.

In the ball and racket games the company was usually divided into two groups. Poles were erected a mile apart. Several balls were used, and all the players had rackets and started from the center of this mile distance. The object of the game was to drive the balls to the opponent's goalpost. This game was played from Florida to the Northwest. No doubt each tribe had variations as to rules and form of racquet and ball used.

Lacrosse was played by many of the Indians of the northern Plains and Great Lakes region, and seemed to have originated among them. They had two different ways of playing this game.

The first way used a curved stick with a net attached, similar to a racket. In this game, a ball was used. In the other game, they used only a curved stick

FIGURE 19.2: EQUIPMENT FOR TEAM SPORTS

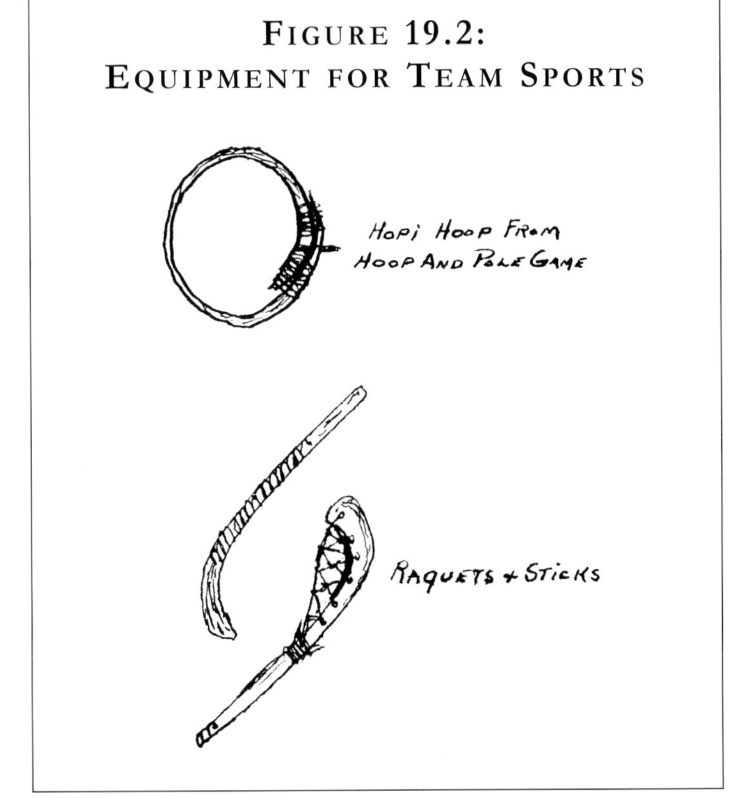

Above: Gaming pieces included chips and dice from non-native sources (25-27), Pima stick dice (28-29) and Makah Beaver teeth dice (33).

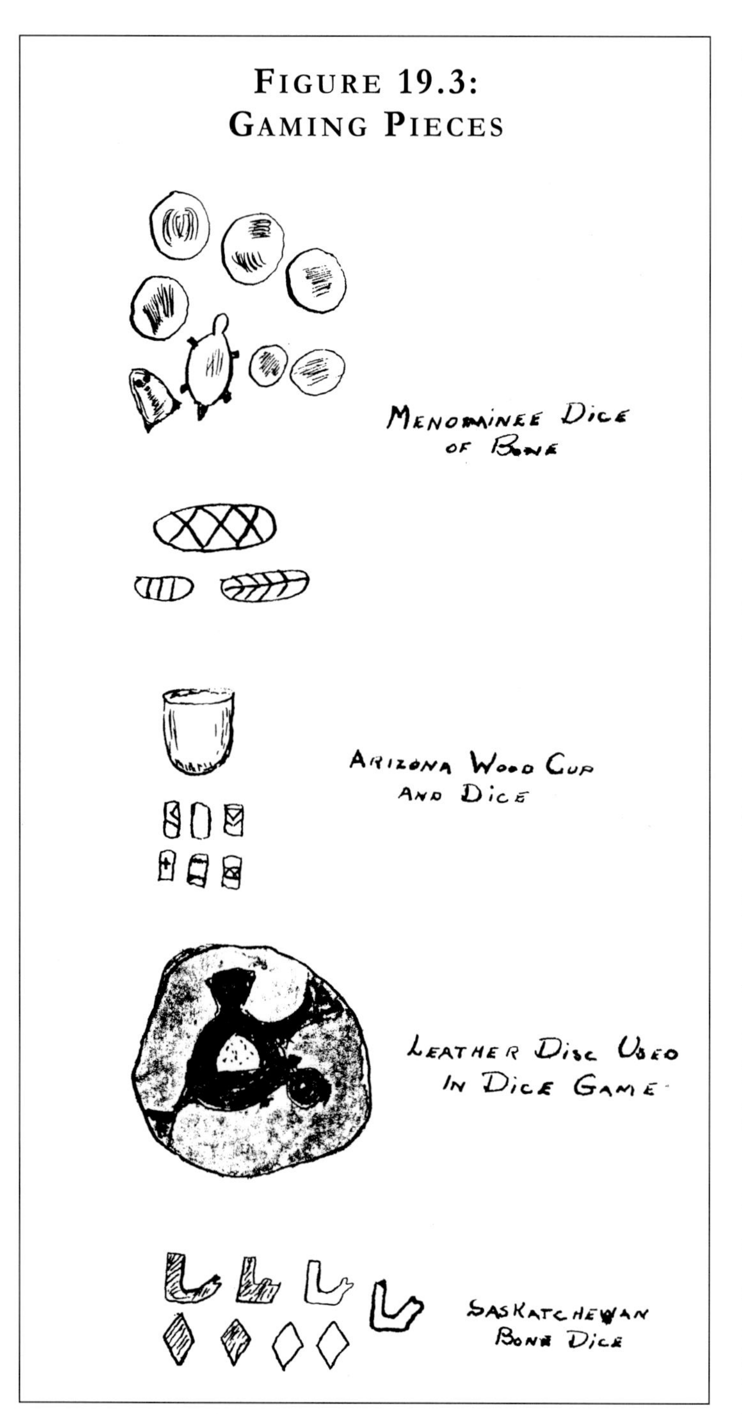

FIGURE 19.3: GAMING PIECES

and played with stones or wooden pegs. In either case, it was the object of both games to drive the object over the opponent's goal line.

A woman's game, called "uhpuhsekuhwon," was played with double balls having a neck between them; the players had poles about six feet long. The object was to throw the balls with the sticks, but the hands must never touch the balls. The object was to get them to the opponent's goal line.

In ho'kiamonne, the Indians used a ball of closely wound yucca ribbons. Each player had a dart made of a hard wooden peg, which was placed in the end of a corncob. From the other end projected two hawk feathers. The players threw it, hitting the moving ball. If they both hit, it was a tie and they started again.

A game which the men and women both played in the evening was the ring and pin game. A peg was set in the ground a foot high. Around this a circle was inscribed at a distance of some four yards, and the players sat around the circle. A woven grass ring about six inches in diameter was used to throw over the peg. Near the foot of the stake the beginner placed some article of value and the players in turn tried for this. He who succeeded took the article and placed another of a different kind. In this way a sort of trading went on. Each player had but one trial.

"Si'kon-ya'mune-ti'kwane" was played for the Rain God in order to exhort him to bring rain. A long, slender reed, with the lightning symbol in black, and a yucca fiber ring were used. The women used these sticks to propel the ring a distance against 10 others, who were kicking a small stick similarly painted. The women seldom won. Chukee stones or discoidal stones were used in games in various ways. In one form of playing, a smooth place was prepared, where the stones were shuffled with a forked stick, much like the game of shuffleboard. They were rolled as in bowling, and also were pitched as in horseshoes.

The discoidal stone lent itself to many purposes and there has been much debate as to its use. It could have been used as a receptacle for preparing paints or herbs by the medicine man; some of the stones show evidence of such use. They also would have served as game stones for both pitching and rolling. In some burials they have been found in a singular position next to all skeletons; and they have also been found in the mounds and refuse heaps where they were placed haphazardly.

Stilts were used by children in many tribes. Among the Mayans there was a high-stilt dance. This was in honor of the bird deity Troano Codex. The Wichita called stilts "hak-i-avits," or walking wood. The throwing of darts through a round hoop was a game of adults and children of all tribes and localities.

Our jack straw game is the modernized splint game of the Eskimo children. They used 50 small sticks, all the size of a match stem, and the playing ceased when one dropped or moved another stick. The fingers were the method of picking up the sticks, although in later times they made hooks of ivory.

When gambling pieces were made of bone, the American Indian preferred the leg bone of the wildcat or the mountain lion. These two animals were the cunning ones. Gambling pieces made from their bones would surely impart some of the animal's deftness to his game. They were both a hard, smooth bone and took a good polish. Players played a guessing game using two bones. One had a cord run through lengthwise and then wound several times around the center. The object was to guess in which hand the bone with wrapping was. In this, as in the majority of the other games, the players had a pile of counting sticks to keep score.

The Shoshone used the vertebrae of the fish as gambling pieces. They worked the sides of the pieces like filigree, and the surface of each piece had a different number of holes pierced through.

FIGURE 19.4: BALL GAME EQUIPMENT

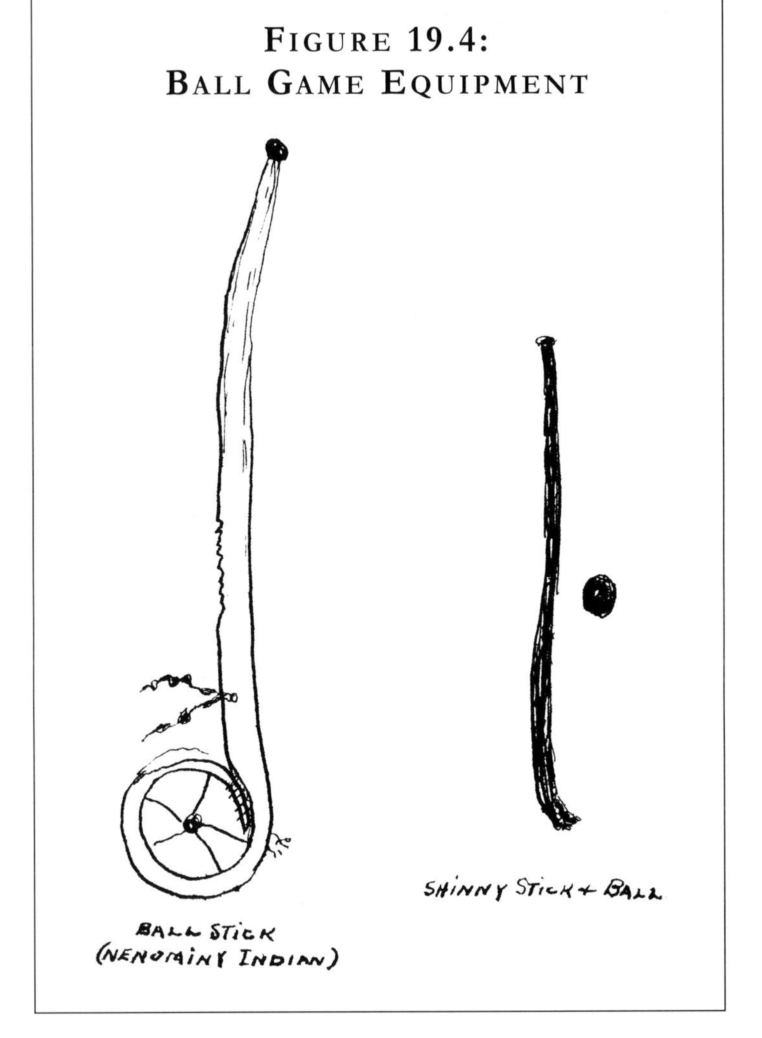

Above: A group of Creek men playing a ball game, as photographed in Oklahoma in 1938.

FIGURE 19.5: GHOST GAME PIECES

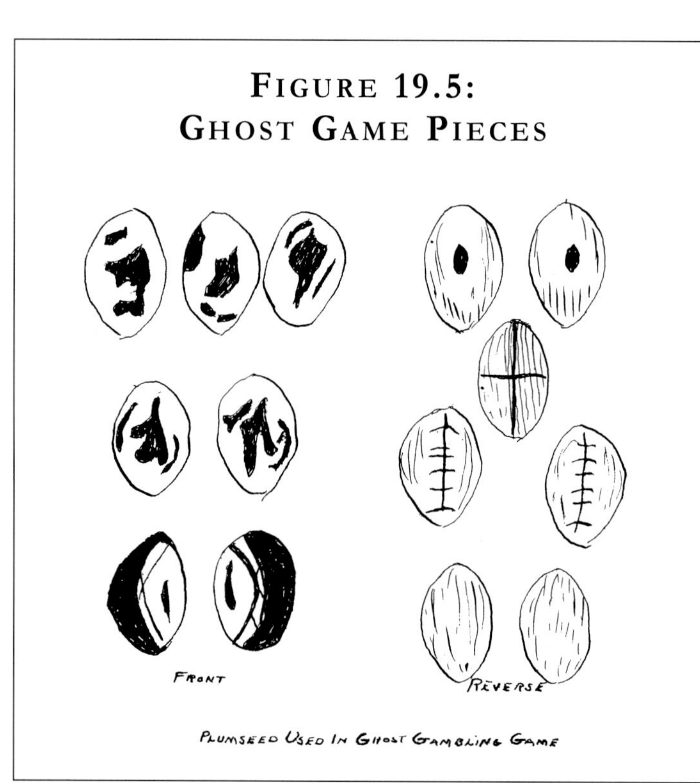

FIGURE 19.6: SPORTING EQUIPMENT

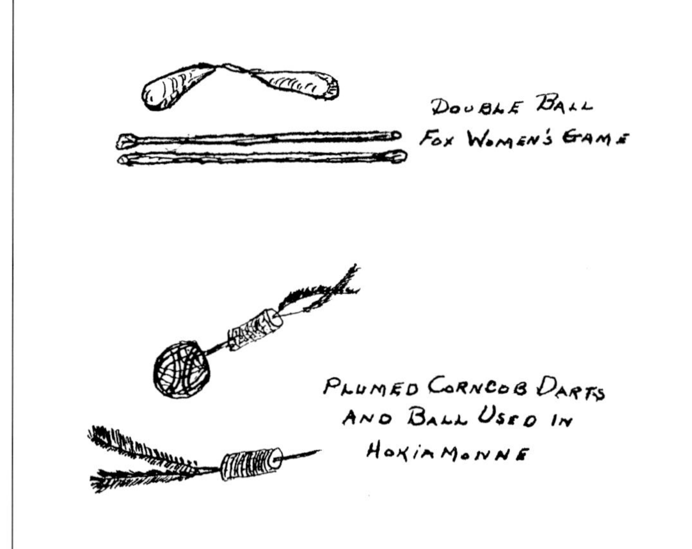

THE RECORDING OF TIME

Time was not reckoned as years among the American Indians but by winters, and was known in recording as Winter Counts. Months were calculated by the cycle of the moon, and other terminology applied to other blocks of time. Short journeys were often referred to as so many "sleeps" away, with a sleep being an overnight encampment, and hence the number of sleeps would be equal to the number of 24-hour days. The American Indian never referred to time as days or by calendar time as we do. They recorded some important event annually on the skin of buffalo or elk, with each drawing representing a year.

The seasons were referred to as they revolved around their daily life — winter was known as "the month of cold," spring as "rain" or "first growth of grass," summer as "heat" or "wild fruits," fall as "acorn and nuts," late fall as "bear and hunting." Their calendar record, the Winter Count, was kept by the chief and carried on by his son or successor. In some instances as many as 125 years were shown on a single skin.

The following dates were shown on the Kiowa calendar pictured herein for the years 1833 to1892:

- In an encounter with Americans, a quantity of silver coins were captured and Black Wolf was killed.
- Winter 1833-1834, the stars fell.
- Winter 1837, the Cheyenne Massacre.
- Winter 1840, the smallpox epidemic.
- The year 1848, initiation of Sun Dance.
- The year 1849, cholera.
- The year 1850, dance over slain Pawnee.
- Winter 1852, women frozen.
- The year 1854, Black Horse killed.
- The year 1856, Prickly Pear Sun Dance.
- Winter 1858, horses stolen.
- The year 1859, Cedar Bluff Sun Dance.
- Winter 1867, Medicine Lodge Treaty.
- The year 1868, Ute fight.
- The year 1871, Konpate killed by soldiers.
- Winter 1873, Pueblo visit.
- The year 1877, camp at Signal Mountain.
- The year 1879, Horse Eating Sun Dance.
- Winter 1880, no dance, Pabote died.

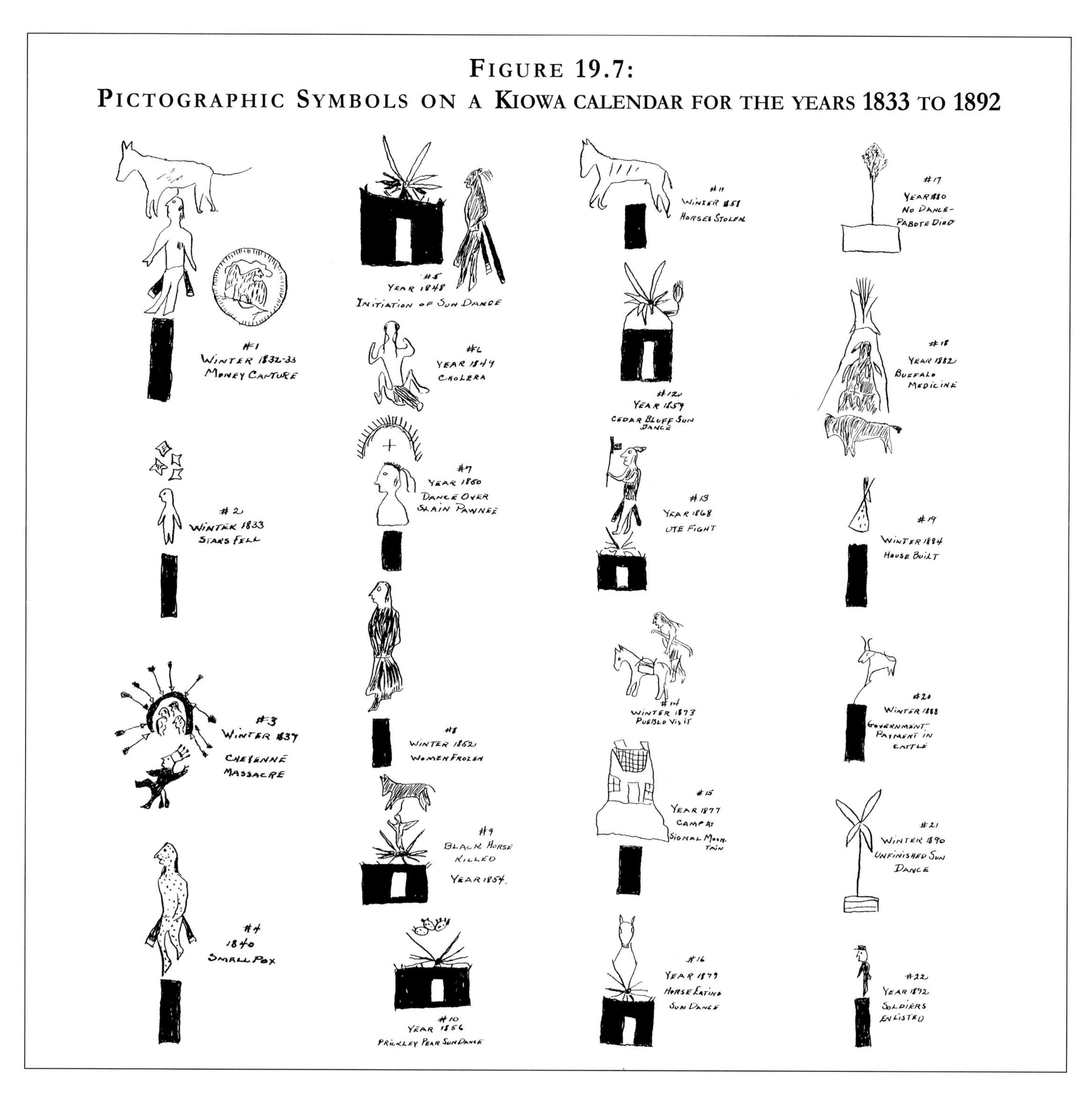

FIGURE 19.7:
PICTOGRAPHIC SYMBOLS ON A KIOWA CALENDAR FOR THE YEARS 1833 TO 1892

- Winter 1882, Buffalo medicine, Patsogate died.
- Winter 1884, houses built, Sioux dance, children taken.
- Winter 1886, camp burned.
- Winter 1888, government payment in cattle.
- The year 1890, unfinished Sun Dance.
- Winter 1892, soldiers enlisted.

The first figure was recorded in the center of the skin and each succeeding figure was placed to form a circle around the skin and outward — each circle larger than the one preceding it, always in a clockwise rotation.

Left: A group of Apache men playing the hoop and pole game at San Carlos, Arizona in 1899.

CHAPTER 20

PICTOGRAPHS AND PETROGLYPHS

This chapter certainly leads one back to the earliest of Stone Age art, when man attempted to express his thoughts in a form that all might see. Some markings were colored, and no doubt the various combinations of colors conveyed a meaning of their own. These records are found on the faces of cliffs, in caves, on boulders, shells, wood, slate and all the materials they had, and in all of the countries of the world.

The pictograph and petroglyph of the American Indian was seldom, if ever, cryptographic, though often conventional, and at times preplanned, as their signals were. All were intended to be understood as written for actual daily use, free from the superstition of remote antiquity.

Some characters or symbols which the American Indian used on the surface of the rocks were also used in making treaties, sending messages and similar purposes. In some cases these were recorded on wood skins and bark. These writings were also used for notices of departure, warnings, leaving records for others to follow, etc.

There were three main types of recording, according to the substances on which they were written: on the human body; on natural objects, such as rocks or trees; or on manufactured objects, such as pottery and baskets. Markings on the human body were painted, tattooed and scarified. The latter left permanent scars.

Bones, stone surfaces or trees were the natural objects on which many records were found. The Alaskans were wont to use ivory and bone a great deal, principally the walrus tusk and the shoulder blade or larger animal bones. The Indians were adept in the use of skins for their character writing. The best specimens of work done on skins were the Winter Counts or calendars. Treaties, alliances and all such documents pertaining to Indian life were written on skins.

Some of the basket makers worked feathers into the baskets in order to make characters, and others did the same with quills. Gourds and shells were used as recipients of such writing in some localities. The art of depicting characters on shells was more highly developed in the South.

Beadwork of characters on skin and cloth should also be included in this group. "Powhatan's Mantle" was one of the best known works of this type. The Navajo sand paintings are another type of character work done with natural objects. These pictures were believed to have been spiritually shadowed or breathed upon by the gods or animals they represented. Consequently, they had to be released as soon as the ceremony was over, so that they might return to the spirit land.

The effigy mounds of the Ohio Valley were another source of recording. So much has been written of

Above: These petroglyphs photographed by Johnston in the Mojave Desert include a thunderbird and a complex maze-like structure.

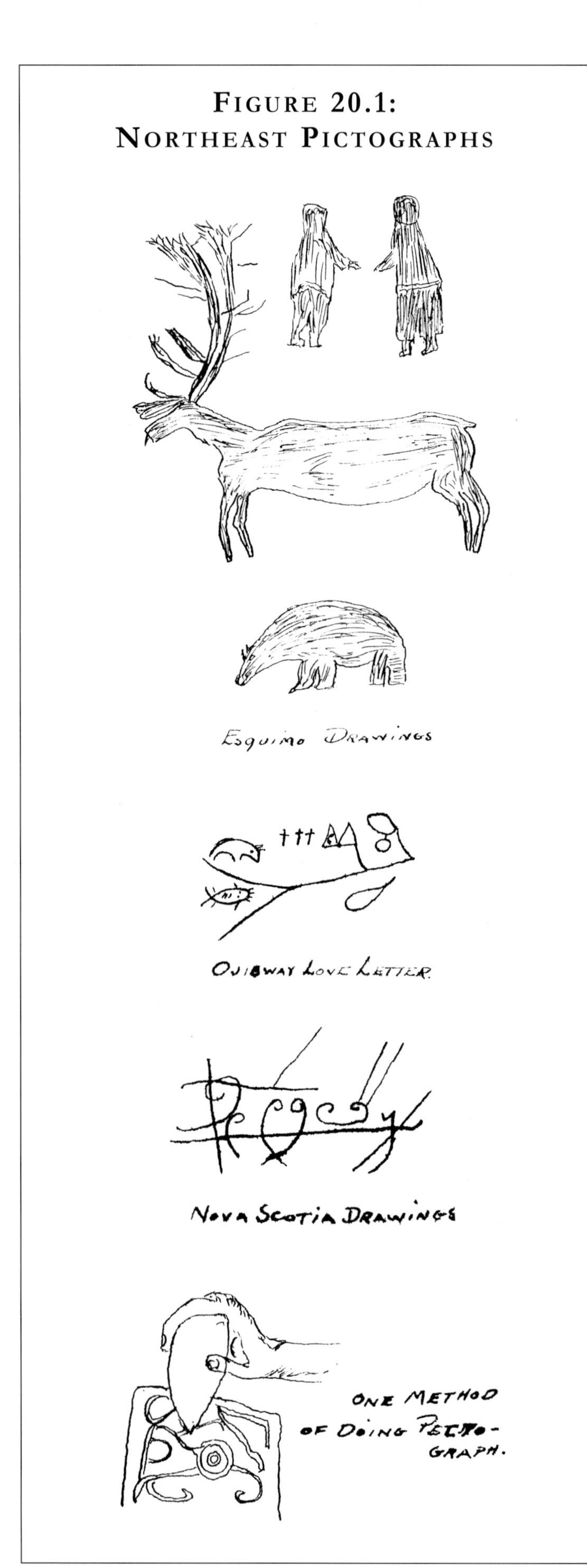

Figure 20.1: Northeast Pictographs

them that there is no need to discuss them further; however, some of the later figures were more baffling. The recent find of outlined figures on the California-Arizona border, and the turtle outline discovery in one of the Dakotas (with the group of circular mounds around it), were two of the best known of the later group.

The Indians of the Great Lakes district mined copper, upon which they did most remarkable character work. One of these tablets, which had been kept by an old Ojibway and which was viewed in 1842, showed the history of his family. It indicated that there had been eight generations of this group. The coming of the white man was in the latter part of the fifth generation. As the old Ojibway stated, his people lived many "moons," and without doubt the tablet is very old.

The Ojibway love letter (figure 20.1) is translated thus: The girl of the Bear Totem live with three girls who are Christians, as denoted by the crosses, and their lodges are on a well-traveled path near a lake. The lodge with the character designates the lodge he is to visit. The recipient is of the Mud Puppy Totem, and the large loops designate the lakes near which he lives.

The Ojibway messenger sends invitations, each for some different person or persons, such as an old man, an old woman, a warrior and a child. Upon arriving at the invited lodge the messenger sticks are returned. If for some reason the invited does not come at the time designated, he must later on return the stick with a suitable answer.

The living tree was used to a great extent by all tribes as a place to leave trail markings and for various other purposes.

The totem poles of certain Northwestern tribes offered a most remarkable display of wood carving. These tribes carved whole scenes on the planks of their lodge fronts; even their pipe stems and bowls had certain characters marked thereon with their various significance. In the bark writing, the surface was scratched and then greased; charcoal was rubbed into the scratch, thus leaving a permanent mark.

Wampum was used for invitations, for the making of treaty belts, for the binding of alliances and all such agreements. The keeper of the wampum, a person of note in the tribe, brought the wampum out yearly and read to the people the messages it contained so that all

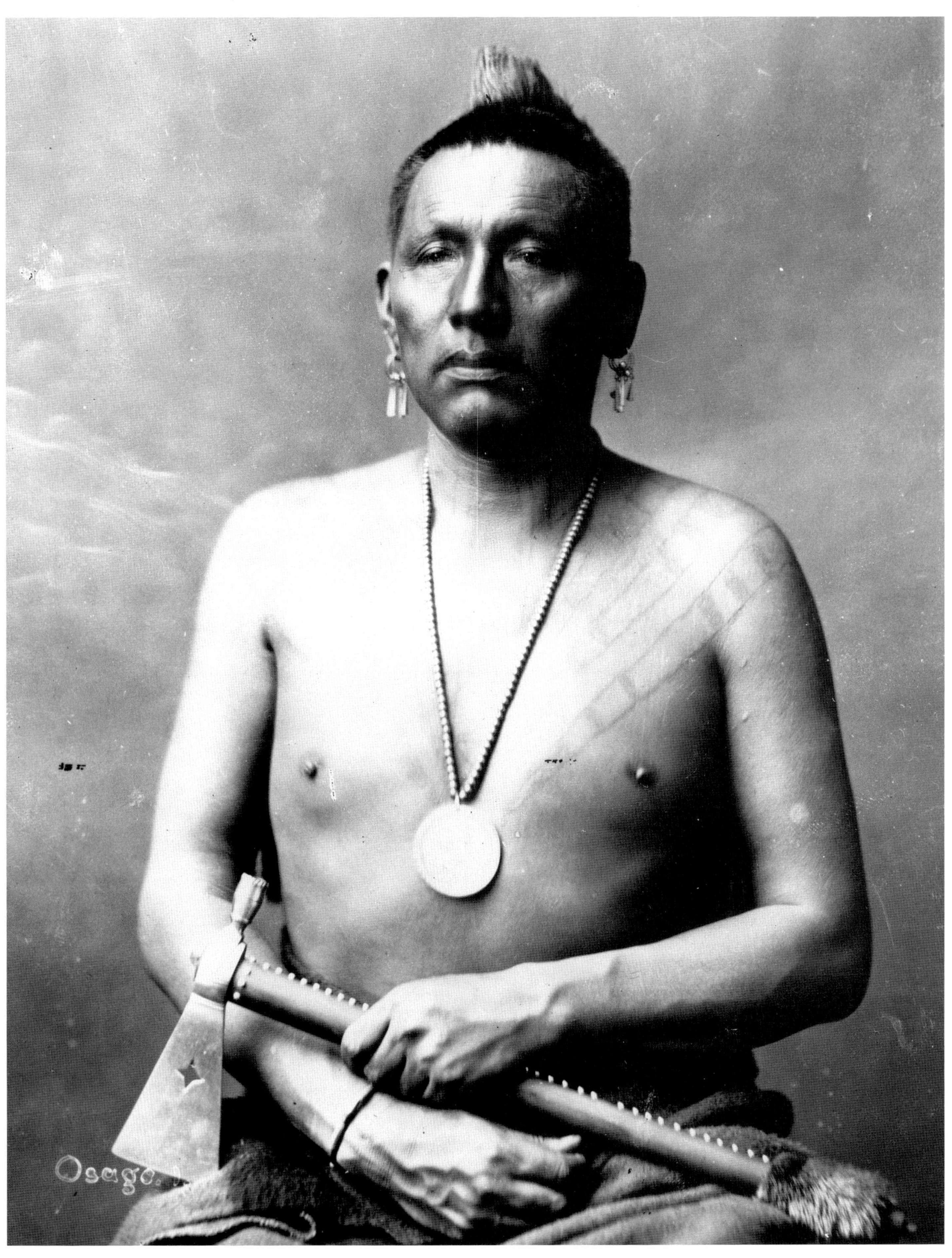

Above: Pathinonpazhi, an Osage leader with tattoos. Johnston considered tattoos as a form of pictograph.

FIGURE 20.2: PIASA AND NEW YORK PETROGLYPHS

Piasa Petrograph (Illinois)

New York State

might be kept posted and have a clear understanding of the obligations or demands made.

The order of songs was usually kept on bark rolls among the Eastern Indians, and these were viewed on certain occasions to refresh the memory.

The Piasa Pictograph (figure 20.2) was first noted in 1675 by Marquette near Alton, Illinois. Since that time, this has been destroyed. In the beginning, it had two similar figures, but erosion had destroyed a great part before the bluff was blasted away. One early account was as follows: On the flat surface of the rock, some fifty feet above the base, were characters in red, black and green; they were as large as a calf, with horns like a deer, red eyes, the beard of a tiger and a frightful countenance; a face something like a man but the body covered with scales; and a tail so long it passed completely over the body and back between the legs and ended like that of a fish. The name "Piasa" is Indian and was translated "the bird that devours men." The above description was one of the earliest taken down, dating back to 1839. At that time one of the figures had eroded away.

The New York State Petroglyph (Figure 20.2) was done after the coming of the settlers. It is believed this work was done between 1609 and 1614. The work of this petroglyph showed the use of metal tools in making it. It was done on the bank of the Hudson River, above the Highlands, probably by the Waranawankongs. The footprints of man, buffalo, turkey and bear were clearly shown, as were many other characters. Some petroglyphs, of course, were never finished. For example, petroglyphs found in Ohio feature parts that had just begun to be outlined. These unfinished parts appear to represent turtle, bird and man.

Declarations of war were made by depositing pictographs on some material near the enemy's village so that they might see them. The sending of bundles of arrows and other methods were also used, and the peace negotiations were carried on in a similar manner.

The third main class of substances on which pictographs were made was the artificial objects. Under this heading comes pottery, on which there was no limit to the characters and designs, and basketry, similar to pottery in that one could go on indefinitely in the weaving of fabrics, each piece telling its own story.

Above: A petroglyph showing a lake, a stream and birds. Photographed in the Mojave Desert by Johnston.

Above: A petroglyph interpreted by Johnston as depicting the goddess of the hunt.

FIGURE 20.3: REGIONAL PETROGLYPHS

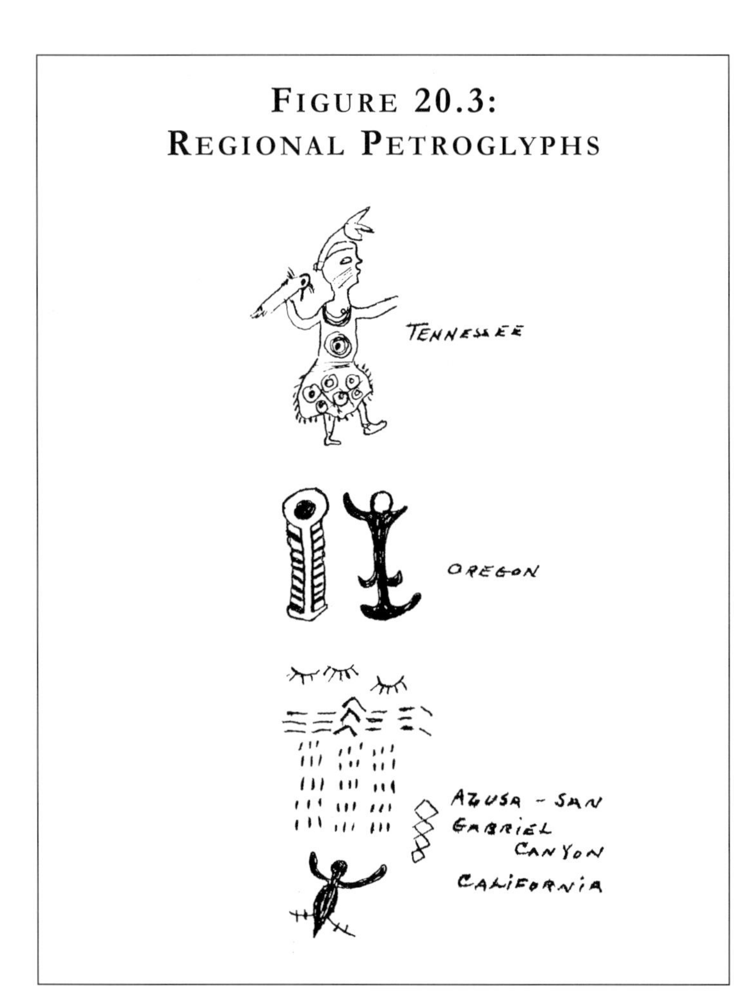

Instruments used in making pictographs, and in their coloring were varied. On skins the Indians used either shell or bone to outline their work, and in painting them they used a wooden stick, the end of which had been chewed to a fiber-like tip. This was used as a brush to apply their pigments, which were mostly made of colored earth or roots and the bark of trees. Work on bark was done usually with a sharp bone. The rock writing depended on the hardness of the stone.

In Nova Scotia (see figure 20.1), the inscriptions on the slate cliffs were no doubt made by flint, as the lines were thin and sharp.

On some of the flat surfaces the writing appears to have been accomplished by rubbing with a stick and using sand as an abrasive. Most of the recording was done either by pecking with a stone hammer or using a flint pick and striking with a stone hammer.

The greater part of the rock writing was uncolored, although some was done in many colors. In some cases it is no doubt true that time has worn away the color. From examinations of the work and tests made of pigments and their penetrating effects, the results lead us to

Above: A petroglyph showing a hunter shooting an arrow at an antelope. The bent arrow always indicated a successful kill.

Above: A detail of the view seen below, showing two hunters about to shoot their arrows into a herd of antelope.

Above: A petroglyph depicting a herd of antelope, one of whom has died, followed by deer. Photographed by Johnston.

FIGURE 20.4:
AN OJIBWAY SONG RECORDED ON BARK:

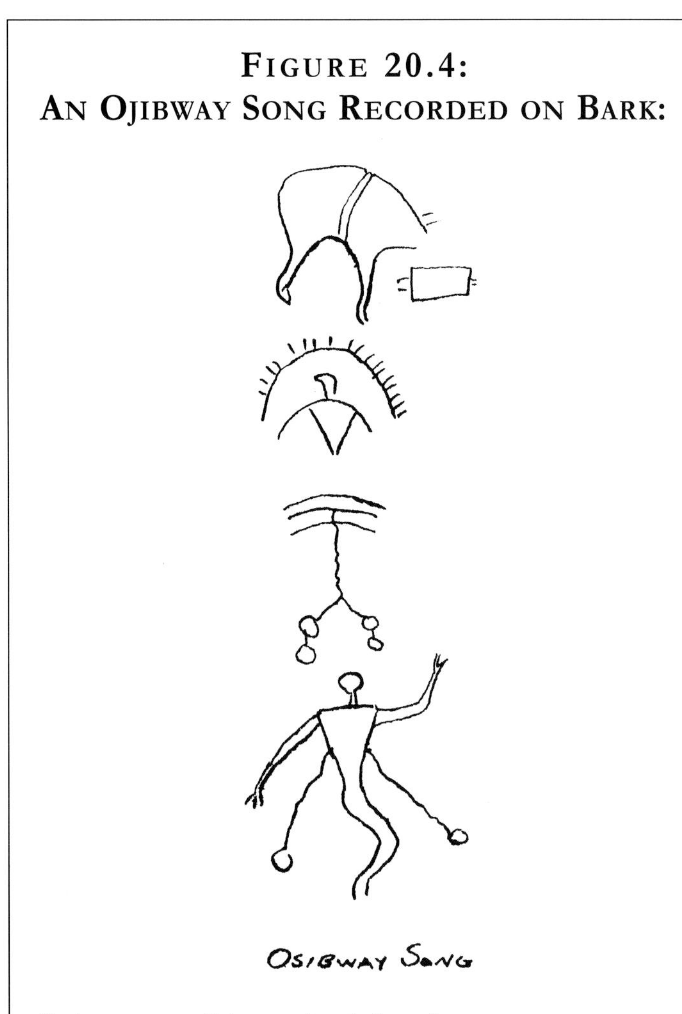

I give you medicine and a lodge also.
(The midge, as the impersonator of Makwa'Man'ido, is empowered to offer this privilege to the candidate.)

I am flying to my lodge.
(Thunderbird deity flying to the Man'idos abode.)

The spirit has dropped medicine from the sky where we can get it.
(The line from the sky diverging to various points indicates the sacred objects fall in scattered places.)

I have the medicine in my heart.
(The singer's heart is filled with knowledge related to sacred objects from the Earth.)

believe that the majority of the uncolored writings were always thus.

Prophecies were also sketched on the side of tepees and all belongings. Other petroglyphs were found on the walls of the inner chamber at Hanlipinkia, near Zuni, which was one of the shrines of the diminutive gods of war long before the coming of the Spanish.

SIGNS AND MARKINGS

When traveling in the woods, the American Indians were wont to use whatever means were at hand to leave suitable messages for those who followed. For example, a sketch could signify "I have gone east as the direction of the stick is pointing"; or "I have not gone far." Another stick could be stuck in the ground across from the former and close to the ground. The number of days of the journey was signified by the number of sticks across from the first. To smoke a piece of bark and leave it on the trail meant "I am sick."

The sun was shown in as many different signs as any one universal thing. No doubt the similarity of the symbols would allow another to read the meaning.

The cloud sign was also significant. All representations had the same general outline. The universal meaning of rain was indicated by lines dropping from the bottom of the sign. Likewise in sign language, to hold the hands with fingers spread apart and pointing down meant rain.

One Apache pictograph meant a party with five pack mules had passed through the country and were eleven days in crossing by the main sun and the successive smaller ones. Connecting lines represented the number of nights.

The signs for lightning were somewhat varied. The serpent's head was often connected with lightning; therefore the combination was a most natural one.

One sketch indicated a warrior returning. He had taken one scalp, while the head sketch was the "Own Marking" of a certain Dakota. The depiction of four plain pipes meant he had led four war parties.

A warrior standing with arms up and spread, with his bow and arrow on the ground, was a sign of peace.

Above: A petroglyph depicting mountain lions chasing down a herd of antelope. Photographed in the field by Franklin Johnston.

Above: A petroglyphic representation of a man and a pair of antelope caught in a rainstorm. Photographed by Johnston.

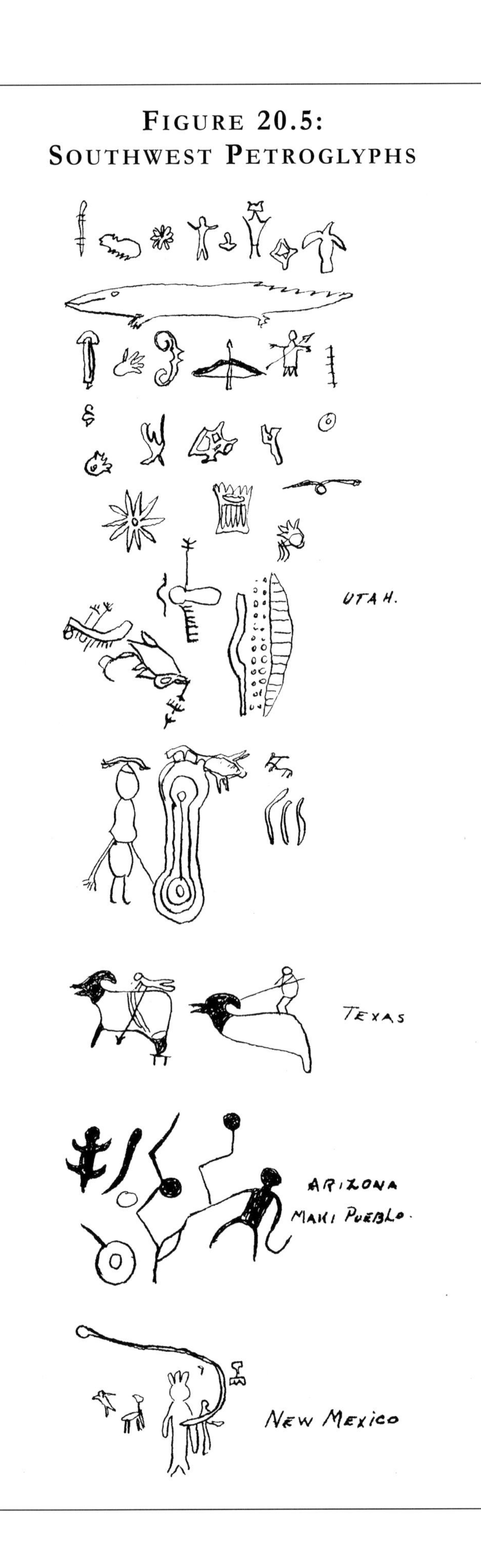

FIGURE 20.5: SOUTHWEST PETROGLYPHS

A warrior with hands up and two fingers pointing meant "Who are you?" The Abnaki Indians used a sign which meant, "I am going hunting, will be gone all winter."

Communication was often accomplished by smoke signals. A fire was kindled and then, as the smoke started to rise, a blanket was thrown over it and then lifted, thus allowing the smoke to come up at intervals in clouds. Each group of clouds and their spacing meant different things. Signal fires were used at night and the drum was also used. The rapidity with which messages traveled is unbelievable. The Pony Express riders were no match with them for dispatching news.

Two methods of keeping records of time were to cut notches in sticks, and to tie knots in a cord. Such notches or knots might be a day, a week or a year, according to the keeper of the record.

A SIGN LANGUAGE ALLEGORY

Franklin Johnston was a gifted and legendary storyteller, but, of course, his stories were always told to instruct, enlighten or explain. The following is a story which Johnston used in explaining the importance of correctly interpreting pictographs and sign language. His admonition upon telling this story was always: "Be careful in reading and interpreting sign language at all times."

King James I, desiring to play a trick upon a Spanish ambassador of great erudition and who had a determined bent for sign language, informed the gentleman that there was a distinguished professor of science in Aberdeen. The ambassador went to Aberdeen, preceded by a letter from the King, with instructions to make the best of him. In the town lived Gregory, a butcher blind in one eye, and a fellow of wit and drollery.

Gregory was to play the part of the learned professor; having been warned not to speak a word, he was gowned and wigged, and in general placed in a position to play the part. When the ambassador was shown in, they were left alone together. When the ambassador left he was greatly pleased with the experiment, and stated that his theory had been demonstrated perfectly.

Above: Petroglyphs depicting an owl, a male hunter and a deer with an arrow through his body. Photographed by Johnston.

Above: Petroglyphs showing a coyote, a coiled snake and a warrior in buffalo dance regalia. Photographed by Johnston.

FIGURE 20.6: THUNDERBIRD REPRESENTATIONS

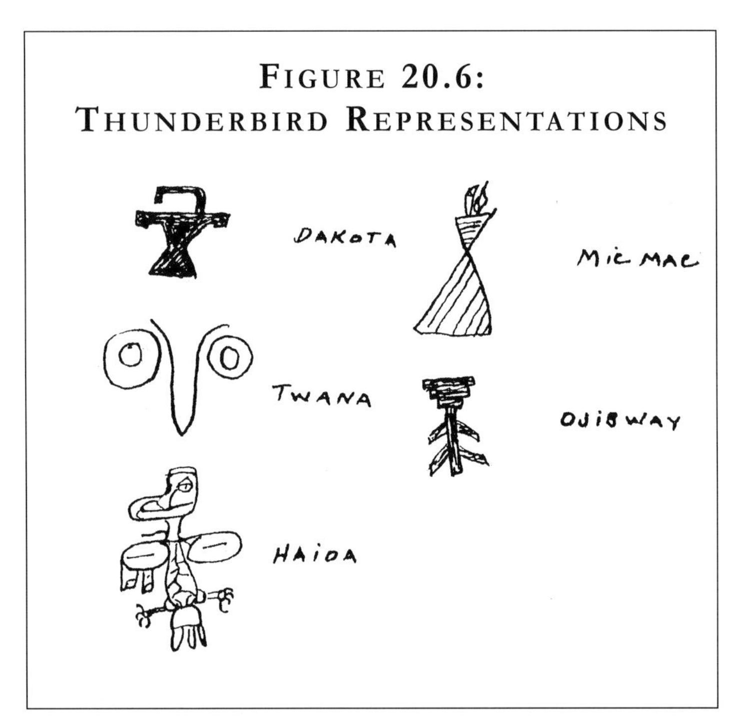

He said: "When I entered the room I raised one finger to signify one God; he replied by raising two fingers to signify that this being rules two worlds, the material and the spiritual. Then I raised three fingers to say there are three persons in the Godhead; he closed his fingers, evidently to say these three are one."

After this explanation, the butcher was sent for and asked for his version of what took place.

He was very angry and said: "When the crazy man entered the room he raised one finger, as much as to say I had only one eye; I raised two fingers to signify that I could see as well with one eye as he could with his two. When he raised three fingers, as much as to say there were three eyes between us, I doubled up my fist, and if he had not left at that time I would have knocked him out of the room."

Above: Complex petroglyphs depicting deities, including a sun deity (*bottom*), a rain cloud (*upper right*) and possibly shaman's bags.

Above: A petroglyph interpreted by Johnston as portraying a person praying or beseeching a deity.

Above: A petroglyph depicting three bodies prepared for burial. Their resting place may be nearby. Photographed by Johnston.

Above: Outline petroglyphs in the form of lizards and coyotes. Photographed in the Mojave Desert by Franklin Johnston.

Above: Among these petroglyphs is one depicting a shore bird, possibly a curlew, eating a frog. The frog image was associated with rain.

Above: The petroglyph that seems to depict a person holding a barbell may actually have been a reference to a chain of lakes.

Above: Many petroglyph sites show evidence of having been reworked by Native Americans. In later years, vandalism also occurred.

Chapter 21

Cave Dwellers and Mound Builders

Cave Dwellings

The cave dwellings of America have not been as rich in archeological finds as has been hoped for; the artifacts found being meager in comparison with those in the caves of Europe, which reveal the early life there. For archeological work, the best early cave finds in America have been made in the Ozark regions. The artifacts from the caves in this section are not dissimilar to those from the burials and camp sites of other parts of the country.

Pipes, bone and antler objects, grinding stones and mortars have all been found. Pottery, next to flint, was the main item of construction in this district.

The specimens taken from one of the caves gives a fair representative list of the finds: 11 skulls of adults, ten partial skeletons (mostly children), six fragmentary skulls, 64 shell objects, 700 flint items, 90 axes, eight mortars, 15 pestles, rubbing stones and hammer stones, 413 worked objects of bone and antler, two clay pipes, some pottery fragments and a few miscellaneous objects. The layers of charcoal with the sediment and the refuse from the midden show a long occupation. Bones of many kinds of animals, some of early species, were also discovered in these shelters.

For a cave to have been used by primitive man it must have easy entrance, be dry, furnish suitable shelter from prevailing winds, and be near water. With these conditions filled, it might become a permanent abode, while the caves of other types were only used as temporary shelter or a place of retreat.

Mound Builders

The work of the Mound Builders of our country is of exceedingly great value to the antiquarian in illustrating the habits, customs and conditions of early Indian life. The grave tumuli surpasses all others in this respect. With the artifacts found we can rearrange their lives quite completely, although their origin still may remain unsolved. The enormous mounds erected by them equal the pyramids, and the variations in shape and form would lead one to suppose they were occupied by different clan groups. Each had a variation in worship and in culture.

The variation of artifacts in animal form, as well as the mound form, tell of a people who must have had a connection with distant countries. While some of the forms may have been taken from the isthmus country, some at least were foreign to the Americas.

Right: Arrow points unearthed at Cahokia Mounds, a sophisticated prehistoric site near Collinsville, Illinois. According to archaeological finds, the city of Cahokia was inhabited from about 700 AD to 1400. At its peak, from 1100 to 1200, the city covered nearly six square miles and had a population as great as 20,000.

Each student of their cultures has a different opinion as to their origin, though it seems quite probable that they were connected with the groups from Mexico and Central America at some early time. It should be clearly understood that it is not my intention to try and establish the fact that the Mound Builders were of a different race than the North American Indians.

Some of the artifacts found have created much speculation among archaeologists. The examination, identification and correct classification of these artifacts is of great importance. The conclusion reached with respect to some of the animal carvings is that some forms of animals are foreign to this country.

There have been pieces of fine cloth found which show they knew weaving; their earthen pots are as fine as any found in other Indian mounds; and their other artifacts show they had quite an advanced culture.

Bones of indigenous animals were found; they had been worked into daggers, awls and implements, and also worked into ornaments and beads. The teeth of many animals have been found, including the bear, wolf, panther, alligator and shark. Five types of shell from the Gulf of Mexico have been found, as have pearls that are not of fresh water origin. All of the above provides enough evidence that these people had been in direct contact with tribes further south and further west. The large mounds throughout the southern states were of a remnant of an earlier culture (and one that had a similar nature) that had once lived there.

The artifacts may be divided into three general divisions: those antiquities that are fixed or stationary and of

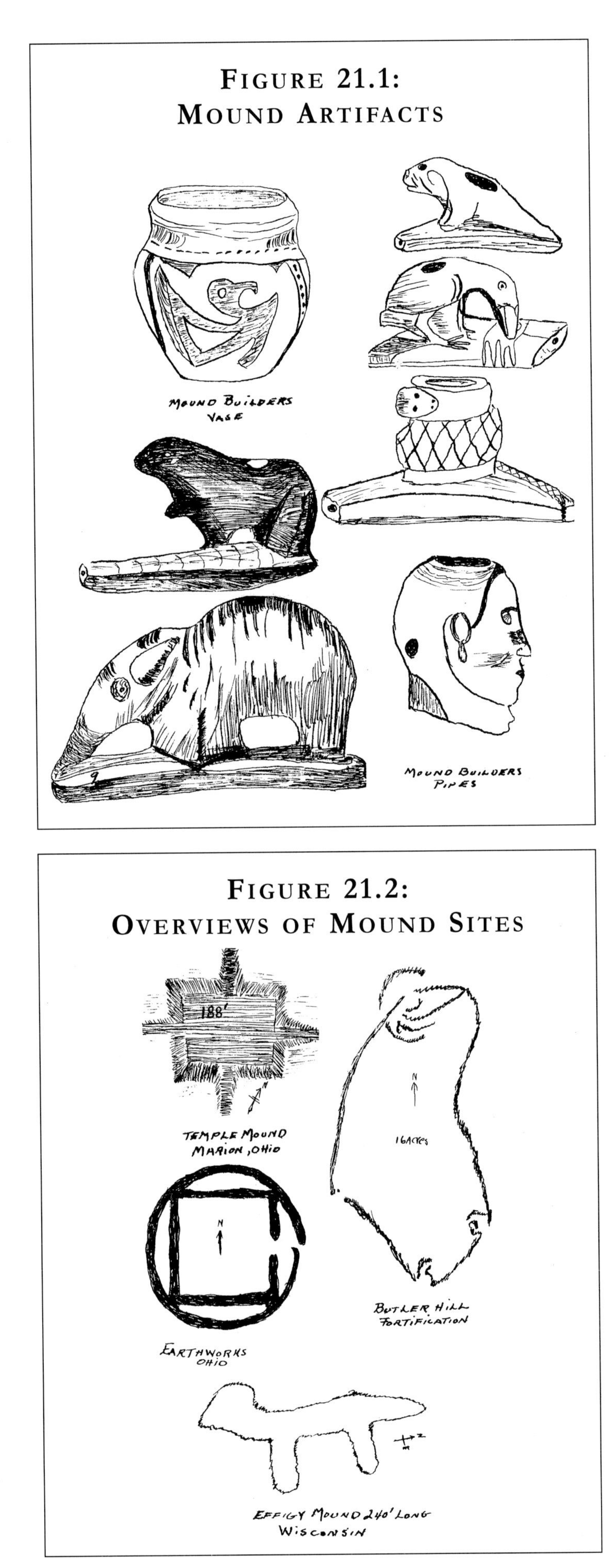

FIGURE 21.1: MOUND ARTIFACTS

FIGURE 21.2: OVERVIEWS OF MOUND SITES

necessity of a particular locality; those movable objects which have no necessary permanent connection with the place, such as animal and human remains; and the planographic objects, such as inscriptions, rock writings, etc., that may be either fixed or movable objects.

The earth works come under the first heading as do cave deposits and quarries, house sites and hut-rings, refuse heaps and evidences of cultivation and graves. In the last group were incised tablets large and small and petroglyphs and such (some of which cover enormous areas of rock, while others are on stone and easily transported). The mounds come under two classifications:. sacred enclosures and fortifications.

The use of copper was greater with the Mound Builders than any other group or division of Indians. They wrought this material into knives, axes, awls, spears,

arrow points and daggers, besides using it to make articles for personal adornment, gorgets, beads, bracelets and pendants. In fact, almost all the items that other tribes had made of shell and stone they also made of copper.

Some of these items have been found in conjunction with the mastodon and other early animals, though not enough to establish evidence that they date from that age. They may have been found thus only by chance. That the manufacturers of these copper implements had some general knowledge of hammering and working metal can be proven by the finely wrought items found. There has been considerable speculation as to whether they were hammered out entirely or cast and then hammered. Some evidence of molds have also been found in the excavations.

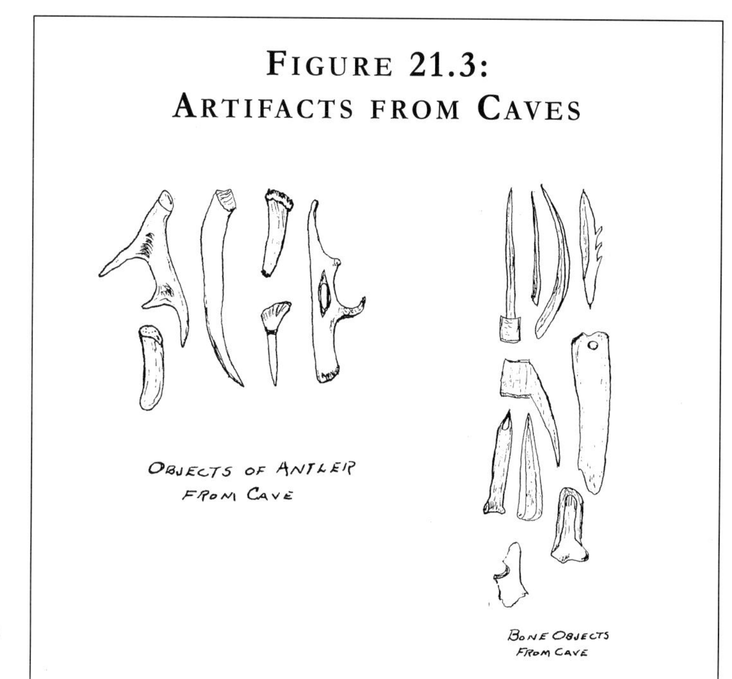

FIGURE 21.3: ARTIFACTS FROM CAVES

Above: Copper beads and utensils unearthed in a mound project in which Johnston was involved.

CHAPTER 22

BURIALS

Among the Indians there were almost as many different methods of disposing of the dead as there were tribes. The majority buried their dead in the ground, although this depended upon the conditions in the particular section of the country, such as the hardness of the ground and the facilities for digging. Some of the graves were lined with wood, while others were lined with slabs of stone; in some cases, regular shaped coffins were formed of both materials.

Cremation was practiced among many tribes as the principal means of disposal; and among tribes which usually buried their dead, cremation was also occasionally used. Often the closest members of the deceased's household would throw themselves upon his funeral pyre until they almost suffocated.

Occasionally there would be a human sacrifice as a part of the rites. If a slave was sacrificed, it was at the burial ceremony of the chief or some important man; the women were not considered worthy of such a sacrifice.

After the cremation, the ashes and some of the bone fragments that had not burned were gathered and placed in some sort of an urn. These urns were anything from a skull to a beautifully wrought steatite or pottery jar, incised or colored until they were works of art. Other containers were just plain bowls or mortars.

Tree and scaffold burials were common, and cave burials were a regular practice among certain tribes. In some cases the bodies, together with their possessions, were placed in rows around the interior of a cave; then stone and brush were piled up to keep animals away.

There were various customs regarding the disposal of the deceased's property. Some tribes buried or destroyed it all at the time of the final ceremony; other tribes permitted tribal members to take everything, leaving the immediate family in want. In a very few instances the widow and daughter inherited all the property. In the majority of cases, however, food and personal belongings were placed in the grave with the departed to assure his being equipped in the beyond. The amount of possessions placed in the grave varied, depending upon the particular tribe.

The Kodiak people seemed to pay more immediate attention to the dead than to the living. The survivors cut off their hair and blackened their faces, and remained in such a state for a year. They did no work for 20 days and did not bathe for five days. If a husband or wife died, the other often withdrew and joined another tribe. It was a part of many Indian legends that in the future the women should join their husbands.

Tree burials were resorted to in tribes that had a dread of the body touching the ground. They considered

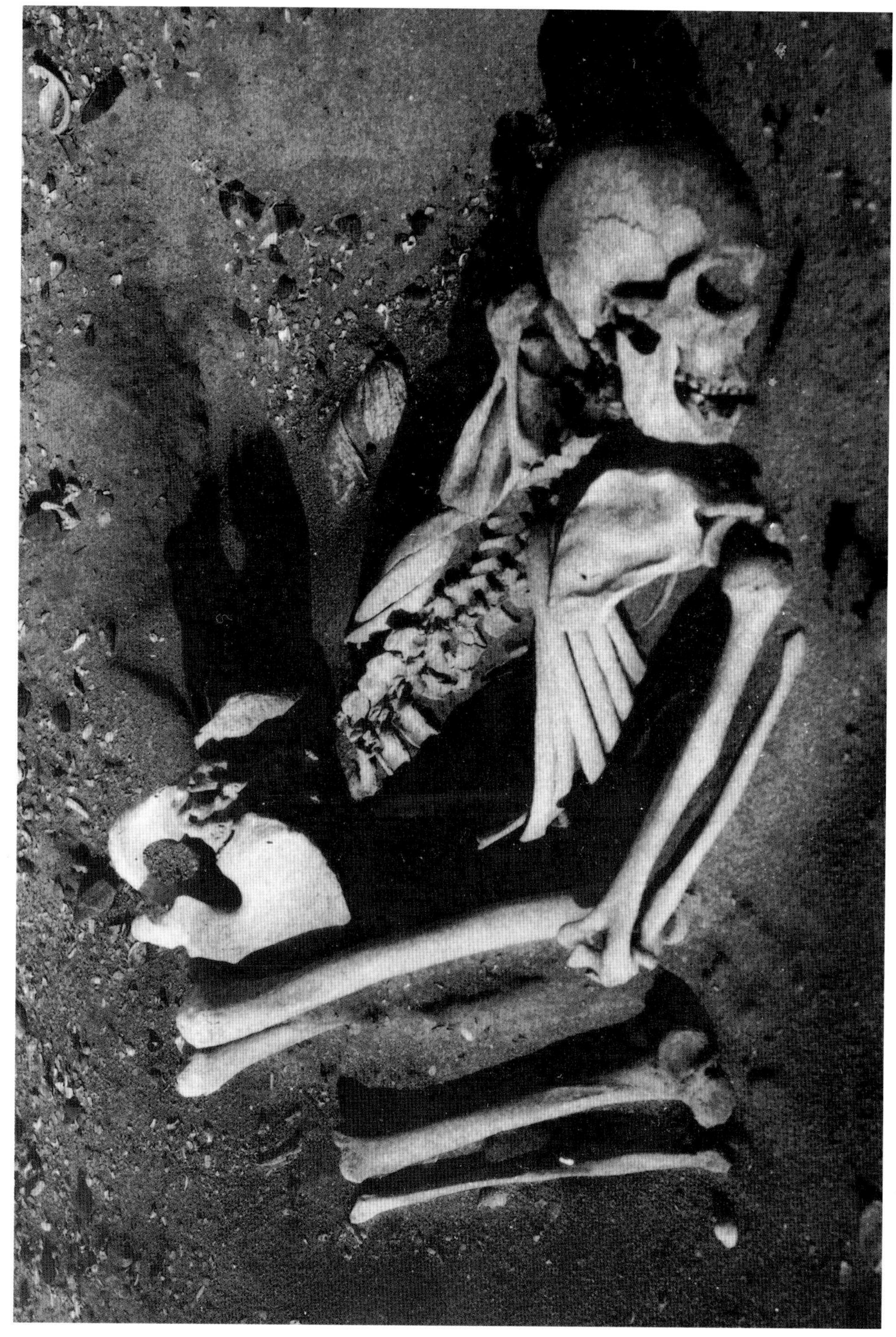

Right: Charcoal was present in the sandy soil of this interment site on San Nicolas Island, California.

this burial practice a sacrilege. In such cases the bodies were suspended in trees. Canoe burials come in this class; the bodies were placed in the canoes and either suspended from a tree or set adrift. Scaffolds were built by some of the Indians, but they used this method of disposal not because of the dread of contact with the ground, but to keep coyotes and other animals from the body. This entailed added labor, since poles for scaffolds were scarce. The body was wrapped in many blankets and placed upon a scaffold 10 to 15 feet above the ground. The tree burial was similar to the scaffold burial in details; however, it was practiced in the timber country where no scaffold had to be built. In both methods the body was prepared in the same manner, and the personal effects were wrapped in the bundle with the corpse.

When a chief of the Okens died his body was disemboweled and the flesh scraped from the bones. The bones were then dried and burned, and the ashes placed in a small, decorated vessel. The remainder of the body was then dressed and adorned with numerous beads and bracelets. His pipe and his most cherished objects were placed with the remains. This was wrapped in a skin and tied, then placed in matting, and more wrappings were tied about it. The body was then placed on a platform in the tomb, along with the former chiefs who had died. At his feet in baskets were placed his riches, so that he might have wealth in the beyond. The Indian chief's

FIGURE 22.1: INTERMENT PLATFORMS

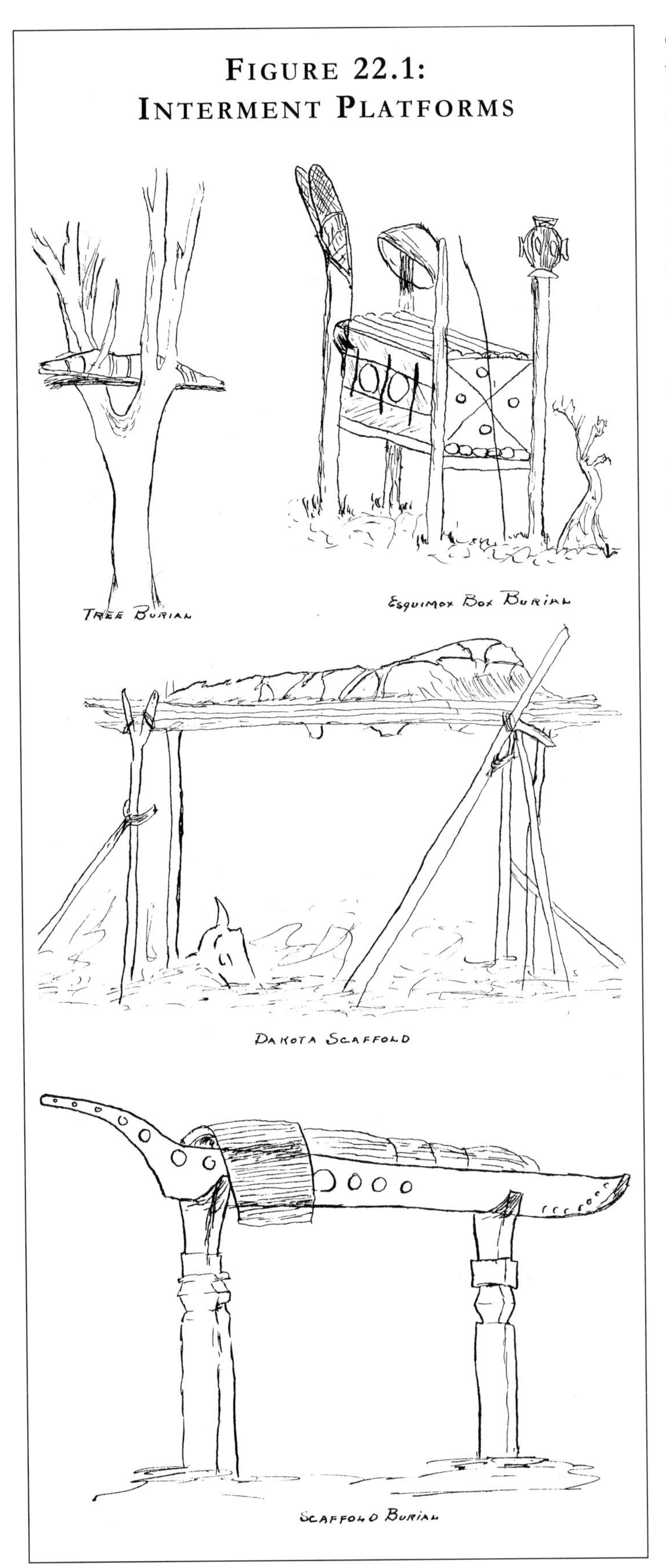

corpse was embalmed and had no bad odor. The chief's body was placed in a well-constructed wooden box, with the covers and sides well fitted and sewn together with twigs or fibers, and then placed on a bench or scaffold a few feet from the ground. Trinkets and personal adornments of the deceased were placed inside the coffin in separate boxes or baskets. The boxes were often beautifully carved and painted.

In a burial ground at Chama, New Mexico, all the skeletons were buried face down with the head pointing south, and with an olla at each head. Some of the tribes in Tennessee dug a shallow grave and placed stone slabs in the bottom, ends, sides and top, forming a stone coffin in which the body was placed, and then covered with earth, thus making a small mound.

In a cemetery in Jefferson County, Missouri, bodies were found that had been buried with no uniformity in regards to the placement of the grave or the position of the corpse in the grave. This happened in many localities, and was no doubt due to different tribes occupying the land at different times.

On the Willamette River, many early burials were found where a shallow excavation had been made and slanting roofs placed over it. In this vault, many bodies were placed in tiers, one above the other.

In the adult burial tombs at Wickliffe, Kentucky, one crematory pit has been found, along with numerous bundle or basket burials, and prone dorsal burials, all intermixed. Charcoal which had been prepared elsewhere was placed over and under the burials, but to a greater degree under them.

The prone dorsal burials faced the sun in its course from east to west. The time of day and the period of year indicated the direction or orientation of the burial. No tombs have been excavated to date which do not conform to this analysis. Grave markers, when used, were made of various materials, including stone and wood, and were often decorated or carved.

The Pima doubled the body to the position in which a child is carried before birth and bound it with ropes. They dug a hole about five feet deep, and at the bottom hollowed a vault, pressing the body into this hollow. They then filled the main hole with sticks, stones and earth to keep the animals from gaining access to the body. The Pima used only a blanket as covering for burial, while others placed the body in large baskets. This largely depended on the condition of the country and the people.

In one group of graves found in Wickliffe, Kentucky, the bodies were buried in a sitting position, some three feet below the surface. All were enclosed in a stone slab wall.

The Muskogee dug a hole under their house, about four feet in diameter, in which they interred their dead. This hole was lined with cypress bark, and the corpse was placed here in a sitting position with all his treasured possessions assembled about him, as near to life in placement as possible. All was then covered over. The remainder of his possessions were given to his eldest wife.

In many tribes a child was buried in some part of the house. The Indians thought the child would have no place to go, so they wanted them around the house. In many instances their toys and some possessions were buried with them.

Among the Achomawi, the men were buried in a standing position, the shoulders coming almost to the level of the ground. The head was cut off. Small bundles of fagots were placed over the hole that held the corpse, and the head was placed on this. The pile was then fired and the head consumed. After this, the female relatives of the deceased appeared with their faces blackened with a tar substance. They dipped their fingers in the cremation ash and made three marks on the right heel and the forehead. This constituted the mourning garb. This period of mourning lasted until the substance had worn off the face.

If a group were being buried together, such as after a battle or an epidemic, the grave was made into the semblance of a small house. The deceased bearing the highest rank while living were placed in the center; the others were placed around him, according to rank. Dirt was then thrown over the entire grave. Some of these mounds were enormous, and some took on the fantastic shapes of birds or animals.

The Mohawk of New York state dug a large, round hole. After the body was dressed in all its finery, it was wrapped and deposited in the grave with all the worldly possessions of the deceased. Timbers were then placed over the top to keep the earth from pressing on the

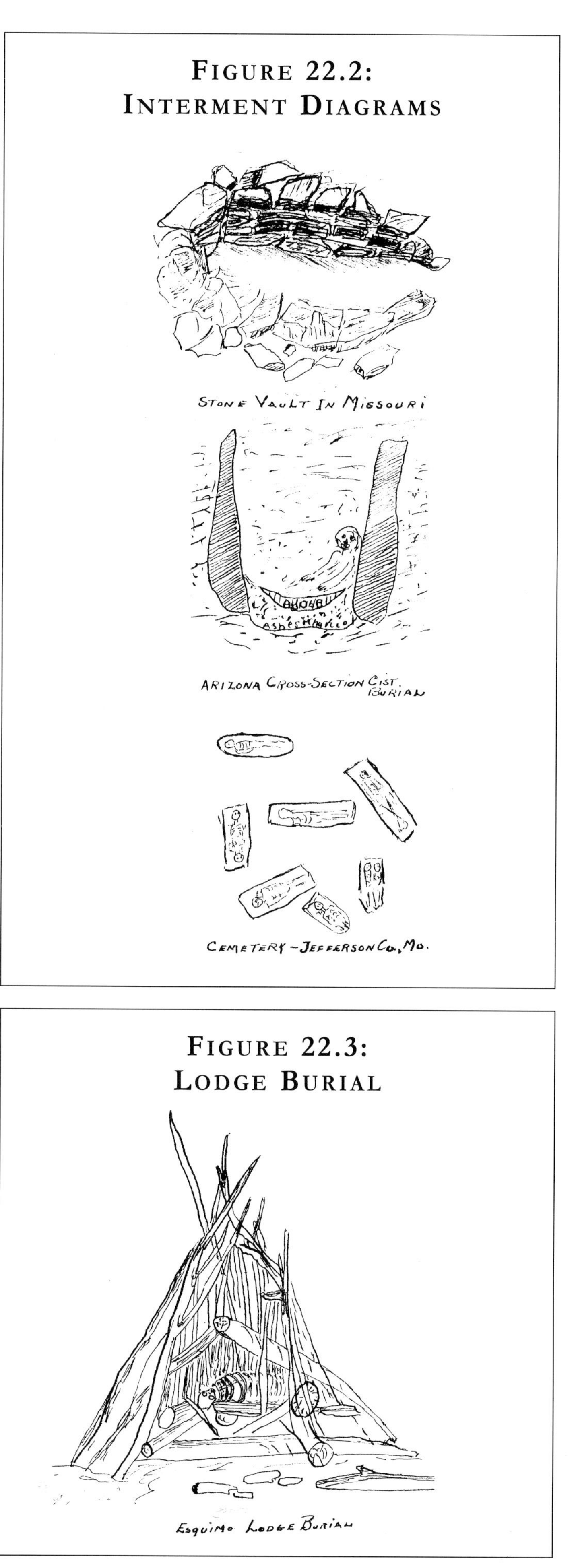

FIGURE 22.2: INTERMENT DIAGRAMS

FIGURE 22.3: LODGE BURIAL

FIGURE 22.4: INTERMENT TOOL

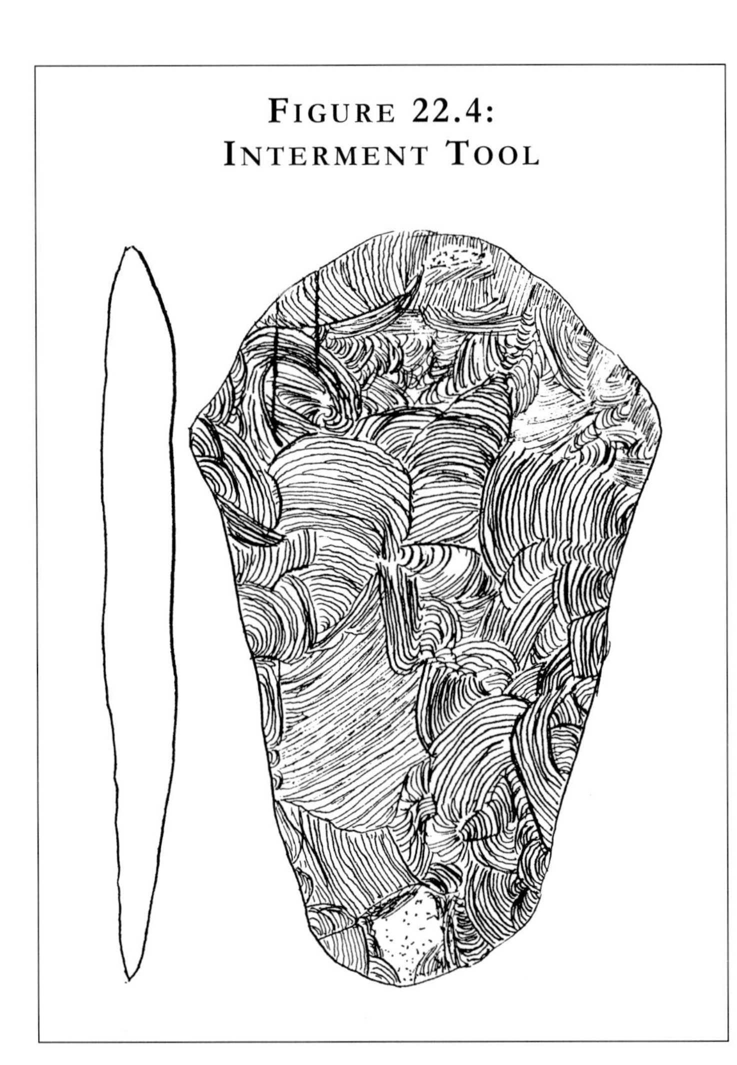

body and a mound was then raised. The height of the mound was in accordance with the man's rank.

The Choctaw deposited the corpse on a scaffold, where it was allowed to remain exposed until the flesh had dropped from the bones or was in an advanced state of decomposition. It was then taken down and the bones were scraped and cleaned. They were dried and placed in a curious wrought chest made for that purpose, which was deposited in the bone house, where it was to remain until it was full of such chests. The whole village then assembled. Each took the chests containing their relatives and, in procession marched, singing and wailing, to a spot selected, where all the chests were deposited in order, according to rank, forming a pyramid. These were all covered over with earth, timbers and wattle, which rose in a conical hill or monument.

In some tribes the bodies were laid full length with a covering of bark, and some even with rudiments of fabric. Other times a coffin was made by placing logs in a crib formation. This was covered over with clay which had been packed hard. This dry form has preserved the timber to such an extent that the kerf marks of the ax are still visible.

Above: Pottery was present in this grave in Arizona.

Above: A grave marker on San Miguel Island, California.

Some give an indication that a type other than the stone ax had been used. Copper was used to some extent, as various finely wrought copper ornaments have been found in the burials from time to time. A dolmen 10 feet x 4 feet x 4 feet was found in the center of a large mound in Illinois. This was built of limestone and in it were interned eight skeletons with numerous ornaments and many artifacts of their daily life. Nothing similar has been found anywhere else.

In many of the cremations the skull was saved and used as a depository for the ashes. This was especially true of tribes in parts of Florida.

While cremation was practiced by many tribes, the Cherokee, at one time, had the most curious way of cremating. The grave was dug and the naked corpse laid in it. The body was then incased with about an inch of plaster which was made of clay. As soon as this had set, a fire was built over the grave and the body cremated. The grave was later covered over, leaving the plaster cast of the form of the front of the person buried. At least five of these have been found, and from what information could be obtained at that time, the custom dated back 500 years or more.

Figure 22.5: Grave Markers

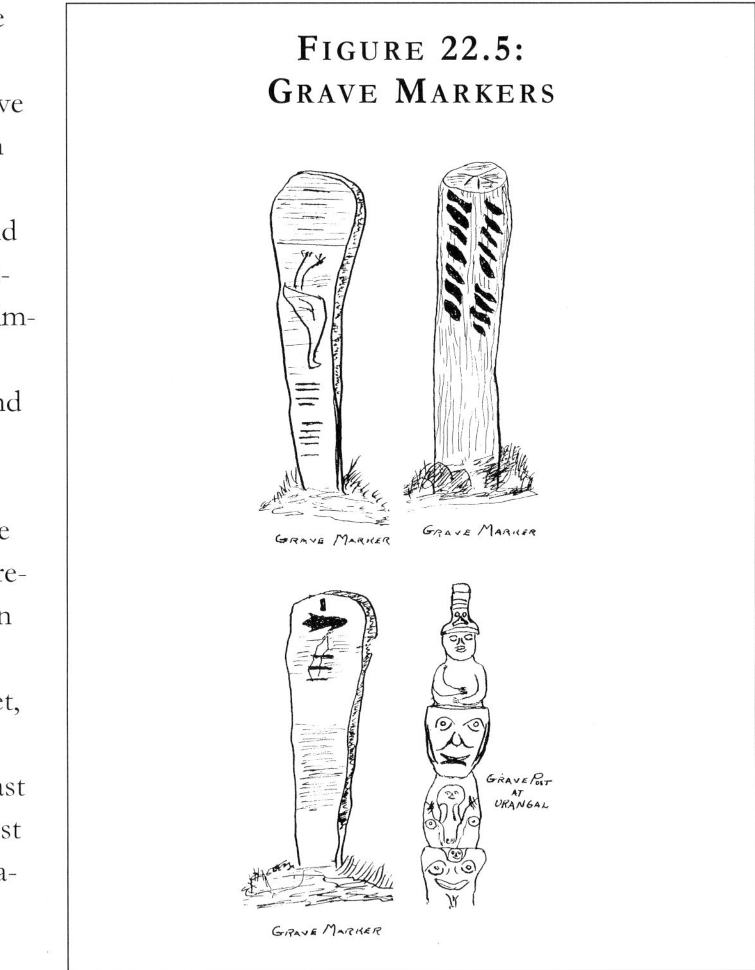

Above: This exhumation site near Wickliffe, Kentucky included a pottery maker buried with his tools near his head (*left*).

Above: The dugout canoe used by this fisherman on the Columbia River in 1897, was based on a deign that had existed for centuries.

INDEX

Right: These petroglyphs photographed by Franklin Johnston at Sand Tank Canyon in the Mojave Desert include strange, almost dinosaur-like, lizards, as well as graffiti mentioning "the days of '49," a reference to the California Gold Rush of 1849. While the petroglyphs date back many hundreds of years, the graffiti was probably left by a prospector in the first couple of decades following the milestone year of 1849.

Above: A woman of the Salish tribe, photographed before a tepee in Montana, circa 1900.

Above: A Shoshone man in full regalia, photographed in about 1880. By this time, non-native influences were present in Indian apparel.